FOUNDATION WATCHER

By

F. Emerson Andrews

FRANKLIN AND MARSHALL COLLEGE
Lancaster, Pa. ~ ~ ~ 1973

Printed in the United States of America
by Princeton University Press

Library of Congress
Catalog Card Number: 73-7398

Dedicated to

THE FIFTH FREEDOM

CONTENTS

PREFACE

One spring day in 1965 I sat with the Program Committee of the National Council on Philanthropy at a luncheon in Longchamps in New York City. The fall meeting in San Francisco would be their first under the new name and broadened mandate; would I make the keynote speech?

No, of course not. Too many people had already heard what I have to say, in far too many speeches, books, and articles. Besides, I had already done that chore three times for this particular organization.

Protests. Flattery, to which usually I am immune. And then I remembered that very soon I would be retiring. I did have nearly a lifetime of experience in the front battle-lines of philanthropy. And now we were newly facing the Great Society and other major changes.

"I'll do it," I finally said. "And I can give you the title right now. It will be 'The Fifth Freedom,' by which I mean the Freedom to Give. I will interpret it broadly, as the freedom we in America possess to use our strengths of mind and body and bank account for our fellow man."

So the speech was given—five times, I confess, but to audiences always a thousand miles apart. And it got printed, and part of it appeared in *Reader's Digest*, so I couldn't give it any more.

The final year before retirement can be a year of terror or delight. All year long the conscious, and subconscious, refrain is, "This is the last time that—" I have seen associates lose twenty pounds that final year, and some of them have shortly died.

For me it was a year of delight. "This is the last time I shall have to get up before dawn in February to shovel out the driveway so as to get to work on time." "This is the last time I shall have to fire anybody." "This is the last time I shall have to arrange for the annual meeting." "Soon I shall be released from administrative chores, and have blessed time in which to visit, and think, and write!"

One of the ideas that grew and began to blossom in that year was an expansion of that Fifth Freedom speech. By a serendipity I shall later describe, I have had the world's most fascinating job: foundation watcher. Indeed, for forty years I have been privileged to sit on the fifty-yard line of all of philanthropy. On rare occasions, when the wrong side seemed to be gaining, I have even myself gone in and tackled somebody.

Perhaps it would be useful, and fun besides, to set down the experiences of those years. This would not be an orderly, balanced history, which an historical scholar should do some decades hence after more facts are in and time lends perspective. This would be a blow-by-blow account as seen by one observer, with names and impressions of persons known, and expression of rash opinions. I might call it, THE FIFTH FREEDOM—AND I.

At this point my severest and best-loved Critic objected. That title would sound as if I were describing my personal philanthropies, presumably in terms of millions; and of course they have necessarily never been large. Maybe the title could be just THE FIFTH FREEDOM. Other critics complained that THE FIFTH FREEDOM was not—certainly not yet—popularly understood as the equivalent of charitable giving. Why not call it PHILANTHROPY?

This is, however, only philanthropy, and particularly foundations, as seen by this particular Boswell during his journey through life. So I have called it, FOUNDATION WATCHER.

During my first quarter century I never dreamed that I should suddenly be plunged into philanthropy, and find it a central and consuming concern. The earlier record is written, but for family and friends. This book condenses the first twenty-six years into a single chapter, Beginnings. Thereafter the record is relatively complete, but sections not related to philanthropy are identified, and can be skipped at will.

When I was retiring people wrote the most outrageous letters. Though I knew that such letters must be discounted at least 90 per cent, it brightened those days to hear that "You have been for all these years 'Mr. Foundation,'" or that "American philanthropy is the sounder and more responsible for your untiring efforts through the years."

It is true that I have happened to be on the scene during many of the more dramatic events affecting philanthropy over some forty years. I shall hope that these views from my privileged window may form a useful part of the record of foundations and philanthropy in America.

F. EMERSON ANDREWS

8 January 1973

Part I

RUSSELL SAGE FOUNDATION

CHAPTER 1

Beginnings

I was born on 26 January 1902 in a small house on South Shippen Street in Lancaster, Pennsylvania. It snowed a little and was moderately cold. The event was of small consequence and no official birth record was made, causing me later problems.

It being Sunday the local newspaper, *The New Era*, was not issued. But copies for some of the surrounding days offer sidelights on conditions and events. A smallpox outbreak was the "widest in fifty years." The Boer Rebellion was headlined as growing. Advertisements promised "$3.00 shoes, now $2.47." The Lancaster Progressive Dental Parlors promised "The 'original' $4 Sets of Teeth. Patent Double Suction. Full Set That Fit."

Some Philanthropic Notes

The week happened to be rich in philanthropic notes. One William McClary of Philadelphia included in his bequests $20,000 for the support of the Home for Aged Masons in Lancaster. Giving for colleges was represented on a diminutive scale. An alumnus of my future Alma Mater, Franklin and Marshall College, sent from Mauch Chunk a check for $250 for the College's new science building, where I later studied. For 27 January *The New Era* carried notice of a larger college gift:

> The descendants of Peter Cooper, Ex-Mayor Edward S. Cooper, his sister, Miss Sarah Amelia Cooper, and ex-Mayor Abram S. Hewitt and family, have given to Cooper Union $300,000, being a sum equal to that given by Andrew Carnegie last week. These amounts, in addition to like donations made by Mr. Carnegie and the Cooper heirs in December, 1899, make in all $1,700,000.

Two days later Andrew Carnegie broke into the local news with broad headlines, and this time on a matter of significance for the whole history of philanthropy:

MR. CARNEGIE'S PLANS
FOR THE NEW NATIONAL UNIVERSITY

The Dispenser of Millions Goes to Washington to Confer with Those Entrusted With the Organization of the New University

---

Andrew Carnegie and the Board of Trustees of "the Carnegie Institution," the new National University of post-graduate studies which Mr. Carnegie has founded with an endowment of $10,000,000 held [their first meeting, at which Mr. Carnegie stated that] he did not wish to influence their judgment in any way.

Under guidance of these trustees Carnegie Institution of Washington chose a different path, not developing as a postgraduate university but as a great operating foundation, advancing research in fields not normally covered by other agencies.

The three-day-old baby then in his crib was later to note that while this was not the earliest American foundation, it was the first large one established on the new principle of wide freedom of action, and to call Mr. Carnegie a "chief architect of these ideas," as expressed first in his essay *The Gospel of Wealth* (published as *Wealth* in 1889) and then in the foundations he established, of which the first important one was Carnegie Institution in 1902.

In the same year General Education Board was set up by John D. Rockefeller, Sr., with Mr. Carnegie an active trustee. The initiating dinner took place on 15 January,[1] concerning which Mr. Fosdick afterwards wrote, "and there one of the most far-reaching philanthropic enterprises of the century was definitely decided upon."[2] The Board was not incorporated until early 1903, but it did not wait for this formality, opening a two-room office in April, 1902.

Mr. Rockefeller was subject of a plaintive editorial in the local newspaper on 27 January, which closed with what may have been the understatement of the year:

---

[1] The modern foundation movement and this foundation watcher were both born in January 1902, but foundations have made the greater progress.

[2] Fosdick, Raymond B., *Adventure in Giving*. Harper and Row, New York, 1962, p. 8.

Hardly a day passes that John D. Rockefeller is not announced as having given a big sum in cold cash to educational institutions throughout the land, but we observe these donations never come to Pennsylvania. Why is this? Do our people not understand the art of asking, or the gift of begging, if it must be so termed? Whatever the reason, the fact remains that Pennsylvania is overlooked when these pleasant gratuities are scattered about. It may not be too late to begin. He still has a little money left, and some of it may be for distribution.

Two other developments in early philanthropy had enough personal relationship—potential or actual—to merit inclusion in this record.

Chocolate Bars

One day, possibly in 1890, Father met Milton S. Hershey on the street in Lancaster. He knew Milton well, for they lived on the same South Shippen Street, he had sold Hershey his first bicycle, and in more recent years, when Father was in the wholesale grocery business, had other dealings with him—not wholly happy dealings, for Mr. Hershey's first attempts at candy manufacture were financial failures. But Mr. Hershey was full of fresh enthusiasms and a new idea.

"I've just come back from Germany," he said, "and now I've got a formula that will really work. I'm going to make a go of this chocolate business now. I like you, and I need a little money. Will you come in as my partner?"

Father said, "No."

He was not the only Lancastrian to say "No" to Milton Hershey. The official biography quotes Mr. Hershey directly: "Some while back I again broached several bankers in town about putting some money into the business, but they turned me down cold. They're still of the opinion I'll go smash one of these days."[3]

In 1903 Mr. Hershey decided to move away from Lancaster and build a vast new chocolate factory in the cornfields adjoining his Old Homestead Farm, near the village of Derry Church. Late in 1904 the first employes arrived, the business began to grow, and soon there were dwellings, a bank, a store, a post office, and the town of Hershey. And then the millions rolled in.

By 1909 Mr. Hershey was able to set up the Hershey Industrial

[3] Snavely, Joseph Richard, *An Intimate Story of Milton S. Hershey.* Privately printed, Hershey, Pa., 1957, p. 27.

School, "a free educational and trade institute for normal, white, orphan boys," with an endowment of 500,000 shares of common stock of the Hershey Chocolate Company and 485 acres of farmland. His reason for limiting the school to boys is a commentary on the times: "There are relatives or outsiders who are glad to adopt girls, for they're useful in the home. Boys, however, are somewhat of a nuisance around the house and no one wants to be bothered with them. So, after talking the matter over with Kitty, we decided to make it a boys' school."[4]

Many years later, when I had become a foundation watcher and had the duty of tabulating grants, it was with wry feelings that I added this footnote for 1964 statistics:

> The 1964 HEALTH is disproportionately high because of inclusion of The M. S. Hershey Foundation's gift of $50 million to establish a medical school in Pennsylvania.

But I am not really sorry Father said "No" that early day in Lancaster. As a rich man's son I might have become a philanthropist, but I suspect life as a philanthropoid has been quite as exciting and perhaps more useful.

Where Atlas Now Stands

On 19 April 1907, when I was five years old, an event was taking place in New York which would greatly influence most of my life. On Fifth Avenue, at about the spot where the great bronze Atlas lifts the world on his sturdy shoulders in front of Rockefeller Center's International Building, the door of a large brownstone house was opening from time to time to admit an extraordinary group of persons. They were Robert W. de Forest, prominent lawyer and president of the New York Charity Organization Society, former president of the National Conference of Charities and Correction; Cleveland H. Dodge, financier and merchant, and an official of the American National Red Cross, International Y.M.C.A., and the American Museum of Natural History; Daniel C. Gilman, organizer of Johns Hopkins University, a trustee of the John F. Slater Fund, Peabody Education Fund, and first president of Carnegie Institution of Washington; John M. Glenn, Baltimore lawyer, president of the Board of Supervisors of City Charities in Baltimore, former president of the National Conference of Charities and Correction; Robert C. Og-

[4] *Ibid.*, p. 149.

den, merchant, associated with General Education Board; Gertrude S. Rice, one of the founders of the New York Charity Organization Society and an officer of the State Charities Aid Association; and Miss Louisa Lee Schuyler, founder of the State Charities Aid Association and of America's first training school for nurses, at Bellevue Hospital. Miss Helen Gould was also invited but was in Europe.

Their hostess was Margaret Olivia Sage, recently widowed. Her husband, Russell Sage, had been a financier and manipulator of railroads, vying with Hetty Green for most of their lives to hold the place of richest individual in America. He was widely reputed to have no shred of interest in the general welfare or in charities. When he died he left his entire fortune, amounting to about $65 million, to his wife. This kindly and generous lady began immediately to give away his hoarded millions.

She had problems. Within six months she received twenty thousand letters from individuals and institutions of all kinds, in addition to countless personal appeals, all wanting some of her fortune. But Mrs. Sage had herself known straitened circumstances before her marriage, and while she was generous, she wanted her money to do as much good as possible. So she asked trusted friends for advice.

They almost unanimously suggested that she use a substantial part of her fortune to set up one of these new-fangled foundations, after the pattern of Andrew Carnegie, John D. Rockefeller, and recently a few others. This new invention seemed to be working well. Moreover, it would provide a paid staff and experienced trustees to handle the flood of requests now inundating her.

She approved the suggestion. A brief, general charter was drawn up, passed by the New York State legislature, and signed into law on 11 April 1907. Eight days later, on the 19th, she invited to her home the persons just named for the first meeting of the trustees of Russell Sage Foundation.

The meeting was opened with a prayer by Mrs. Sage "which brought tears to the eyes of all present," reported Mr. de Forest. Mrs. Sage gave her trustees an even $10 million, nearly four fifths in railroad bonds, one fifth in mortgages on Manhattan real estate, some Provident Loan Society securities, and cash to round out the total. It was to be a perpetuity in honor of her husband, with the income to be applied "to the improvement of social and living conditions in the United States of America."

She then read her Letter of Gift. Without limiting the broad purposes in the charter, she expressed certain preferences:

> The scope of the Foundation is not only national but is broad. It should, however, preferably not undertake to do that which is now being done or is likely to be effectively done by other individuals or by other agencies. It should be its aim to take up the larger and more difficult problems, and to take them up so far as possible in such a manner as to secure co-operation and aid in their solution.
>
> In some instances it may wisely initiate movements, in the expectation of having them maintain themselves unaided after once being started. In other instances it may start movements with the expectation of carrying them on itself.[5]

The new trustees agreed to submit within ten days memoranda on their views as to future plan and scope, and they passed a few appropriations which seemed immediately needed. The Jamestown Exposition (the 300th anniversary was of course in 1907) should have educational exhibits on children's school gardens, children's playgrounds, facts about tuberculosis, and, if arrangements could be made, concerning safety appliances.

"I am nearly eighty years old," said Mrs. Sage at the close of the meeting, "and I feel as if I were just beginning to live."

She had established what was then one of the first of the large foundations. Though now relatively small among the giants that have since been created, it was early in the field, and has continuously tried to be helpful and to accumulate knowledge about effective giving. It has sometimes been called "the foundations' foundation."

It was important, too, to the little boy who had never heard of it but was to become one of its historians. About two decades later I joined its staff, almost by accident, remained on that staff nearly thirty years, and served as a consultant ten years more.

The Years Between

Childhood was a disturbed period. I continued less than well, had a minor operation, and it was thought best not to send me to school for a while. So I did not enter the Ann Street School until the autumn after I became eight. But lessons came easily, then

[5] Quoted in Glenn, John M., Lilian Brandt, and F. Emerson Andrews, *Russell Sage Foundation, 1907-1946.* In two vols., the Foundation, New York, 1947, p. 667.

and always, and soon I had skipped two grades and was with my age group.

Mother died when I was twelve. Father did what he could toward being both parents, and we had a succession of housekeepers to keep the home going.

I went to the local Boys High School and to the local college, Franklin and Marshall, from which I graduated in 1923.

At about the age of six I decided to become a writer. Shortly thereafter my brother Paul and I started a neighborhood magazine called *Sports*. He was the managing editor, being older; I did most of the copy, and we both printed our editions in pencil. The subscription price was one cent. In the midst of the second issue it dawned on us that even if subscriptions increased, income would never catch up with the strains of making more copies by hand. So we gave up that publishing venture.

All through high school and college I turned out stories and articles in an almost continuous stream, sent them out with high hopes, and for a long time got them all back. It was the ninety-seventh submission that finally brought the thrill that comes to a writer only once in a lifetime, that first check. Mine was for $3.00 for a short story in *Grit*, a magazine circulating widely in rural areas.

As college graduation approached it was clear that I could not follow my earlier confident plan of supporting myself as a freelance writer. There had been a few acceptances—articles in several quite reputable magazines, a page on Parkman in *The New York Times* Book Review, even a published playlet, *Hannah Henpeck's Vote*, an item that befuddles my bibliographers. But the actual income would not even rent a garret in which to starve. I would have to seek a job, and a book publishing house might use some of my presumed talents and be a good education for a writer. But I made myself one firm promise. After five years, no matter where I was in the publishing house, I would quit and devote myself to creative writing.

Publishers were remarkably uninterested in my talents. Finally I was offered a temporary job in the shipping department of The Macmillan Company at $25 a week. In September, 1923, I went to New York, rented a room, and became a shipping clerk.

The toe-hold turned out well. One day during a shipping lull I chanced to look at a college text which included a passage from Francis Parkman, on which I was now an authority because of the *Times* paper. The date of Parkman's birth was wrong. A note to the head of the college department correcting this error signed "F. E. Andrews, shipping clerk" led to an interview with that apparently flabbergasted gentleman, word got about, and soon I was in charge of advertising printing.

At the end of five years, in the fall of 1928, I was head of Macmillan's Mail Service Department, with some thirteen employes. Meanwhile I had been so busy selling other people's writings that little time remained to do my own. As the date approached, I began having second thoughts. My diary says:

> I find myself wondering whether I can safely take my desired course. This will not do. I'm five years out of college . . . and am in real danger of drifting on through life in a pleasant, comfortable, mediocre job. Blast this weasel spirit!

On 4 September 1928, five years to the day, I wrote a letter to Mr. Brett, submitting my resignation. It became effective at the end of the month. I laid out for myself a tremendous writing schedule. The idea that I might soon, or ever, enter the field of philanthropy had not entered my mind.

CHAPTER 2

Baptism in Philanthropy

Tㅴ HAT first free-lancing October I shall not forget. Even the weather turned glorious. I wrote mornings, took long walks in the flaming woods afternoons, and in the evenings caught up on my reading, and revised and mailed out manuscripts.

Some Literary Successes

The first day of the new freedom I chanced to look down from a high office window in mid-Manhattan. There, among the drab gray and black roofs was a splash of brilliant color. Two water towers masqueraded as Dutch windmills with golden sails. Chimneys and pipe vents became peppermint sticks striped with crimson. I carefully located the roof as the top of the Prince George Hotel on 28th Street. The manager, with evident pride, gave me a personal tour. Closer inspection of his children's roof revealed an Indian wigwam, a doll house, swings, a seesaw, boat pond, sandbox, a witch riding a weather vane—all surrounded by growing plants and shrubs. Judicious brush strokes transformed an adjoining wall into a forest, and at the entrance to the roof were pictured Old King Cole, Simple Simon, Tom the Piper's Son, and other gentry from Mother Goose.

Intrigued, I did a survey of New York roofs from the Battery to Central Park. They included a small golf course on the old Astor Building with water hazards, sand traps, and bunkers; the weather station on the Whitehall Building; the top of the American Telephone and Telegraph Building fitted out as a sky-land gymnasium with a further large rest area resembling a ship's deck; penthouse gardens galore, some with real trees and even a waterfall; a bandstand on the northern wing of the Municipal Building; pigeon cotes; playroofs on settlement houses and public schools; and promenades and small gardens attached to the dining-and-dancing roof gardens of the swank midtown hotels. *The New York Times* took a long feature article on "New York Roofs Hold a Life of Their Own" and several magazines accepted special stories.

A playlet, "An Evening in India," was a modest success when produced by the young people's group, many of whom I knew, at the Marble Collegiate Church, where the preaching minister was Daniel A. Poling. But the aftermath of my only Fifth Avenue production was slightly catastrophic. While the cast was on stage in the final act and I was in the wings ready to prompt, a sneak thief visited the improvised dressing room and made off with all the purses and jewelry of the ladies.

Articles and short stories poured out of the typewriter in a stream that autumn, and work was proceeding on a second novel. (The first I was abandoning, after many rejections.) But one of the short stories deserves special mention.

The Accursed Cross

On a walking trip in Germany's Black Forest some years earlier I had picked up the legend of Michel the Woodsman. It seems that Michel wanders endlessly through the Black Forest, bearing a burnished ax on his shoulder. Sometimes he hacks into a tree a mark known only to himself. But if a mere mortal afterward cuts down that tree and uses its wood, disaster follows. If its timber planks a ship, she will sink, sometimes in a calm sea. If its wood is built into a house, some night with a ghostly creaking the rafters break and the house comes tumbling down upon the doomed inhabitants.

Haunted by the legend, I began wondering what would happen if wood bearing his curse were used to fashion a cross? The literal fulfillment of one's prayers might be the worst of all curses!

So, in the guise of a priest in whose parish such an accursed cross was unwittingly set up, I told what happened to the three persons who prayed before it for selfish ends. I liked that story, and sent it to *The Dial*, which was still carrying on its extraordinary literary traditions. Back came a discouraging-looking fat envelope, but inside it a letter from Marianne Moore beginning,

"We admire, and should be glad to have for *The Dial* your story, 'The Accursed Cross' . . ." She had minor changes to suggest, but "could not consent to accept concessions made at a sacrifice; the pencil marks are so light that they can be erased without injury to the manuscript."

I have known other considerate and helpful editors, but the experience with Miss Moore, when I visited her in her apartment, has not been equaled for the pertinence of her comments and her precision in word use. As just one example, the manuscript included the word *marriage*.

"Mr. Andrews," she said, pointing to it, "this is a French derivative; since your setting is the Black Forest, would you consider substituting *wedding?*"

The story was published in the March, 1929, issue, and was later triple-starred by Edward J. O'Brien as one of "The Best Short Stories of 1929."

A Publishing Survey

A different sort of writing assignment came from Russell Sage Foundation. While I was still with The Macmillan Company a young New Yorker whom I had met at a Phi Beta Kappa meeting sought some publishing advice. Lawrence M. Orton, who became vice-chairman of the New York City Planning Commission, was then an assistant to John M. Glenn, general director of Russell Sage Foundation. The librarian and director of the Foundation's publications was then in terminal illness, unable to perform his duties. So Mr. Orton would invite me to lunch, and as a favor to him and to a foundation that I admired from afar, I gave him advice on its publishing problems.

This slight personal philanthropy had for me two tremendous consequences. First, one of the "conferences" was in Mr. Orton's home, where his wife had invited as another dinner guest a delightful Cornell classmate of hers, Miss Edith L. Severance. I escorted the young lady home that evening, and later married her.

Mr. Orton apparently profited from our conversations, for in October 1928 he invited me to do a survey of the Foundation's publishing program, with recommendations for the future. I protested that I was done with publishing, but he pointed out that this could be done as a writing job, on my own time schedule, and would be paid.

Later that month I submitted my 37-page *Report*. Russell Sage

Foundation at that time (and now) differed from the typical foundation pattern of making grants to outside agencies by using a large portion of its funds to conduct research with its own staff and publishing the findings under its own imprint. There were no author royalties, since authors were salaried staff members. Profit was not a consideration; books and pamphlets were priced to return approximate costs of printing and distribution, and actually seldom did even this. Individual department directors and authors took a large hand in publishing and publicity, with quite varying skill.

The *Report* was frank and hard-hitting. It found a good bit to commend. Even before the rise of the commercial book clubs, Russell Sage Foundation had begun its own Standing Order Plan, sending its publications automatically to libraries and individuals who signed up. But the list had dropped to 358. Because at this time substantially all the publications were in the specialized field of social work, I saw great possibilities in this device, suggested as the title for a promotional booklet "Your Share in $15,000,000," and predicted an eventual membership "ranging between 1,200 and 2,000." (In a few years it was 3,000.)

I was not happy with the approach taken in most circulars of asking people to "help" in distribution of Foundation publications out of their general interest and good will. The only effective appeal in obtaining actual orders, I firmly insisted, was to point out the specific value and helpfulness of the advertised publication to the circular recipient. To make ordering easy, I advised using the then-new government reply card. Bookstore discounts needed drastic revision. Foreign sales, which were only 190 in the surveyed year, should be much larger for such pathfinding books in the social field; sometimes special British and foreign language editions could be negotiated. In view of the heavy costs of research which the Foundation wholly absorbed, the meager promotion budget ought to be much enlarged so that findings could be adequately translated into public understanding and usefulness. Very costly authors' alterations suggested a need for more care in original preparation and editing of manuscripts.

Publicity and promotion were sometimes excellent but in other cases "very spotty. So far as one can judge from the outside, this is due to the lack of a responsible and centralized publicity department." Circulars and ads appeared often to be designed by the department heads and therefore lacked a "house" style which would help readers identify RSF publications. Centralization of both publishing and publicity activities in a director of the Publication Department was recommended.

A few weeks later I was invited to lunch at the National Arts Club for further discussion of the *Report*. Those present were Mr. Glenn, the vice-general director Shelby M. Harrison, Lawrence M. Orton, and myself. In general they approved of the *Report*, in spite of its sometimes severe criticisms. But theirs was not commercial publishing, and only actual experiment could determine whether some of the suggestions would work. Would I join their staff on a temporary basis and try out my own recommendations?

I protested that I had just quit a good publishing job, and assumed I was done with publishing forever. They pointed out that by my own assessment, with only four or five books a year, the publishing operation was about a half-time job; I could write half time, making my own time schedule, and give half time to them.

By this time I had learned that one does not indeed write regularly more than three or four hours a day. So I expressed interest but disclosed a new complication.

When the newspapers had recently reported that Gifford Pinchot, former governor of Pennsylvania, was purchasing a large sailing vessel for an eight months' cruise in the South Seas, with exploration of unknown islands in view, I had written the Governor suggesting his cruise needed an official scribe and submitted my qualifications. He had expressed interest, and together we had visited his ship in a Brooklyn dock and I had been introduced to the dour-visaged Captain he later fired. He would be sailing in late March and needed more time to consider my proposal. So now I felt committed, until the Governor made his decision.

Mr. Glenn suggested that even a few months would be enough to get things started and to test some of my proposals. After further conversations it was so arranged, and confirmed by Mr. Harrison in a letter dated 17 December 1928:

> ... We wish you to take charge of the work of our Publication Department for the period beginning today and running to March 15, 1929, on a half-time basis. In view of the possibility that you might have to be away from New York City after the middle of March, I understand that you do not wish to commit yourself beyond that date. This is a satisfactory arrangement with us as we regard the special promotion work on our publications more or less in the na-

ture of an experiment. The offer, therefore, does not carry any commitment on your part or on ours after March 15....

Prosperity Unlimited, U. S. A.

The double assignment worked well. Writing in the morning and being chiefly a department administrator afternoons were different enough to bring zest to both jobs. Actually, the writing production fell off scarcely at all, and may have profited by new stimulations.

The 1928-early 1929 period was one of unrivaled prosperity in America. To the few Cassandras the financial moguls confidently replied that stocks, now at five times their 1920 values, were not too high; we had simply reached a new level of prosperity. Even foundations were not immune to this doctrine. Julius Rosenwald made this pronouncement from a sadly clouded crystal ball:

> Men accustomed to investing a large part of their private fortunes in sound common stocks have felt that as trustees they must invest only in first mortgages or bonds. Of late a good many boards of trustees have enjoyed a change of heart, to the vast benefit of the institutions they serve.[1]

If ever there was a time when the nearly hopeless job of supporting one's self by free-lancing might succeed, that was the year. Almost everything I wrote brought in a check. By coincidence, in a single week in March, four items were published, three of them major. My diary for 11 March has a smug note:

> A few years ago America's best newspaper, its most important religious paper, and its highest-standard literary magazine would have represented dizzying thrills indeed for a single week! But as usual, having arrived at a once-envied stage, my aims shoot higher and satisfaction is not yet—nor ever.

In this initial writing year, instead of having to invade my slender capital, I was adding to it. So I conferred with my Lancaster banker, asking his advice about investing in stocks.

"I know that nearly every financial expert says we are on a new level of prosperity, and stocks will go up and up. But I don't believe it. We're in for trouble. If I were you, I would stay out of the market."

[1] Rosenwald, Julius, "Principles of Public Giving," in *Atlantic Monthly, May, 1929*. (Date italics mine.)

A few months later when Wall Street collapsed I did not have a penny in stocks or in an unsafe bank. My checking account is still in the bank where I received such sage advice.

Baptism by Immersion

One writing project failed. Mr. Pinchot wrote me in late February that there was no room for me in his expedition.

No other of my many failures has been so fortunate. Had I gone on that expedition, I would have returned just after the market collapse, jobless, with magazines failing right and left, and the skinny survivors buying no new materials.

As it was, I promptly notified Russell Sage Foundation of the Pinchot declination, and they as promptly informed me of their "wish to continue the present arrangement with you indefinitely."

Whenever I have an interest in a subject, some inner compulsion drives me into finding everything about it that can be known. I was now involved in philanthropy, and no spot in America could have offered a better place for learning about it than "the foundations' foundation."

Now it was baptism by immersion.

CHAPTER 3

Russell Sage Foundation, 1929

IT may be worth while to record a newcomer's impressions of Russell Sage Foundation in 1929, before the Great Depression struck and wholly changed its program.

When I took charge of publications the Foundation was located in its own impressive Florentine building at the corner of Lexington Avenue and East 22nd Street. Mrs. Sage, allegedly against the preference of most of her trustees, had had this fine building, designed by Grosvenor Atterbury, constructed as a memorial to her husband, Russell Sage, though that tight-fisted gentleman died before the Foundation was established and probably never would have consented to committing income from his millions "for the improvement of social and living conditions."

The Foundation at this time, and for many years previously, was disbursing about half its net income in grants to a wide variety of social agencies, some of which had also free office space in the Sage building, and the rest on its own staff-conducted operations. There were some eight departments representing various aspects of social work, a large library specializing in this field, and my Publication Department.

Charity Organization and Mary E. Richmond

"Charity" in the sense of giving needy and "worthy" people food, clothing, shelter, or sometimes money had been an American practice from Colonial times. As life grew more complicated it began to be clear that Christmas baskets and the ministrations of Ladies Bountiful were not enough, and indeed could be actually harmful. Helping people *in* trouble (relief) sometimes merely confirmed them in habits of laziness and dependency. It was essential to help people *out* of trouble (rehabilitation, cure).

And it might be even more constructive to help people *avoid* trouble (prevention, research into causes), and to provide for them the means for climbing to their own highest potentialities.

So, first in England and then in America, charity organization began to be the order of the day. Voluntary societies with workers specially trained in dealing with families, children, the sick, the criminal, and other social problems took over from Lady Bountiful. There was still place for the dedicated volunteer (and certainly for his money!), but under professional guidance. In bringing social work toward professional status, Russell Sage Foundation had perhaps the key role in the United States, and within the Foundation Mary E. Richmond, head of the Charity Organization Department, was the acclaimed leader and prophet of the movement.

Miss Richmond died just before I came to the Foundation, and I never saw her. But her reputation was world-wide, and my publication survey had acquainted me with her *Social Diagnosis*, sometimes called the "bible" of social work. Published in 1917 as the first book under sole Russell Sage Foundation imprint, in an edition of 1,500 copies, its Preface asked for corrections "in the remote chance of there being another edition." For many years it was the Foundation's best seller, and it is still in print.

Its insistence upon complete knowledge about people with whom one deals must deeply challenge case workers dealing with real persons, for it pricked even the conscience of this dealer in paper characters. Says my writing notebook on a first reading of *Social Diagnosis*:

> What a stupid dilettante am I, pretending to create men and women and knowing less about them than the greenest social worker demands to know before granting a dollar of relief! Hereafter every character is going to have more than name and sex and one distinguishing trait. He is going to have mannerisms or lack of them, parents, education, a previous life history completely known to me, opinions and beliefs, a salary of definite size, a place where he was born, surroundings in which he grew up, people and events which influenced him. Until he is alive I will not touch him.[1]

Marriage and the State

I did have the pleasure of handling Miss Richmond's final book, *Marriage and the State*, written in collaboration with Fred

---

[1]Expanded for writers in "Three-Dimensional Characters," *The Writer*, February, 1931, pp. 40-41.

S. Hall and published early in 1929. Miss Richmond had been finding that "a considerable number" of the more difficult problems case workers had to treat "could be traced to ill-devised and indifferently administered marriage laws." So for ten years the Department had been studying the laws themselves in the various states, and their actual administration.

Their study revealed fifteen minutes as the average time for obtaining a marriage license, with some states issuing licenses by mail; the license clerk usually a political appointee, with his salary often dependent upon fees collected; nearly 700,000 persons in the United States who participated in a child marriage; and not fewer than 57 marriage-market towns, making a regular business of runaway marriages with special profits from ceremonies performed at odd hours and without awkward questions. In one such town a clergyman improved his share of the business by dividing his fees with the taxi drivers. In another, six marrying justices of the peace emblazoned MARRIAGE PARLOR across the front of a rented store, taking turns in attendance days and evenings; they charged a standard $3 for an ordinary service, but an additional $3 to keep it out of the papers.

The study's chief constructive recommendations were establishment of a minimum marriage age of sixteen in all states; five days advance notice before a license may be issued; abolition of the fee system for license clerks; better control by religious denominations; and establishment of a bureau of marriage law supervision in every state. In addition to securing wide press publicity for the book's revelations and recommendations, I did a special article for *North American Review*.[2]

Social Work Year Book Department

Though he helped Miss Richmond with her final book, Fred S. Hall had for some years been developing an idea of his own, which turned out to be brilliant. This was creation of what was first proposed as a social work annual and Who's Who for the emerging profession. The Who's Who part of the project was abandoned, and the successive volumes never appeared more frequently than biennially, but the name *Social Work Year Book* was adopted and stuck. The new project was announced in January, 1929, just after I joined the Foundation.

---

[2] "The Mills of Marriage," *North American Review*, July, 1929, pp. 17-23.

"Mr." Hall (I never learned he had a Ph.D. until assembling material for his retirement notice) was a slender, goateed, distinguished-looking gentleman, with a fine sense of humor, considerate of others but never sparing himself. Extreme absorption in his work resulted in certain incidents of absent-mindedness, which, in confession, brightened many of our luncheons. On one occasion the usher taking up the offering in his Montclair, New Jersey, church was a little startled to find Mr. Hall handing up a commutation ticket to be punched. Another day, having enjoyed the sunshine on the forward deck of the ferry across the Hudson, he walked briskly to work, and then remembered he had left his automobile on the ferry. On still another occasion he proudly announced to Mrs. Hall that he remembered he was to be home early this evening, and here he was. "Yes," she said, "but where is Mother?"—whom he was to have picked up in Grand Central Station.

On that first *Social Work Year Book, 1929* Fred Hall took personal responsibility for nearly every detail, from selecting the experts for its 195 articles to final proofreading, and as we saw him lose weight and grow more haggard week after week, we worried. But it was published in 1930, immediately became an indispensable tool in its field, and the Department began to work more smoothly on its successors. Mr. Hall also edited the volumes for 1933 and 1935, in which year he retired—first to his beloved garden in Montclair, and then to Winter Park, Florida, where soon he was engaged in five volunteer assignments related to his social work skills. His successor, Russell H. Kurtz, edited the biennial volumes from 1937 through 1947, and Margaret B. Hodges edited the tenth, 1949, volume. This encyclopedic reference was then taken over, in slightly changed form, by the American Association of Social Workers.

Remedial Loans

Mrs. Sage, within two years of her husband's death, had received sixty thousand letters from individuals, appealing for aid. Many of these were from victims of loan sharks. Unbelievable interest rates were often charged, and the borrower was kept impoverished and in the toils of the loan shark by unconscionable methods, including use of force:

> The rates charged by the loan sharks were exorbitant: 120 percent a year, 260 percent, 360 percent, 650 percent, or even 1,300 percent

a year. A wage-earner securing a loan at such excessive rates could, of course, not easily extricate himself from debt. Often he dared not appeal to his employer. He could but pay his periodic assessment to the loan shark; he was, in effect, a peon. . . . The best procurable evidence showed that in the American cities of over 25,000 inhabitants about one family in five was a victim of loan sharks.[3]

Mrs. Sage's advisers suggested attention to this problem. As early as 1908 the Foundation published a first pamphlet[4] in this field, and in 1910 set up a Division of Remedial Loans.

The crux of the problem was interest rates. It was easy to get state legislatures to pass laws setting low maximum rates, usually 6 percent. But of course small loans for needy borrowers could not possibly be handled profitably at such a charge, due to office overhead, collection costs, and high risks. Studies were made of actual costs of this business, and a Uniform Small Loan Law proposed that would permit rates high enough to attract legitimate lenders, but with careful protections for the borrower.

Opposition came from a strange source, the loan sharks. These scoundrels piously supported the economically impossible 6 percent rate. So long as legitimate agencies could not afford to lend small sums to the needy, they, always working outside the law, had the whole field to themselves.

When I joined the Foundation in 1928 the battle was still raging. Careful studies were being made covering small loans in all forms, credit unions, "salary buying," moneylending in Great Britain, and explorations in consumer credit. But the ebullient Leon Henderson, director of the Department, was also engaged in vigorous campaigns, almost state by state, to secure legislation more nearly in accord with the latest revision of the Uniform Small Loan Law.

These activities preceded amendment of the Internal Revenue Code which denies tax-exempt status to an organization if a substantial part of its activities "is carrying on propaganda, or otherwise attempting, to influence legislation," which might have blocked Henderson's activist program. But problems aplenty developed from other sources, including charges that Russell Sage Foundation was promoting these higher rates because it had heavy investments (it had none) in the small loan business. Rolf

[3] Gallert, David J., Walter S. Hilborn, and Geoffrey May, *Small Loan Legislation.* Russell Sage Foundation, New York, 1932, p. 54.

[4] Wassam, Clarence W., *The Salary Loan Business in New York City,* 1908, 143 p.

Nugent, Mr. Henderson's assistant, received personal threats to his life, secured a pistol permit, and for a while thereafter went armed.

Leon Henderson's explosive transfer to the national scene in a Depression emergency is later detailed. Rolf Nugent was appointed director, with legislative work in the small loan field minimized and research brought to new emphasis. Installment buying and consumer credit in its national economic implications became a new focus of interest.

Rolf Nugent was a young, energetic, able executive whom I grew to know well. His careful studies, and his personal commitment to full disclosure of all costs of lending (including the true costs of bank discounted loans, which brought him bitter opposition from even those institutions), might have accomplished much more, except for his tragic death in 1946.

The Department was not reconstituted, but in 1969 the Congress passed a "Truth in Lending" bill.

Delinquency and Penology

Hastings H. Hart was in his late seventies when I joined the Foundation. He had come to the Foundation in 1909, taking charge of the work concerning dependent, defective, and delinquent children. But his interests were swinging into the field of penology, and his department's name was changed to Delinquency and Penology in 1924.

When I met him he was still a hale and vigorous man, a social-work patriarch whose views were listened to with respect by prison authorities and legislative committees. Reform of the prison system, with a particular concern for adapting prison architecture to patterns conducive to rehabilitation instead of merely security, was a keen interest of Dr. Hart in his final years. He was still a traveler; in one of those latest years he visited thirty-five reformatories and jails all over the United States. But in 1931 he had a serious operation, and died in 1932 in his eighty-first year. Two days after his death we published his final small book, *Plans for City Police Jails and Village Lockups.*

Surveys and Exhibits

When I joined the staff there was still a Department of Surveys and Exhibits, though the title no longer fitted the program. One of the earliest interests of the Foundation had been the pathmaking Pittsburgh Survey, begun in 1907, as the first comprehensive city survey in America, and recipient of one of the Foundation's very first grants—for $27,000, in June, 1907. Convinced of the importance of such surveys, the Foundation organized its own Department of Surveys and Exhibits in 1912, headed by Shelby M. Harrison with Evart G. Routzahn as associate director. Both of these gentlemen had been on the Pittsburgh Survey staff. A third very important addition, at first on temporary assignment as a special agent, was Miss Mary B. Swain, who became Mrs. Evart Routzahn in 1914.

The Department conducted, or participated in, a large number of civic surveys within the next decade, with Mr. Routzahn being particularly concerned with the exhibit side, attempting to bring home to the citizens the findings concerning their towns.

By 1929 Mr. Harrison was engulfed in administrative duties as the Foundation's vice-general director, and heir apparent to the directorship. Formal surveys were not being undertaken, but the Department was moving in two quite divergent directions because of the special talents of its members.

Mr. and Mrs. Routzahn formed a unique team in the whole broad field of social work interpretation. Evart in his green eyeshade, hammer in hand, gave earthy, practical advice wherever any organization was setting up an exhibit to inform the public about health, or social work in all its ramifications. Mrs. Routzahn was the better writer and a skillful consultant.

They had just published their compendious *Publicity for Social Work* when I came on staff, and it was not doing as well as anticipated; what did I have to suggest? Recognizing that making suggestions about their own book to two publicity experts was toying with dynamite, nevertheless I did devise a new circular stressing the practical values of the book for specific purposes, proposed a new mail campaign, and had their generous and warm approval.

Evart and Mary Routzahn and I were often involved in conferences on publicity for Foundation projects, and I remember only one brief difference of opinion. We were about to publish the first *Social Work Year Book*, and I had proposed, both to introduce the entirely new volume and to put some of its special articles promptly into the hands of people who needed them, that we offer nearly all the articles for prepublication to specially selected periodicals. The general idea had full approval, but for one of the articles in the health field I had suggested Bernarr Macfadden's *Physical Culture*, a journal of wide circulation and less than scholarly reputation. There was objection.

I reported a recent meeting with Harry Emerson Fosdick, at which he had ferreted out my interest in writing and told me of some of his own experiences.

"I have many requests for articles," said Dr. Fosdick, "and usually I must refuse. You may be surprised to learn that I am now doing a piece for *Physical Culture*. I know that most people would think *Harper's* or *The Atlantic* more suitable, and better for my reputation; but you see, many of the readers of those magazines do come to Riverside and hear my sermons. I have things to say that I think would be helpful to readers of *Physical Culture*, and I must try to reach them where they are."

The point was won, not merely for that article but as a matter of policy. The Foundation also would "try to reach them where they are."

Evart Routzahn's handwriting was, to say the least, unique, and became historic. Russell Sage Foundation had early established an Education Division, which took a pioneering interest in educational measurement. The Division's director, Leonard P. Ayres,[5] published in 1912 his first *Scale for Measuring the Quality of Writing of School Children*. (We were still selling it by the many thousands when I came to the Foundation.) Mr. Ayres believed that the then-prevalent practice of teaching "Spencerian" writing emphasizing beauty, was not good, and adopted the sensible principle of grading on the basis of ease and speed of reading.

His scale was based on accurately timed readings of samples of children's writing from 40 school systems in 38 states. It used a portion of Lincoln's Gettysburg Address, and proposed to display samples in eight gradations, marked from 90 down to 20. But among the many thousands of collected samples, none seemed poor enough for Grade 20. Just then Mr. Ayres received a penciled note from Mr. Routzahn. "Eureka!" he exclaimed, and promptly asked Evart to write the Grade 20 sample of the Gettysburg Address.

Another important member of the Department was Allen H.

[5] Mr. Ayres resigned in 1920 to become a vice president of the Cleveland Trust Company, with the president of which, Frederick H. Goff, he is believed to have earlier worked in setting up The Cleveland Foundation and helping Mr. Goff develop the community trust idea.

Eaton, who came nearer to artistic genius than anyone else on our staff. He had conducted a book and art store in Eugene, Oregon, after graduation from college, and had become acquainted with Robert W. de Forest, then both president of the Foundation and of the American Federation of Arts. Mr. Eaton was appointed a field secretary of the Federation, and in 1920 joined Surveys and Exhibits "to bring into the field of social work a greater appreciation of the vital relation of art and beauty to life."

Allen Eaton was small in stature, gentle voiced and kindly, but, like many persons with artistic temperament, with little regard for practicalities and no willingness to adjust to the views of others. My printers begged me not to let him into their press-rooms. He would hold up a giant press for hours, waiting until the outside light was just right for judging the depth of ink tone on a particular illustration being run.

On one occasion his office was frantic because he was due in minutes for an important radio broadcast, set for eleven o'clock, had left home at the usual commuting hour, but had neither appeared in his own office nor the broadcasting studio. Two hours later he wandered in, aglow with the beauty of the naked steel arches of the George Washington Bridge, which he had stopped to watch them build. "But your broadcast—"

He had an eloquent address, "Woodpiles and Haystacks," celebrating the simple arts of country life, which won him wide plaudits. When I joined the Foundation he was especially busy with exhibitions of immigrant art[6] which grew into his 1932 book, *Immigrant Gifts to American Life*.

It was he who suggested to workers in the Southern Mountains that an organization be formed to promote arts and crafts in the homes and schools of the region. As a result, the Southern Moun-

[6] How many of us knew that these are immigrant gifts: the notable sculptures of Augustus Saint-Gaudens, born in Ireland; among our coins, the 1893 half-dollar and the 1916 dime by Adolph Weinman, native of Germany, the 1915 silver dollar by Anthony de Francisci from Italy, the $10 and $20 gold pieces again by Saint-Gaudens; among painters, English-born Thomas Moran famous for his landscapes, from Germany a large group including William Ritschel, William Wendt, and Gustav Wiegand, and the former director of the Art School of Petrograd, Nicholas Roerich; graphic artists include Timothy Cole, the London-born pioneer wood engraver, Rudolph Ruzicka from Czechoslovakia, and wood-block printer Gustave Baumann from Germany; among illustrators, W. T. Benda (noted also for his masks) from Poland, Willy Pogany from Hungary, Joseph Urban from Austria, Hendrik Willem van Loon from Holland; perhaps greatest of the cabinetmakers was Duncan Phyfe of Scotland; and so the list grows, almost endlessly.

tain Handicraft Guild was organized in 1929. Much later, this interest flowered into his lovely book, *Handicrafts of the Southern Highlands* (1937). "What we thought was just common," wrote a farm girl who had just seen it, "Mr. Eaton thought was beautiful enough to put in his book."

Statistics

A single copy exists—it used to be in my own locked Publication Department file—of a book that was never published. An advance copy fell under the eye of an alert staff member who detected a number of mathematical errors and found the author arriving at conclusions not at all supported by the statistical evidence. The book seemed beyond retrieval, and was destroyed. That experience was in part the reason for especially careful statistical review of all subsequent Foundation publications, with setting up of a formal Division of Statistics in 1912, under Leonard P. Ayres.

Mr.—soon Colonel—Ayres was loaned to the government in World War I, took all his Foundation staff with him, and was put in charge of a statistics branch of General Staff. Soon he was furnishing weekly confidential statistical summaries to President Woodrow Wilson, and every morning at 8:30 gave General Pershing in France an up-to-the-minute report on the disposition and condition of troops, on arrivals and losses, and on equipment and supplies.

At the end of war duties he returned in 1920 to find his Division now designated "Department." But he shortly resigned, as already noted, and his wartime assistant, Ralph G. Hurlin, was appointed director.

Ralph Hurlin occupied that important post from 1920 until his retirement in 1958. Dr. Hurlin is self-effacing, able, and accurate. A chief function of his Department was the careful review of statistical aspects of all Foundation studies, and he extended this service, on request, to many organizations in the welfare field. The reliability of statistics prepared by, or reviewed by, Dr. Hurlin became proverbial.

Such supportive work, however important, does not make headlines. But when the Depression broke upon the country, bringing into astronomical figures expenditures for relief and the number of the unemployed, the Department began performing new functions discussed in the next chapter.

Industrial Studies

The Department of Industrial Studies was throughout its history under the able and autocratic direction of Miss Mary van Kleeck. My contacts with the Department were few, for Miss van Kleeck was one of the only three or four persons in the field of philanthropy with whom I could establish no rapport. Her earlier studies, chiefly on the conditions of women's work, were admirable. By the time I joined the Foundation it seemed to many of us that the Department's studies had become not so much objective pieces of research as platforms from which to express sweeping opinions on economic and political questions.

For instance, her first book after my arrival was *Miners and Management*, which concluded that "socialization of all natural resources as part of a planned economy is the only solution for the breakdown of the coal industry in the United States."[7] It was certain that most of the trustees, and perhaps all of them, disagreed with this conclusion, but it is a tribute to the spirit of academic freedom in foundations that the book was duly published under the Sage imprint, and Miss van Kleeck remained on staff until retirement age. It may have been more than coincidence, however, that *Miners and Management* was the first Russell Sage Foundation book to contain the "disclaimer" notice which then became general:

> While the general responsibility for management of the Foundation is vested in a board of twelve trustees, the responsibility for facts, conclusions, and interpretations rests with the research worker alone and not upon other members of the staff or upon the trustees. Publication under the imprint of the Foundation does not imply agreement by the organization or its members with opinions or interpretations of authors.

Recreation

In 1907, that year of beginnings, Lee F. Hanmer was enticed into the Foundation's Committee on Playground Extension from his job as New York's first Inspector of School Athletics. By 1913 a full Department of Recreation was formed, with Mr. Hanmer its director.

This genial, energetic man and his associates had a very sub-

[7] van Kleeck, Mary, *Miners and Management*. Russell Sage Foundation, New York, 1934, p. 228.

stantial share in the growth of playgrounds in America, both through the Foundation's original committee on this subject and subsequent aid to the Playground Association of America and its successor, the National Recreation Association. By the time of Mr. Hanmer's retirement in 1937, and discontinuance of the Department, playgrounds had grown from 90 in 1908 to 2,204, with a budget of $37 million a year.

Another early enterprise of the Department, this time the special concern of Mr. Hanmer's assistant, tall, blond Clarence A. Perry, was to investigate and stimulate the use of school buildings and grounds outside of school hours for recreation and other social and civic purposes. When in recent years bright-eyed innovators have come to me with their brilliant idea that since the taxpayers own the school plants, we ought to make full use of them for all sorts of public purposes, I take delight in agreeing enthusiastically, and suggest that as background information they get hold of Perry's 423-page book, *Wider Use of the School Plant*, published in 1910.

Recreation, however, was not really a book-publishing department. It issued more than a hundred pamphlets treating immediate situations, but few books. Messrs. Hanmer, Perry, and their associates were engulfed in programs the *History* was to call "kaleidoscopic." Interests included continuing cooperation with the playground organizations, efforts for a "safe and sane" Fourth, help in organizing Boy Scouts, Camp Fire Girls, sand-lot baseball, folk dancing,[8] improved movies, amateur dramatics, music as treatment for the insane, recreational surveys for cities . . .

When Mr. Hanmer was retiring in 1937, I said in the *RSF Bulletin*, "On the 1st of July Lee Hanmer retires from recreation to work on a farm. . . . And we, who have seen Mr. Hanmer's productive capacity in other fields, feared for the future of the AAA Crop Control Program until we learned this was to be a fruit and dairy farm."

[8] They induced a manufacturer of hurdy-gurdy music to produce one roll of folk dances, hired an organ-grinder for a day to use it when he refused to experiment at his own expense, and he drew crowds that interfered with traffic.

The Great Depression

AND THEN it happened.

Books about the Great Depression often imply it struck all in one black day. It was not quite like that. Losses were unbelievably terrible, then came reassurance and even some improvement, then it was worse, and then the bottom fell out. Here are main headlines from *The New York Times* for the closing days of October, 1929; of course the *Times* is a morning paper, so that the dates represent stock market gyrations for the previous day.

Wednesday, 23 October. STOCKS GAIN SHARPLY BUT SLIP NEAR CLOSE

Thursday, 24 October. PRICES OF STOCKS CRASH IN HEAVY LIQUIDATION / Total Drop of Billions / Paper Loss $4 Billion

SAYS STOCK SLUMP IS ONLY TEMPORARY / Professor [Irving] Fisher Tells Capital Bankers Market Rise Since War Has Been Justified

Friday, 25 October. WORST STOCK CRASH STEMMED BY BANKS / 12,894,650 SHARE DAY SWAMPS MARKET / LEADERS CONFER. FIND MARKET SOUND / Five Wall Street Bankers Hold Two Meetings in Morgan Office

Saturday, 26 October. STOCKS GAIN AS MARKET IS STEADIED. BANKERS PLEDGE CONTINUED SUPPORT. HOOVER SAYS BUSINESS BASIS IS SOUND

Sunday, 27 October. STOCKS HOLD FIRM IN NORMAL TRADING

Monday, 28 October. WALL STREET HUMS ON THE DAY OF REST TO CATCH UP WITH WORK

Tuesday, 29 October. STOCK PRICES SLUMP 14 BILLION IN NATION-WIDE STAMPEDE TO UNLOAD. BANKS TO

SUPPORT MARKET TODAY / Unexpected Torrent of Liquidation Again Hits Market

Wednesday, 30 October. STOCKS COLLAPSE IN 16,410,030-SHARE DAY, BUT RALLY AT CLOSE CHEERS BROKERS. BANKERS OPTIMISTIC, TO CONTINUE AID

My own diary for Tuesday the 29th has this note:

> This is the day of the greatest stock slump in history. At noon I went to a broker's office and watched the debacle for a while. Atmosphere heavy with smoke and stale air. Men crowding the room solid. No hysteria, just heavy hopelessness. "The market will not close," someone announces. "They must have discovered a few of us have got a little money left," mutters someone behind me. Prices jump unaccountably ten points one way or the other. New lows are announced as they come, over the bond ticker—the stock ticker is too far behind to matter now.

No one who did not himself go through those years can learn from any written record what it meant. An attempt at description is from the outset a lost cause, but since philanthropy sharply shifted its course to meet that flood of misery, an attempt must be made.

Background Thoughts

To recapture some of my own reactions to those days I have been reviewing diary entries and the few writings I managed to have published. Excerpts from one of the latter may be pertinent:

> Most of us have been so utterly dazed by the crash of the stock market and the attendant disappearance of fortunes and jobs that we have failed to notice other and far more significant crashes. We have not even observed that a whole new philosophy lies shattered about us, its fragments still brilliant but showing now their lacerating edges. . . .

> It had seemed a philosophy based on realities, and for a while it had seemed to work—even to work magnificently. . . . If it had any one name, that name was materialism . . . a brand new Enlightened Materialism which could have arisen in no era other than our own one of sudden and stupendous scientific advance. It was, so we thought, an entirely new basing of life on sure realities. . . .

> Science was in the midst of its comet-flare of progress and discovery. . . . Here, obviously, was the thing on which to found a philos-

ophy of realities—here, and in the trade which financed scientific discovery and brought its results to our own hands.

We turned our colleges largely into laboratories and schools of business. Our sages and philosophers were expert accountants and specialists in trade. We gave our new god Science most of our first-rate brains. . . . We were dazzled by authentic miracles, performed more reliably than those of the regularly canonized saints which had won the faith of earlier generations.

Meanwhile the gentlemen of trade, for reasons of their own, set about bringing these discoveries into every household. They hired an army of paid prophets, called advertising experts, to help them. . . . Heaven here and now was promised in terms of motor cars, cigarettes, tooth paste, sun-lamps, radios, rowing machines. . . .

We are now reaping in personal and general misery the results of the philosophy we followed. . . . Since the bright, hard philosophy of science and trade has so dismally failed, what shall we erect in its place? . . .

Human engineering, the effective use of power in man and for man, is catching the stride of that earlier miracle-worker, mechanical engineering. . . . A modern philosophy will base its values not upon supernatural revelation but upon human experience, including in that experience the whole realm of man's spirit as well as the data of his physical senses. [It] will recognize that a rich emotional life is as important for personality as intellectual achievement; that much concern for material advancement is definitely stunting; that the economic rules of the physical universe do not operate in all realms, but personality grows best by a generous giving of itself, is most intensified (paradoxically enough) not by centering attention upon itself but by broadening that attention to include a wide variety of other persons and other interests.[1]

I did not myself suffer severely financially. As already related, none of my modest assets was in common stocks. My half-time job with the Foundation was secure, though for some years no salary increases were granted.

Of course income from regular free-lance writing practically disappeared. In the three deepest depression years, 1931 through 1933, I sent out, including resubmissions, 406 manuscripts. All but 13 returned. Most catastrophic was 1933. Of 132 manuscripts sent out, all but two were returned or lost in the files of expiring

[1] In "Toward a Modern Philosophy," *World Unity Magazine*, March, 1934, pp. 361-372.

magazines. Of these two, one was published, but paid nothing. For the other I received $50, but the magazine died before it could be published.

Remembering how narrowly I had missed going on the Pinchot expedition and returning in late 1929 without a job, I could identify with the jobless who sold apples on the street corners. For apple-selling is not a mere colorful invention of popular accounts of depression days. That, and its equivalents, were all about us, and the experience of able personal friends. I hired as shipping clerk one such friend who was an Annapolis graduate. *The R S F Bulletin*[2] carried this note:

PRIVATE FLOWER SHOW. If you see an array of gay flowers attended by a smallish man on the R S F corner, it is more than likely Mr. Pete Carnatti [who] was chased by the police so often that the Foundation has now given him permission to put his wares on the private property of our Lexington Avenue coping.

But also, two issues later, this note:

UPSETTING THE APPLE CART. The apple woman, who won the sympathies of many R S F staff members in her long vigils at the corner of Fourth Avenue and 22d Street, is no longer at her post. Kindly inquiries elicited a new address for her—the Women's Prison. It seems that her apple selling was only camouflage for one of the regular dope stations of a N Y vice ring.

Financial Effects on Foundations

During the Depression many foundations lost a substantial part of their assets, at least in terms of market value, and a few perished.

One of the more drastic experiences was that of Julius Rosenwald Fund. Mr. Rosenwald's confidence in common stocks as late as May, 1929 has already been noted.[3] His Fund's investments in the 1930s were chiefly in the common stock of Sears, Roebuck and Company, which dropped from close to $200 per share in 1928 to a low of less than $10 in 1932, with complete suspension of dividends. If the Fund had met all its pledges, made when the

[2] A mimeographed house organ I originated in May, 1932. Its purpose was "keeping the various departments informed of each other's activities and letting us all know of the more important personal events and adventures of each of us." It was published "spasmodically," but usually quarterly, into 1948.

[3] See p. 18.

market was high, with cash and on time, it would have been wiped out. But fortunately—

In careful financial arrangements to meet this crisis, sister foundations helped generously. The General Education Board gave a number of emergency grants to Negro schools and colleges, thus making possible postponement of payment on the Fund's current pledges without hardship to the institutions concerned. The Carnegie Corporation, long interested in library service, appropriated a total of two hundred thousand dollars in 1932 and 1933 to support the program of library extension in southern counties. By agreement with the beneficiaries, interest rather than capital was paid on large pledges, and payments for current expenses were spread over a longer period than originally planned. These measures enabled the Fund to meet all its pledges and to continue active work for another sixteen years. Following this experience the Finance Committee regularly sold securities sufficient to cover all commitments for eighteen months in advance.[4]

Many foundations had conservative investments and suffered less severely. The record of Russell Sage Foundation, with which I had reason to be intimately acquainted, was not untypical. In 1929 the portfolio, consisting chiefly of bonds and real estate, had produced an income of $737,000, the highest thus far in its history. It was still $730,000 in 1932. But as the Depression deepened and continued, and later other factors drove down interest rates, income declined with disturbing regularity to $501,000 in 1944.

In view of declining income and other considerations, a steady effort was made to reduce the outside grants program. But the same stringencies which forced effort toward such reductions were also creating financial emergencies for most grantees. Their general contributors fell off drastically; at the same time depression-induced demands for their services skyrocketed. So some grants were increased rather than reduced; but the trend was downward. From $349,000 in 1932 grants dropped, fairly regularly, to $129,000 in 1946. Declining income also made it necessary to curtail some of the activities of the Foundation's own departments, and prevented a desired renewal of interest in such fields as community surveys and penology. Depression-induced drastic changes in the nature of programs of surviving departments are later discussed.

[4] Embree, Edwin R., and Julia Waxman, *Investment in People: The Story of the Julius Rosenwald Fund.* Harper and Bros., New York, 1949, pp. 206-207.

The Depression and New Foundations

With the collapse of many large fortunes in the Depression it
was assumed that for the foreseeable future few new foundations
would be created, and certainly none like the giants of the past.
This assumption proved completely in error.

Of the ten largest foundations now existing in the United
States, all with assets exceeding $300 million, five were created
in the 1930-1939 Depression decade. Some of these Depression-
born foundations were initially small, but they include The Ford
Foundation (initial assets only $25,000 but rapidly increased),
The Robert Wood Johnson Foundation, W. K. Kellogg Foundation, Lilly Endowment, and Alfred P. Sloan Foundation. In fact,
when Edition 4 of *The Foundation Directory* was published in
1971, 29 percent of the assets of all American foundations were
in the hands of the foundations established in the Depression
decade.

Shifting the Gears

Nearly every foundation, of course, found the new emergencies demanding changes in program. In the first years of the Depression private efforts tried to find jobs for the unemployed and
feed the starving. Prosperity was asserted to be "just around the
corner," and emergency drives were organized in all principal
cities to care for immediate needs. New York City in the fall of
1931 set up the Emergency Unemployment Relief (Gibson)
Committee with thirty thousand solicitors, which collected $18
million. Such committees, manned by civic and business leaders,
brought heavy pressure upon foundations to abandon programs,
whatever they might be, in order to meet the present emergency,
presumably for "just this year."

By this time experienced foundation executives had accepted
the doctrine that the limited and peculiarly free funds of foundations should not be given for relief or other palliative programs
but should be more adventuresomely expended for research, efforts to find cures, and prevention. Should this accepted doctrine
be modified in light of the present emergency? Many foundations
decided that it should. The Rockefeller Foundation made a 1931
appropriation of $750,000 to the New York City Emergency Un-
employment Relief Committee.

This was an especially severe problem for Russell Sage Foundation, with its central concern in "organizing charity." A meeting of the trustees was called in November, 1931, for sole consideration of this question. Advance memoranda presented both sides. In the midst of the meeting an urgent telephone call conveyed word of the Rockefeller action, and reportedly added biting words to the effect that no real man could stand up for a mere institutional policy while people were starving in the streets. After extended discussion this resolution was passed:

> Resolved, that the policy of the Russell Sage Foundation in the present emergency, as always, is in its permanent contribution to the improvement of living and social conditions by its studies and its wide cooperation with agencies, rather than by contributing directly to relief. Therefore, be it resolved that the Russell Sage Foundation make no contribution to the Emergency Relief Committee.

It was a difficult decision. Soon, however, New York City alone was spending from public funds some $18 million a month on relief. At that rate, the Foundation's income for a whole year would have paid the relief bill in New York City for hardly more than a single day, and its contribution might have done no more than delay for a day the necessary transfer to public auspices. Meanwhile, every department made contributions in its own field toward meeting Depression needs.

A Mountain Woman

A little later in the Depression I had finished an exhausting week at the National Conference of Social Work, listening to the concentrated miseries of the nation. To recover, my wife and I spent a few days in the Great Smoky Mountains in Tennessee, climbing each day a new peak.

We based ourselves at the Wonderland Club Hotel, and in that depressed year were the only guests in that vast hostelry except for a government agent in the farm allotment program, who one evening had dinner with us.

The agent had just returned from visiting a mountain woman who, all alone, managed somehow to scratch survival from her two acres, mostly on end.

"If the government could allot you two hundred dollars, what would you do with it?"

The woman thought a moment. Her cabin had no floor but the

packed earth, and light came through chinks in its wall. Finally
she said:
"Reckon I'd give it to the poor."

Charity Organization in the Depression[5]

Miss Joanna C. Colcord had been appointed Mary E. Richmond's successor as director of the Charity Organization Department just before I joined the Foundation, but could not leave her
duties as general secretary of the Minneapolis Family Welfare
Association until August, 1929.

Joanna Colcord in the years I knew her was a somewhat
buxom, usually jolly, able lady. With five generations of sea-
captain ancestors, she was born on shipboard in the South Seas,
and as a pleasant avocation collected and published lusty capstan
shanties in her *Roll and Go* and *Songs of American Sailormen.*
Ashore, she had studied under Miss Richmond in the New York
School of Philanthropy in 1910-1911, was author of one of the
Department's earliest books, *Broken Homes* (1919), had come
up through the Charity Organization Society of the City of New
York to her present Minneapolis position, and was Miss Richmond's own recommendation as successor. Experience with gales
and hurricanes, and the need to change course in heavy weather,
was useful background for piloting her Department through a
tumultuous fifteen years.

During the interregnum, under Miss Colcord's supervision *in
absentia*, the Department prepared a collection of Miss Richmond's speeches, with biographical notes, which we published
in 1930 as *The Long View.* The title came from this very quota-
ble section of an included letter:

> We have learned to take the long view, to realize that the very
> stars in their courses, not our small army alone, are overcoming the
> weakness and misery of the world.[6]

By the time Miss Colcord was actually on the scene the Depression was affecting all phases of the Foundation's work, but
none so intimately as that of the Charity Organization Depart-

[5] This and following sections borrow liberally from the Russell Sage Foundation history, previously cited. Since I wrote the sections dealing with the Depression through 1946, these borrowings, even if verbatim, are usually not identified.

[6] Colcord, Joanna C., and Ruth Z. S. Mann, *The Long View*: Papers and Addresses by Mary E. Richmond. Russell Sage Foundation, New York, 1930, p. 6.

ment. Provisions for relief and social welfare, the core of the Department's interest, underwent changes in the decade which can only be described as revolutionary, and in their extent unequaled in any other period in this country.

At first it was generally believed that this Depression, like many predecessors, would be brief. To meet the immediate emergency, nearly every city organized its special mayor's committee, or citizens' committee. Private welfare societies conducted special drives for funds and tried to carry the load. It was a time of improvisation and experiment, all on the local level—breadlines, commissaries, share-the-work, subsistence gardens, work relief, self-help cooperatives. President Hoover did appoint a national committee (in November, 1930) named the President's Emergency Committee for Employment, but merely for coordination and stimulation of local efforts.

One of Miss Colcord's first actions was calling a Conference on the Coming Winter in September, 1930, for executives of family welfare societies and financial federations. Her Department's own first project for meeting the new needs was the pamphlet, *Community Planning in Unemployment Emergencies*, summarizing the best experience that could be found. We got wide publicity on it, distributed over 9,000 copies free, chiefly through the President's Committee, and sold some 1,800.

By mid-1930 it was evident that a major emergency faced the country, though its duration was not yet guessed. The Department cleared decks for an intensive three-part study on how communities could organize unemployment relief.

The first part was historical, recovering the experience in earlier depressions, often buried in dust-covered files and out-of-print publications. It seemed silly to repeat the worst errors of the past, or flounder about when previous experience might point a clear path. The record was published as a 384-page book[7] in 1936, but some of its findings could be brought into earlier use.

The second part was a continuous study of developing relief methods in selected cities. This was based on field visits, correspondence, copies of regular reports, and newspaper clippings in some thirty selected cities. The field visits were made chiefly by Miss Colcord herself and her new assistant, Russell H. Kurtz —who later became editor of the *Social Work Year Book*.

[7] Feder, Leah Hannah, *Unemployment Relief in Periods of Depression*. Russell Sage Foundation, New York, 1936, 384 p.

These field visits uncovered such unusual relief expedients as fitting out a disused brewery as a barracks, issue of temporary currency printed on wood, and establishment of an Unemployed Citizens League which used its own unemployed barbers, machinists, fishermen, coal miners, and other workers to supply these services and materials to its own members.

It proved impossible to limit the field visits to fact finding; community leaders were eager to hear what was being done in other communities and to submit their own plans for comment and advice. Miss Colcord's 1932 Department Report included examples of such services:

> Advice was given in Seattle to chest and family society representatives on difficulties in co-operation with the Unemployed Citizens' League; in Portland on the avoidance of a commissary system; in Salt Lake City on distribution of Red Cross flour, and on plans for the care of the homeless. . . . [Mr. Kurtz] was able to assist the chest executive [in New Orleans] in marshaling the vital factual information from other cities that helped to put across a $750,000 bond issue.

The third part was a special study of work-relief methods and results, and much of the information gathered on the field visits was directed toward this particular project. Early findings were released in magazine articles, speeches, conferences, and correspondence. The complete study was hurried through the press and issued in August, 1932.[8]

Many improvisations of the early Depression period received special study. One of these was subsistence gardens. During 1932 quite a few communities set aside vacant lots where the unemployed could raise some of their own food. The Department published a pamphlet on community experience with such projects early in 1933.[9]

Certain other measures to meet the emergency called for disapproval and opposition. In spite of long experience with the evils of commodity distribution, breadlines and commissaries cropped up early in the Depression, and for a time spread and flourished. The Department advocated relief in cash instead of "in kind," and the evidence it supplied resulted in several of the larger cities abandoning giving relief in kind or grocery orders,

[8] Colcord, Joanna C., William C. Koplovitz, and Russell H. Kurtz, *Emergency Work Relief*. Russell Sage Foundation, New York, 1932, 286 p.

[9] Colcord, Joanna C., and Mary Johnston, *Community Programs for Subsistence Gardens*. Russell Sage Foundation, New York, 1933, 74 p.

and going over to cash relief. Later, the Department published a study on the subject, a quotation from which does much to present this case from the recipient's point of view:

> I got a check for $4.66 and I can tell you truly it was the best two weeks I lived since I've been on the Relief. I got about twice as much groceries for that money as I could get on a grocery order and besides I felt a different man. . . . In the last two weeks I always had a nickel or a dime to put in [the church collection box] when it came around. I tell you it made me feel good, that I was living like a man once more. And besides, I could buy myself some razor blades and little things I wanted and still have money left.[10]

The need for record forms during the emergency period resulted in a new social worker's "face sheet" and a financial data card which, with other similar forms earlier issued by this Department and Department of Statistics, sold nearly half a million in 1932. Everything was rush-rush—face sheets, pamphlets, publicity, books—which placed heavy but welcome burdens on the Publication Department. Books like *Emergency Work Relief* sometimes sold out almost by publication day and had to be speedily reprinted.

When Government Moved In

As the Depression deepened local communities were finding they could no longer meet the bare subsistence needs of their citizens. Many states set up emergency relief administrations. In a political upheaval Franklin D. Roosevelt and the New Deal came to Washington. Federal loans to states were succeeded in 1933 by outright federal grants for relief.

The Civil Works Administration mushroomed briefly as a gigantic federal experiment in work relief, to be succeeded in 1934 by national programs of work and direct relief under supervision of the Federal Emergency Relief Administration (FERA). While assistance from voluntary agencies continued at about usual dollar levels, it represented a rapidly decreasing proportion of total relief. Workers—trained, semi-trained, and untrained—flocked to the public agencies. State and federal government assumed vastly increased responsibilities for relief.

In 1935 was launched the Works Progress Administration

[10] Colcord, Joanna C., *Cash Relief*. Russell Sage Foundation, New York, 1936, p. 230.

(later called the Work Projects Administration, but in either case the WPA). In August of the same year the Social Security Act became effective, constituting the most important single act of social legislation in American history.

This massive move of government into areas that had been the prime responsibility of voluntary agencies and private philanthropy raised sharply what is perhaps the fundamental question for private philanthropy: what is its proper place, or does it have a place at all, in a developing welfare state? As early as 1921 Cornelia J. Cannon[11] had hoped for the day "when our philanthropic obligations will be brought to our attention, not by an appeal from boards of directors, but by a tax-bill from the properly constituted authorities." The winds of change still blow strong in the direction of tax-supported services, but in my view the "appeals from boards of directors" have not notably diminished, and the removal of the burden of mere relief has opened to private philanthropy widening opportunities for useful and creative service.

Certainly, as government moved in, calls for service to government itself came to Russell Sage Foundation, involving not only Charity Organization but nearly all of us in the Foundation.

Some Other Departments

Mr. and Mrs. Routzahn had a large share in helping the public understand the rapid changes in social work occurring during the Depression. Contributors were usually aware only of the primary needs for food and shelter; social workers had moved on to a concern with the maladjustments of family life, vocational training, and many other secondary problems. As the Depression deepened, more and more people came into direct contact with social work and social workers; they frequently distrusted and disliked their methods and were bewildered by the differences between public and private social work. Significantly, one branch of the original Department of Surveys and Exhibits was shortly named Department of Social Work Interpretation.

Ralph Hurlin's statistical services to various governmental relief bureaus would alone have justified the Foundation's refusal to contribute to direct relief, if such a contribution entailed—as indeed it would have—a reduction in those services. The Depart-

[11] Cannon, Cornelia J., "Philanthropic Doubts," *Atlantic Monthly*, September, 1921, pp. 289-300.

ment of Statistics became a center of advice, information, and sometimes operation in the whole field of statistics of relief.

One early project was an unemployment survey undertaken by some sixty temporary workers loaned by Civil Works Administration. They were directed by Dr. Hurlin, housed in one of our exhibition halls, and were on a three-day-a-week schedule to "spread the work." One day when I reached the Foundation pickets were on parade. Big black-lettered signs conveyed this demand of these part-time relief workers:

TWO WEEKS' PAID VACATIONS FROM WORK RELIEF

A vaster project was done for New York City itself, which by 1934 was spending some $18 million a month for relief purposes. On Welfare Commissioner William Hodson's urgent requests, Dr. Hurlin and his assistant, Miss Anne E. Geddes, were loaned to the city's Emergency Relief Bureau to organize and conduct for a time a new statistical service. The task proved "herculean." Full weekly reports were issued to the commissioner, administrative heads of all divisions, and some 45 large district offices. At its peak the statistical project was employing 341 workers.

Play for All

A report of the Department of Recreation just before the Depression had proclaimed that "Leisure is no longer the gift to the rich, but is rapidly becoming the possession of all economic classes on an extensive scale." Mr. Hanmer was being prophetic in a sense he neither desired nor intended. The rest of his service with the Foundation was a period of deep depression, with many millions of the unemployed desperately needing recreational outlets for their enforced leisure.

The program of the Department was profoundly altered to meet these emergency needs. Mr. Hanmer and other members of his Department contributed ideas, advice, material, and frequently personal service to recreation programs which were in many areas expanding rapidly to supply profitable occupation for the increased "leisure."

Loans and Credit

The Department of Remedial Loans of course found the problems of the needy borrower multiplied as the Depression deepened. It had also a small official part in one of the most colorful events of the early Depression.

On Friday, 3 March 1933, just before Roosevelt's inauguration, I was conferring with Mr. Harrison when a secretary came in with an urgent note. There was a run on New York savings banks. The next day all New York banks were closed, as well as those in many other states. On Monday the new President declared a national banking holiday. Mr. Nugent was at that time secretary of the New York State Credit Union League, and he had to sit up most of the night the moratorium was determined and then order all credit unions closed, since they were regarded as banking institutions.

For about a week checks could not be cashed—not even travelers' checks, as some of our field people discovered—nor savings deposits be withdrawn, but we managed with what we had, and the general spirit was surprisingly good. My diary for 15 March notes:

> It is now a little over a week after the beginning of the first "bank holiday" in my experience. . . . It was all very jolly, taken in good spirit by everybody. Stores still did credit business and at first the movies were crowded—people were making a Roman holiday of it. Now, after more than a week, many banks are open again. Savings banks usually allow withdrawals of only $25. What in prospect would have been a black panic week was for most people (not bankers, perhaps) a week of vivid, interesting living, when each person had his tales of how he managed.

Because of the broad economic interests of its successive directors, Leon Henderson and Rolf Nugent, the Department took an even keener interest in the effects on our total economy of borrowing in all its forms, and particularly consumer credit.

Pursuing one of these broader interests, bouncy, aggressive Leon Henderson confronted swearing, table-pounding General Hugh S. Johnson, National Recovery Administration head, in behalf of consumers who were also borrowers. As editor of *The R S F Bulletin* I interviewed Henderson and published this "exclusive account" of the conversation:

Gen. Johnson: "Xpq! Xxx! Blank-Blankety!"
Mr. Henderson: "ZXT! Xxx and XX! Blank-blankety-BLANK!"
Gen. Johnson: "I need a guy like you on my staff!"
P. S.: Next day Mr. Henderson got a telegram reading: "EXPECT NEXT MOVE FROM YOU BY REPORTING FOR DUTY— JOHNSON"

Leon Henderson joined the General on 2 January 1934 as assistant to the administrator in charge of consumer aspects of all NRA codes, "for a limited period." He never returned to the Foundation, but in the next few years occupied a succession of important government posts, including consulting economist, WPA; executive secretary, Temporary National Economic Committee; Securities and Exchange commissioner; member, Advisory Commission to the Council of National Defense; and administrator, Office of Price Administration. "It is only a matter of time," Leon predicted when he took the last of these jobs, "till I shall be the most damned man in the country."

After Mr. Henderson officially resigned, Rolf Nugent was appointed department director, and in 1938 the name was changed to Department of Consumer Credit Studies.

Public Welfare

With the expansion of both state and federal programs for relief, the Charity Organization Department's chief concern began to be public welfare. Wrote Miss Colcord:

> The Department's program became a breathless rush to keep abreast of the changes and their implications. Constant field work, and much public speaking, all with promotional as well as research emphasis, became necessary. The output of periodical articles by members of the staff doubled and trebled; there was no time for the preparation of books and pamphlets which would have been out of date before they saw print.

One of the co-authors of *Emergency Work Relief*, Russell H. Kurtz, was her chief help in this period of stress. Mr. Kurtz, lean, energetic, imaginative, and always to be counted upon for at least one good story or outrageous pun at our informal luncheons (45 cents plus a nickel tip in those years), had previous experience in personnel work in industry, and both private and public social work experience as general secretary of the Family Welfare Society and director of the Department of Public Charities in Akron, Ohio. One of his early and prophetic projects under Miss Colcord was a pamphlet, *Looking Toward a Public Welfare Plan*.

When Mr. Hall retired as *Social Work Year Book* editor, the very able Mr. Kurtz was appointed to this post, in 1935. But the

Year Book also was necessarily deeply concerned with public welfare, and effective cooperation between the two departments continued.

Moreover, the energetic editor, remembering that his "year book" was biennial, thought he could also manage another related publication in the "off" year. Noting how ill-trained were many of the new workers in public agencies, he brought together a group of able writers, wrote an Introduction, and in 1938 we published *The Public Assistance Worker.* I carried this note on Publication Department's experience with it in the April *R S F Bulletin:*

> We had premonitions about *The Public Assistance Worker,* edited by Russell H. Kurtz, and printed 4,000. Then Miss Bailey up and said it was a musty book of social work, or maybe a *must* book, and we told a few people she did, and before we knew it 3,200 of those few wanted the book, so we got pretty mad and ordered 3,000 more even before it was published. Somebody in Chicago (the body called the Amer Public Welfare Assn) wanted 800, and in an unguarded moment we let the NYC Emer Relief Bur. know about it, and some of their employes began strolling into the office, cash in hand; since the elevator operators *would* bring them up, we had to take their money—1,376 moneys from this one group. We sent out some postcards. Then the first 4,000 were gone before the next 3,000 got in, so we sent more postcards telling people we couldn't fill their orders right now, and please not to order any more for a bit. But they just wouldn't listen. So we got even madder and ordered 3,000 more, which will make 10,000 in print within 2 months of publication. . . .

> It has averaged more than a thousand a week the first five weeks, broken all R S F records for fast production (idea to book in seven months), for first *year* sales (and still has eleven months to go), and when the reviews begin to come in, it ought to start to sell right nicely.

Miss Colcord took on a new research assistant in 1936, Donald S. Howard, formerly area statistician for the WPA in Colorado and director of research and statistics for the Colorado Relief Administration. Appropriately, Mr. Howard's chief task was to do a definitive study of the WPA. A demon researcher, he spent years digesting the voluminous materials already on file, collecting new data by field visits and correspondence, conferring in Washington (he did not always see eye-to-eye with the administrators), and then revising and updating manuscript as the many administrative changes occurred. He was also frequently interrupted by calls for special service growing out of his fund of knowledge. As a result his 879-page tome was not published until 1943, when the WPA program was being liquidated in view of heavy employment (and draft calls) in World War II. It remains the substantially complete record of federal relief policies during the latter half of the Depression decade, and the definitive report of the largest works program undertaken by any government for the relief of unemployment.[12]

Bigger Man, What Now?

As the Great Depression grew to a close, I began to wonder what lessons it might have for persons above the relief level. The American little man was having his day in court. Social Security laws had spread over him a protective cloak, though still a thin one. But what of those of us who have the dubious privilege of charting our own course to security? Once that was believed to be mainly a matter of foresight and character. The Depression had blasted that belief.

I began asking my friends in all walks of life what the Depression had taught them about their own security. Many of them had been pondering the problem, and answers were fascinatingly varied. (The names used below are fictitious.)

Mr. Nathan was a stock salesman. The initial crash left him untouched, for though it ruined his customers, he had been canny enough not to trust the stocks he sold but to stow away all his own assets in a bank. And then that bank folded. Now he trusts "nothing, especially not banks. Next time I have some money, I'll put some in gold in foreign countries. Some in the best form of cash I can find in safety deposit vaults. No promise of high income will coax it into any new shell game."

Mr. Lang, a city planner, feared chiefly inflation. He would invest in common stocks in basic industry, to have a "solid percentage of possession in industrial plants." But nothing on margin.

An elderly lady I met on a train in Montana pointed out that she had no dependents, and the best investment was "in yourself. If I was younger, I would take courses, buy myself books—and spend some just for fun. But I'd spend most of it so that I could

[12] Howard, Donald S., *The WPA and Federal Relief Policy*. Russell Sage Foundation, New York, 1943. 879 p.

make a better living afterward. Since at my age there's no point
in that, I'm traveling."

A book publisher, concerned for an only daughter, did not
plan to save up money for her, "but if we can give her right now
a little better education than usual, she is certain of having that
asset all her life."

Others emphasized high insurance, or mutual savings banks,
or laying away nonperishable consumer goods, with the excess
probably tradable for perishable necessities. Alice Foster thought
real security consists in getting rid of needs instead of storing up
property.

Land was the choice of several, one proposing two farms, one
in the United States, one in Canada. In a bad depression one
could retire to the farm and at least have food and shelter.

A sailor friend proposed a boat. One could live aboard,
go South in the winter where few clothes would be needed, perhaps have a vegetable garden on a deserted island, use the wind
for power, and pay no taxes.

The manager of a large New York department store, after
scorning diamonds—if Great Britain should release all the diamonds already mined in Kimberley, the world market would be
flooded and diamonds would be nearly worthless—came out for
art objects. "They are the only things I know which have in-
trinsic value and are a natural monopoly." Rembrandt will paint
no more. True, sales would be difficult in the depth of a depression, but only in the rarity of genius is there permanent value.

Another suggestion, appropriate for this book, was the value
of pure philanthropy:

> Help your friend who is in temporary financial difficulty. Give
> your chore man better-than-usual wages and a special unexpected
> gift when he is up against it. If a promising young chap you know
> wants to go through college and can't afford it, advance him the
> money. Invest in such ways not only your money but your time and
> interest.
>
> How often have you seen a simple kindness bring in a legacy? Not
> every day, perhaps, but I'll wager more people cash in on kindness
> than on sweepstakes tickets. You will miss the best results if you in-
> vest in other people selfishly, but for the moment consider it solely
> from the selfish viewpoint. Granted that half of the people you help
> will be ungrateful, or never in a position to return your favors; the
> remainder may return them with more interest than you are likely to
> get from any of your so-called practical investments.

Besides, we are in a social world now. Your other solutions are nearly all of the kind that seem to work out for the individual but are likely to ruin society as a whole. If any considerable proportion of us invested in people, a serious depression would have no chance of starting.[13]

[13] I published these responses at greater length in "Bigger Man, What Now?" *Liberty*, 2 January 1937.

CHAPTER 5

A Note on City Planning

M Y FIRST CONCERN with professional city planning began almost as soon as I joined Russell Sage Foundation. For just then it was launching the Regional Plan of New York and Its Environs, the most ambitious single enterprise it had ever sponsored.

City planning was not new to the Foundation. The Forest Hills Gardens experiment begun in 1909 was a suburban planning project. A number of grants had been made for planning projects elsewhere and to the National Conference on City Planning.

The Regional Plan

Then in the early 1920s trustee Charles D. Norton, a former associate of Daniel H. Burnham in the planning of Chicago, became greatly concerned about the situation in New York. Politics had brought in an administration which, to put it gently, had "a complexion unsympathetic to planning." Moreover, a sound plan for New York would necessarily involve its environs, and these included territory in three states, New York, New Jersey, and Connecticut. It would be useless for New York planners to start a trans-Hudson bridge on Washington Heights unless New Jersey planners agreed on its termination in Fort Lee. In the absence of interstate compacts, it seemed necessary that a private agency formulate the needed regional plan.

Mr. Norton took his vision to his fellow trustees in February, 1919. A 1921 committee considered this project, later described as "almost terrifying in scope," and decided that the work might take some four years and cost "as much as $300,000." (It came to over $1 million, plus free office space.)

In spite of the death of Mr. Norton in 1923, the project grew rapidly. Frederick P. Keppel became the first secretary to the Committee on Regional Plan, but shortly resigned to become president of Carnegie Corporation of New York. Engineering studies were begun by Nelson P. Lewis, and upon his death in 1924 were continued by his son, Harold Lewis.

The services of Thomas Adams were obtained in 1923 for general direction. Mr. Adams was a Scotsman, and already prominent in planning circles in Great Britain and Canada. I knew this short, solidly built, pipe-smoking gentleman only in his later years, at the very end of his work on the Regional Plan and still later when we were publishing his *Outline of Town and City Planning*. He was competent, widely experienced, and a good administrator, but I did not think him strikingly original or imaginative.

The Plan was a Sage Foundation project, though for better public acceptance it was actually not published by the Foundation but by the Committee on Regional Plan, which was given separate status and received "grants" from the Foundation. But to house the Committee the Foundation built a tenth floor onto its own building, most of the Committee members were Sage-related, and the Foundation staff contributed heavily to the work and to the published volumes. Since it was not merely a physical plan, but embraced "the commercial, the industrial, the social, and the artistic values and possibilities" of the region, the assistance of the departments in such areas as recreation, population statistics, the arts, industrial studies, even penology, were pertinent and helpful. Indeed, when it was finished James Ford said of it:

> There can be little doubt that this series of ten volumes is the most comprehensive and valuable urban study yet made in America. . . . The Russell Sage Foundation, by underwriting nine years of comprehensive study by a large staff of competent professional men and technicians, has made a contribution to constructive thinking and action which is notable in the history of American philanthropic foundations.[1]

Although my Publication Department was not actually responsible for promotion and sale of the eight Survey and two Plan volumes in which the Plan was presented, I was called in as consultant and needed to be closely familiar with content. It was a

[1] *The American Economic Review*, Vol. XXII, No. 3, Sept. 1932, p. 539.

mind-stretching experience. Here was a Plan looking ahead forty years (1925 to 1965), covering a region with a population of already 10,000,000 but with density variations per square mile from only 45 persons to 104,000, and with land values ranging from $57 to $460,000 per acre.

Looking back at it now, more than forty years after its formal presentation, one finds most of the proposals sound, and many realized. The George Washington and Whitestone Bridges, the around Manhattan "continuous highway for the most part on or adjacent to the waterfront," circumferential highways, came about in substantially the positions suggested. Some of the recent population shifts, and the presently severe racial problems, were not foreseen. Perhaps the greatest contribution was the popularization of planning itself.

For the Foundation had no intention of foisting upon the public a finished, final plan, to be followed in every detail. The Letter of Presentation itself said:

> Those who have been engaged upon its preparation have realized from the beginning that they have no power to impose their ideas on the community and that all they can do is to bring forward well-reasoned proposals in the hope that these may arouse interest and commend themselves to public opinion and to the judgment of experts.[2]

As one step in popularizing the Plan, the Foundation commissioned Robert L. Duffus, distinguished free-lance author and longtime editorial writer for *The New York Times*, to prepare a single-volume presentation of the Plan's more important features. When the manuscript was completed I sat in on the title conference, which came up with *New York Tomorrow* as a catchy description. We informed Mr. Duffus of our unanimous choice, and met violent objection. We expostulated that the people who paid for the book ought to have at least some say in its titling, and we really believed this was an excellent choice.

"Ah," said Mr. Duffus, "but I also write other books, including a new Latin-American novel. If you insist on this title, the book lists will this year read thus:

Duffus, Robert L., *New York Tomorrow*
Duffus, Robert L., *Tomorrow Never Comes*."

The title was changed to *Mastering a Metropolis*.

[2] *The Graphic Regional Plan*, Vol. One, Regional Plan of New York and Its Environs, New York, 1929, p. 8.

The Plan was formally presented at a large public meeting on 27 May 1929. At the same time a Regional Plan Association was formed as a citizen organization, charged with its promotion and further development. The Foundation gave it an initial $25,000 grant "to enable it to get a proper start and secure contributions from other sources." But the date was 1929, and the Depression intervened. Some substantial contributions were obtained, but the Foundation was to continue its contributions for a long period, the most recent being made in 1947.

Working with Mr. Orton

Lawrence M. Orton, who as Mr. Glenn's assistant had brought me to the Foundation, had on two occasions worked with the Regional Plan Committee, and in 1929 was its secretary, with major editorial responsibilities in publishing the exhaustive Report. When development of the Plan was turned over to the Regional Plan Association, Mr. Orton had to choose between remaining with Russell Sage Foundation in some other capacity or going to the new private organization. The planning virus had bitten deep and the disease was already chronic. He went to the Regional Plan Association in 1932 and by the next year was its secretary and general director.

On 1 January 1938 New York City entered a new era with government under charter. Along with other reform features, the Charter provided for a City Planning Commission of seven members, charged with not only the usual functions of preparing a master plan, advising about zoning changes, and the like, but in New York with setting up the budget for capital expenditures in an attempt to remove school buildings, libraries, and all permanent improvements from the area of local pressure groups and political patronage into the regularized planning development a great city should have.

Probably no other living person knew so much about physical conditions in New York City, or had so intensively considered the planning aspects of its future, as Mr. Orton. His appointment to the Planning Commission was inevitable, and he assumed office as Commissioner in 1938. In 1969, he was the only member who had continuous service, and was vice-chairman. He has since retired.

Because of our acquaintance and mutual confidence, I was early drawn into operations of the Regional Plan Association,

sometimes with voluntary advice on publicity problems, sometimes with paid writing assignments.

Then as the Depression deepened, Mayor Fiorello LaGuardia
appointed a committee on city planning, which offered relief employment to a small army of investigators, draughtsmen, and
skilled workers who made detailed studies of traffic, zoning, population density, and other aspects of planning for America's
largest city, to a total expenditure of $1 million. Mr. Orton
served as secretary and was in fact directing head. I functioned
as special writer to the committee. One task was to analyze in
great detail some thirteen diverse New York areas. The technicians would make careful studies and detailed maps. I would sit
in on a number of conferences in which the technicians and planners would consider changes desirable for these neighborhoods
in the light of past history, present situation, and reasonable future. Then, great rolled maps in hand, I would retire to my Tenafly home[3] and draft a report. After conference and revision, it
was issued as a mimeographed booklet. The titles name the
neighborhoods and suggest the varieties of problems we
encountered:

East Harlem, a Deteriorated Neighborhood
West Harlem, a Crowded Area
Riverdale—Future of the Separate House
Long Island City, an Industrial Center
Greenwich Village, a Transition Area
Bay Ridge, and the Two-Family House
Forest Hills, a Suburb in the City
East Bronx, a City in the Making
Yorkville, Rebuilding an Old Section
Sutphin Boulevard, and Racial Changes
Woodside, Possible Self-contained Area
Gravesend, Some Topographical Influences
Flushing, and the Moderate Priced Home

A Few Speeches

A more interesting assignment, done for Mr. Orton and the
Regional Plan Association but with Depression overtones, was

[3] Shortly after our first son, Frank, was born in 1935, we moved to Tenafly, New
Jersey, where a third-floor office has been the setting (in both senses of that word)
for nearly all my writing since. The children—there were three boys—early learned
that Daddy was not to be disturbed when at work. If the house caught fire, they
could come up and remove the typewriter, in which case I might follow.

preparation of a series of "speeches" on aspects of planning in the
New York region. Some of this material was incorporated into
Association publications, but its chief use was with teams of lecturers in schools and before men's service clubs, women's clubs,
and public meetings, the lecturers being paid, I believe, by WPA
but working under Association supervision.

I prepared basic lectures on such topics as "Finding a Place to
Live," "You and Highways," "A Place to Play," "Moving Moun-
tains," "Planning for Quiet," and a view of the Plan as a whole,
"Looking Forward." The research included the full Regional
Plan documentation, later studies of the Regional Plan Association, material from the Port of New York Authority (which
proved only too helpful with detailed statistics and then further
statistics to prove how inaccurate all statistics must be), the U.S.
Department of Commerce, Bureau of the Census, Real Property
Inventory, and much else. The problem was to condense these
masses of data into story form that might interest untrained
adults and children.

In "Planning for Quiet" I was able to point out that in Herald
Square the ordinary noise level was so high that an African lion
could roar his loudest roar without being noticed by people as
much as thirty feet away—unless they saw his tail waving. Writing in 1936 it was possible to note that the Depression, assumed
to have benefited no one but bankruptcy lawyers, had in fact
helped recreation. Unpaid taxes brought into public ownership
land needed for playgrounds, and the tumbling land values
made possible purchase of other required plots. Relief workers,
instead of raking leaves, were beginning to be used in fixing up
neglected parks, building brand new ones, and converting vacant
lots into bustling, useful playgrounds. In 1934-35 New York
had an average of 40,000 such workers so employed, and created
112 new playgrounds.

"Moving Mountains" compared New York's problems in moving goods to the Great Pyramid, which covers 13 acres and
weighs 4,883,000 tons. As to food, each of us eats about one ton
a year. With the Region's population then about 11.5 million, it
was necessary to move into the Region more than two Great
Pyramids of food a year. Coal was the equivalent of six Great
Pyramids, oil products another eight. And then manufactures,
land and ocean freight. . . .

The effort was not to stun or impress, but to lead the individual to realize that sound planning was necessary, and for his benefit:

> The purpose of city planning is not to create something vast and imposing and probably useless, but to arrange all the city's shuttle-cock of movement, all the cogs and gears of its industry, all its humming life, so that you and I may find it a comfortable, healthful, happy place to live.[4]

Zoning and Mr. Bassett

There are "inventions" in the social sciences no less than in the physical sciences, and presently they may be more needed. One of the most useful of those social inventions, at least in preserving human and economic values in cities, is zoning, and in America Edward M. Bassett, "father of zoning," is chief inventor.

In some respects zoning is not new. Ancient cities in India regulated heights of buildings in accordance with street widths, Augustan Rome restricted industries to certain districts. But we Americans are a queer people, usually more concerned about property rights than human rights. So for a long time we "protected" the owner's right to use his property for anything he pleased, no matter what happened to the neighbors. A boiler factory might start up next door to a nursery, without any regard for the health and welfare of the babies.

Mr. Bassett, lawyer trained, knew that the courts would scarcely uphold what would seem the sensible basis for zoning—restrictions we accept in order to have like protection from our neighbors. But he saw that the advent of the skyscraper and the subway were in New York making degrees of congestion physically possible—and profitable for the individual landowner—which were a real threat to health and safety.

Health and safety—those were the words with which to charm the court! With a few other farsighted individuals he had an ordinance drawn up regulating the height, area, and use of buildings, and use of land, as an extension of the police power in the interest of health, safety, morals, and the general welfare. This first comprehensive attempt at zoning became a law in New York City in 1916. The courts upheld it. The Foundation made grants

---

[4] "Looking Forward: Planning for the New York of the Future." Manuscript, April, 1936.

for a number of years to the Zoning Committee of New York City, chaired by Lawson Purdy but of course including Mr. Bassett, which supported this pioneering zoning law and promoted the principle elsewhere.

In the 1930s Mr. Bassett asked the Foundation to sponsor a definitive volume on zoning which he proposed to write. We published not only *Zoning* (1936), which speedily became the chief authority in its field, but a later brief treatise of his on *The Master Plan*, issued in 1938. I worked with Mr. Bassett in these years, and grew greatly to admire his selfless devotion. As the recognized chief legal authority in the field, one would assume he might have had a very lucrative practice; but big money would have been in cases trying to upset or skirt the zoning laws. Mr. Bassett was not interested. He conducted free zoning clinics at conferences, and many other of his services were unpaid.

Zoning flourished. By making the shoe-box skyscraper with its maximum density illegal, it changed the skylines of our cities more effectively than architectural precept. Perhaps because judges also have homes which need protection, the courts approved ever stricter zoning laws, stretching the principle as far as residential districts requiring as much as two acres for a private house. To spread the idea, I tried to stimulate articles which would reach the interested citizen, and myself did several such.[5] But in spite of its obvious advantages and the clearing of legal obstacles, surprising gaps and deficiencies remain.

Tenafly Planning Board

When we moved to Tenafly we found our new house numberless. It was built on what had been a large estate, and was reached by an extension of an existing street where houses were already numbered, beginning at 1. We did not favor a minus number or a decimal, so I attended an early meeting of the Tenafly Planning Board, seeking a solution. They heard me, and rashly asked my views as a new local citizen on some of the other problems they had been discussing. Fresh from my planning studies, I had some quite definite views.

Soon they wanted me to serve on the Planning Board. I was willing, but there was a problem. The Tenafly Planning Board

[5] Including "Want to Insure Your Home Free? Then get a zoning law which will restrict property use and protect your neighborhood," *The Rotarian*, October, 1940; "When Is a Restriction Really a Protection?" *House Beautiful*, December, 1943.

is nonpolitical, with party affiliation never asked; but the incumbent Mayor had a personal friend for that year's vacancy. However, the Board possessed a small budget, so they elected me executive secretary in early 1937. Later, when a regular appointment was available, I became an unpaid citizen member and so served as long as I was willing, which was some twenty-five years.

This viewing of planning at the local, highly personal level was most enlightening. Our Board consisted of six citizen members, and three *ex officio*: the mayor, a councilman, and the borough engineer. We met regularly once a month, and in special session when business required. Weekends we not infrequently had informal sessions, tramping over proposed subdivisions to see for ourselves the lay of the land and the possibilities of proposed new streets.

Tenafly is a suburban community, a little north of the then newly opened George Washington Bridge. Most of the still unoccupied land was on the steep western slope of the Palisades which rise to as much as 400 feet above the Hudson in this area. There was a zoning ordinance, but it needed revision.

So we had, *in parvo*, most of the problems of planning everywhere. When we tried to put half-acre restrictions on houses on the difficult Palisades slope, lawyers for developers threatened suit for property confiscation, and even a former mayor argued that we were impoverishing the Borough by reducing taxes— though studies have shown that extra school and other costs result in higher taxes in denser population areas. We won that battle.

Sometimes we lost. Public hearings, in particular, were disappointing. However much a proposal might benefit the general citizen, he usually failed to appear at hearings; but the developer, or proposer of a new gas station seeking a variance in a residential area, was there armed with legal talent and loud voices, and sometimes he won.

In efforts to inform the public we arranged special program meetings, got reasonably good press coverage, offered prizes for high-school essays on planning subjects, and had one meeting a year when high-school youths served as the board. In my work with foundations I had learned of The Eno Foundation in Connecticut, devoted to "study and research on highway traffic and related problems." With the aid of their studies, we added to our zoning ordinance a new off-street parking section. Every busi-

ness establishment, hotel, restaurant, theater, or similar structure
thereafter constructed was required to provide off-street parking
appropriate for its expected employes and customers. Every
private house had to provide a garage or off-street parking area
for at least one car. It was one of the earliest and best such ordi-
nances in the country. To this day no overnight parking is permitted on any street in Tenafly. Streets are for moving vehicles,
they are not garages. (New York, please copy.)

We were not always unanimous, even as a Board. One of our
regulations required that no new street could have a grade of
more than 10 percent; anything steeper would entail severe hazard, particularly under winter driving conditions. A developer
on the steep Palisades slope presented a subdivision which, to
maximize profit by getting the most lots, was gridiron in pattern,
with a street running straight up the slope at much more than 10
percent grade in some sections. The afternoon before the meeting I had taken a walk and seen the bulldozers already cutting
in the street.

At the meeting I objected violently, and mentioned the bulldozers. Our engineer member said the developer just had
to rush, and we would have to approve the plan anyway, for on
that steep slope any other scheme would lose several lots and
make the development uneconomic. I may have been a little
angry. I said that if the street went in, sooner or later we would
have a severe accident, with possibly a life lost. Whatever the
extra cost to the builder, I hoped none of us would vote
approval, and suggested that if the engineer was also receiving
pay from the builder as his surveyor, he had better disqualify
himself from voting.

We won that one, and now Churchill Road slabs up the Pali-
sade slope at safer grades. The gash in the hillside for the proposed road is still visible, but nature is healing it.

As a part of personal philanthropy, perhaps even more important than the giving of money, I recommend the giving of personal service—as a volunteer in a hospital or elsewhere, service
on boards in churches, schools, libraries, official town bodies, or
wherever else one's interest and talent suggest.

CHAPTER 6

World War II

As war clouds gathered in Europe in the late 'Thirties my concern increased, particularly as many of my compatriots seemed almost pleased, for munitions orders from foreign governments and our own "preparedness" were bringing an end to the Great Depression. We, of course, would have sense enough to stay out, though we might be the profitable arsenal of democracy. My contrary view failed to get a hearing.

Hitler invaded Poland on 1 September 1939. I saw the scare headlines in extras from town to town as I drove to our summer home on Isle La Motte, Vermont, to bring back the family. Again, my world of hopes was crashing down.

Memorandum to the General Director

In early October a luncheon meeting of department directors of Russell Sage Foundation discussed future program. As the youngest department head and not in charge of a research division, my proper role was observer, and during the meeting I managed to preserve it. But the next day I boiled over, and sent this brash note to Mr. Harrison, the general director:

I listened with the greatest interest to our luncheon discussions yesterday . . . It seems fair to draw these general conclusions.

(1) Although one or two of the directors wish we might be drawn immediately into the war, there is a general feeling that the United States should be kept out if at all possible.

(2) There is a justifiable pride in participation by most of the staff members in the past war, although probably many of those present believe that the existing condition of Great Britain, France, and others might be better at this moment if the United States had

stayed out the last time and the war settlement had been made on a less conclusive basis.

(3) There is already a feeling that we might do well to begin preparing for similar types of service on the part of the Foundation in case we again become involved.

One significant omission in all this discussion has interested and concerned me. We are apparently willing to sacrifice nearly all of our current programs of general research in favor of an emergency which we agree will be socially disastrous—whatever its termination —if it occurs. On the other hand, we as a Foundation had not so far as I know sacrificed any of our current programs or devoted any of our time except possibly individually to implement the peace which we assert is so desirable and important.

I appreciate that this is a general attitude. Even the word "preparedness" always means willingness to sacrifice and spend money for war; we never "prepare" for peace. In our Federal Constitution six of the eighteen powers assigned to the Congress relate to war, and the remaining twelve are supposed to take care of taxes, coinage, commerce, naturalization, post offices, sciences, arts, and the social welfare. Our Cabinet has two War Secretaries and no Peace Secretary unless occasionally the Secretary of State functions in that field.

This may all be a cry in the wilderness and completely out of order but I wonder if it might not be possible to have at least a discussion as to what the Foundation might and could do toward implementing peace. If we are willing to devote six years of the work of one department for studying a series of relatively minor economic fluctuations might not the major fluctuations of a war economy be worth some advance study? Might not labor conditions in the past war and the prospect in a future one be a matter of immediate concern? Might not some study of existing propaganda agencies in the United States and their operations be useful?

I appreciate that Carnegie Endowment and the several other peace organizations have this as their special field. I also believe that we shall not have peace until and unless there is a general sacrifice and a general effort in that direction somewhat comparable to efforts we seem willing to make in a field whose final result we recognize in advance to be futile, and dangerous to the liberties we enjoy.[1]

I remember no reply.

However, many staff members did participate in one useful

[1] Memorandum to Mr. Harrison from F. E. Andrews, 10 October 1939.

prewar organization. Set up in 1933 as "an unnamed committee on the plight of German social workers," it was christened Hospites in 1934 and its work was concentrated in Miss Colcord's Charity Organization Department. It raised and disbursed funds from American social workers and their friends, mostly for the relief of displaced or refugee social workers still in Europe, sometimes in concentration camps. The program within Germany necessarily employed secret channels. Aid was given in bringing displaced workers to America and finding positions for them.

The War Comes

The weather was balmy that first weekend in December, 1941. I was down in Lancaster to help Father celebrate his birthday, and on Saturday we played a little golf. Sunday 7 December about 2:30 P.M. I was waiting for the New York train. A porter came along. "The Japs would do a thing like that!" he mumbled, shaking his head.

The words struck fire on something I had been fearing. But on the train there was no sign of anything unusual. A young sailor stopped to chat with two girls in the seat in front of me, convincing one of them with some difficulty that he knew her. The train drifted into Pennsylvania Station. The extras were out. ATTACK ON PEARL HARBOR NAVAL BASE. ATTACK ON MANILA.

On Monday I lunched with the Foundation air-warden group. We listened first to the President's ten-minute speech calling for a declaration of war on Japan, a foregone conclusion. Then the wardens got down to serious talk. A token German air-raid might come within forty-eight hours. Certain of our interior corridors were designated as air-raid shelters. A room was stocked with first-aid supplies, blankets, some canned food, even water. A number of us had already taken the Red Cross courses in first aid.

At home similar flurries took place. We all bought black-out curtains for our windows, darkened our streets, and at night drove cars with dimmed lights or not at all. I was an air-raid warden, with night stick and metal hat. There were several false and several practice alarms, but in our sector of Tenafly the only casualty was a fellow warden who in the darkness bent to stroke a dark, furry object he mistook for a cat.

That first war year was full of disappointment and frustration. I could not even share the hope that victory was all that was needed to solve the world's problems. Says a year-end diary note:

> I have had to see the hopeful world of yesterday washed away in war, and in a war which I cannot believe will settle the issues for which we spend so much blood and tears and sweat. . . .

> Foundation publications, being practically nil up to now, left me with a feeling of a squirrel in a treadmill; our present staff seems utterly unable to desert its measured pace and do any useful project.

This is not quite a fair statement. There was no general exodus to Washington or major shifts to war-related projects in the early war years, as there had been in World War I. But a great deal of committee work related to wartime problems, and Mr. Harrison delivered a number of addresses (some of which I helped draft) on social work's special tasks in the war.

Mr. Nugent of Consumer Credit Studies had several exciting assignments. Even before Pearl Harbor, at the request of the U.S. Intelligence Service, he visited Hawaii to help arrange safer forms of credit than those offered by Japanese loan sharks, who were worming secrets out of our United States military personnel in their toils. He was also chiefly responsible for drafting pre-war Regulation W, an executive order issued by President Roosevelt giving the Federal Reserve Board power to regulate consumer credit. By shortening the term, increasing downpayments, and regulating charge accounts, this device greatly reduced customer purchases of automobiles and other expensive durables, thus releasing productive capacity for armaments before this was legally possible by direct order. After Pearl Harbor he was put in charge of rationing the half-million automobiles remaining in stock when car manufacture ceased in January, 1942.

The Department of Statistics suffered one very minor war casualty. For some fifteen years it had been distributing packets of tiny symbols to be pasted on maps, representing community facilities ranging from *City Dump* to *Welfare Agencies*. But No. 21, *Meeting Place, Other Religions* happened to be the swastika, which Mr. Hitler was making infamous. We changed it.

With publishing operations at a low level during this period, I tried to make myself useful with more outside activities.

American Institute of Graphic Arts

One of these, with eventually a minor war relation, was a more active role with the American Institute of Graphic Arts. I had been a member since 1936, finding its book clinics and special meetings involving typography useful in my publishing operations.

In 1940 I accepted editorship of the *News-Letter of The American Institute of Graphic Arts,* and from 1942 to 1948 was a member of the board of directors. These offices, and particularly the editorship, acquainted me with many of the colorful leaders in the graphic arts.

Melbert B. Cary, Jr., president of the Institute when I became editor, had his own private Press of the Woolly Whale. This Press issued one of the more delightful spoofs of those years, *The Missing Gutenberg Wood Blocks,* proofs of twenty engravings allegedly spirited out of Germany by a refugee from Hitler and depicting the invention of printing, together with a slightly scandalous episode in Gutenberg's life. A few humorless reviewers took this "find" seriously.

At the May, 1941, annual meeting of the Institute Mr. Cary presided with his customary geniality, and only a few of us close to him noted a slight limp. An operation was required, and he died before the month was out. His presidential successors under whom I served as editor or board member were Arthur R. Thompson, whom I had known for many years as head of the Bureau of Publications of Bell Telephone Laboratories, and Walter Frese, president of Hastings House.

For the *News-Letter* I did a special story on Bruce Rogers ("BR" was probably America's most eminent type designer) when that gentleman was working on the "type" to emblazon Ralph Waldo Emerson's

WE ARE OF DIFFERENT OPINIONS
AT DIFFERENT HOURS BUT WE
ALWAYS MAY BE SAID TO BE AT
HEART ON THE SIDE OF TRUTH

on the south wall of the Hunter College Building, 68th Street at Park Avenue. The largest letters were "3,024 point" in printers' sizes.

I came also to know many other eminent typographers of the

day, including prolific type designer Frederic W. Goudy, the Grabhorns, Robert Josephy, Peter and Edna Beilenson of the Pauper Press, W. A. Dwiggins (who was induced to design the two new numerals needed by The Duodecimal Society, special cuttings for X and E), and Will Ransom.

During the war I was co-chairman of an Institute meeting on microfilm. We duly noted that its first important use was in the Franco-Prussian War of 1870, when German troops surrounded Paris. René Patrice Dagron, a Paris photographer who had been experimenting with microphotography, managed to get out of Paris in a balloon, and in Tours photographed dispatches down to minute size, so that a whole gazette could be rolled in a quill and attached to a pigeon wing. By this microfilm pigeon-post, some 115,000 official dispatches and more than a million private letters were flown to Paris.

With this knowledge freshly in mind, I was ready for a request which came to Russell Sage Foundation from Hung-chung Chang, of China's Ministry of Social Research, who reported that because of Japanese investment China had for some years received no books from the outside world; what were late developments in relief policies, and could not some new books be got to him? A selection committee picked pertinent material (including the whole of the latest *Social Work Year Book*). The Office of War Information was induced to photograph this material onto 35 mm. film, with 1600 pages in each tiny roll. We had no Chinese carrier pigeons, but the State Department let us use left-over corners in the diplomatic pouch. *The R S F Bulletin* carried the story:

> Silence for nearly a year. Then one morning came a sudden telephone call; would your Editor come in to lunch with Mr. Chang, who had just flown in from Chungking? Some fifty books, Mr. Chang reported, had come safely over The Hump. All had been read, and important portions translated into Chinese for further distribution. And from the light in his eyes and his almost embarrassing gratitude we learned anew how much the printed word can mean to a man and a nation starved for it.[2]

Twentieth Century Fund

In mid-1940 Elizabeth Mann, serving on my editorial board at the Institute, invited me to a special luncheon with Evans Clark,

---

[2] "Winged Books for Free China," in *The R S F Bulletin*, June, 1944, pp. 1-2.

director of Twentieth Century Fund. I already knew a great deal about the Fund. It was set up in 1919 by Edward A. Filene, Boston department-store magnate. After an independent survey of foundations it decided that the most important neglected field was economics, and resolved to concentrate its efforts for a period in that area. During its early years, when resources were small, the Fund acted solely as a disbursing foundation making grants to outside agencies. But after 1929 it began itself to survey economic problems of crucial current importance, and after 1938 it ceased to make grants to outside agencies. It did not, however, develop the departmental structure of Russell Sage Foundation; its policies were these:

> For most of the Fund's major research projects the Board of Trustees appoints a special committee composed of representative men and women with varying points of view and a particularly wide knowledge of the problem that is to be studied. Special research staffs are retained to assemble and present to the committees the essential facts bearing on the subject in hand. The committees then formulate constructive recommendations for action to meet the problems involved. . . .[3]

> The Fund believes that its research is not an end in itself but is justified to the degree that it contributes to sound public policy; and that policies are useful to the degree that they result in action, which depends on widespread public knowledge.

> In choosing subjects for investigation, the Fund has sought out, rather than avoided, controversial issues. It does this in the belief that controversy is often an index of the public importance of a subject and of the need for its impartial treatment.[4]

This interest in emergent problems has often been reflected in selection of the Fund's trustees. It has been stated, with some exaggeration, that one could determine the most exciting problem and person in a particular year by finding out what new trustee Twentieth Century Fund elected the following year. The 1940 Board included:

A. A. Berle, Jr., Assistant Secretary of State
Francis Biddle, Attorney General of the United States
Bruce Bliven, editor, *The New Republic*
Percy S. Brown, director, Edward A. Filene Good Will Fund
Henry S. Dennison, president, Dennison Manufacturing Company

[3] *Annual Report, 1946.* Twentieth Century Fund, New York, 1947, p. 5.
[4] *Annual Report, 1949*, p. 3.

John H. Fahey, chairman, Federal Home Loan Board
Oswald W. Knauth, president, Associated Dry Goods Corporation
Morris E. Leeds, chairman of the board, Leeds and Northrup
    Company
Robert S. Lynd, professor of sociology, Columbia University
James G. McDonald, president, The Brooklyn Institute of Arts and
    Sciences
Charles P. Taft, lawyer, Cincinnati
Harrison Tweed, lawyer, New York City

At this time, I learned at the luncheon, the Fund was convinced that the war in Europe, whether or not we became involved, would affect drastically economic life in the United States, and the Fund's entire program was being reshaped to meet the sharpening crisis. Second, certain difficulties had developed in the Fund's relations with Raymond Rich Associates, who had been handling the publication program, and it was now being put in direct charge of Miss Mann. She and Mr. Clark hoped I would do a survey of their publishing operation, and that I might be induced to have an advisory relationship to it.

Since just at that time Russell Sage Foundation publications were at ebb, I saw here a chance to be useful in the threatening storm. A *Memorandum on Twentieth Century Fund Book Promotion* was submitted on 18 June 1940. It reported my "very favorable impression as to the education-mindedness of the Fund," which indeed has always devoted a substantial portion of income, sometimes approximating half, to spreading knowledge of its research findings. It already had a standing order plan, and out of the Sage experience I made detailed recommendations for its expansion. (It eventually climbed to over four thousand.) And I recommended abandonment of the attempt to automate mailing lists on a gigantic Hollerith machine as taking an inordinate amount of staff time for additions and corrections and being wholly unsuited to data changing as rapidly as do addresses.

The *Memorandum* was approved in general, and I agreed to come to the Fund half a day a week as consultant on publications. Husky-voiced, dark-haired, friendly, and extremely competent Elizabeth Mann was chief of the Publishing Division, as well as assistant to the director, Mr. Clark. We had as efficient division secretary Miss Carol Kier, and with such relief from detail I was able even in limited time to direct the bookselling operation and write mail campaigns. General publicity was in the hands of a special Education Department under Thomas R. Carskadon.

It was an exciting program. Even before we entered the war Miles L. Colean and the Housing Committee produced *Housing for Defense* and Lloyd G. Reynolds, under direction of the Labor Committee, *Labor and National Defense*. Also foresightedly, the Fund in April, 1941, commissioned Stuart Chase to write a series of six popularly slanted books under the general title, *When the War Ends*. Economists have not always seen eye-to-eye with Mr. Chase, but no other writer in America possessed his ability to explain economic theory to the layman and make it fascinating. We speedily broke all previous sales records for the Fund with the Chase volumes, reaching these totals by 1947:

The Road We Are Traveling: 1914-1942	(1942)	37,648
Goals for America: A Budget of Our Needs and Resources	(1942)	32,911
Where's the Money Coming From? Problems of Postwar Finance	(1943)	36,722
Democracy under Pressure: Special Interests vs the Public Welfare	(1945)	38,244
Tomorrow's Trade: Problems of Our Foreign Commerce	(1945)	19,297
For This We Fought	(1946)	18,847

Meanwhile a variety of other publications and activities dealt with wartime problems or postwar planning, making my ringside seat fascinating. Also, the Fund was deeply involved in its impressive economic study, *America's Needs and Resources*, edited by the late J. Frederic Dewhurst. Begun in 1943 and published in 1947, it speedily became a chief resource for study of economic trends.

With the coming of peace, the "Fund redoubled its efforts to get before the public the results of its investigations bearing on the reconversion period and the even more difficult years that lie beyond."[5] By 1947 it took a further step, going into the foreign field for the first time, with surveys in Brazil, Greece, and Turkey. Evans Clark, director of the Fund since its inception, retired in 1953 and was succeeded by J. Frederic Dewhurst.

I had expected my tenure to be brief, certainly not beyond the stressful war period. A schedule of half a day a week did not look promising, and could not have been productive without exceptional staff cooperation. Then a tragic event further extended my stay. Overworked Miss Mann, never able to spare herself, one

[5] *Annual Report, 1945*, p. 9.

day in 1954 did not appear for work, and the next day was found dead in her apartment. I remained on, briefly increasing my time, until Miss Kier had the publication reins firmly in hand. But in 1955, with heavy other responsibilities shaping up for me, I had to submit my resignation.

During those fifteen years I witnessed significant changes in the handling of research at the Fund. Whereas in 1942 the Fund's *Report* had stated that "for *each* of the Fund's research projects" a special committee would be appointed, by 1946 the statement read, "for *most* of the Fund's *major* research projects." Moreover, in the original plan the committee with its "varying points of view and wide knowledge" had clearly been central, the research staff simply aiding the committee in finding relevant facts. On paper this seemed a splendid scheme.

In practice, difficulties developed. Committee members, usually leaders in their respective segments of a given field, sometimes engaged in extensive bickering at committee meetings, and if compromise were finally reached, the recommendations for "next steps" were dangerously weakened. Quite as often, the committee report came out peppered with footnotes indicating disagreement, or even accompanied by a contrary minority report.

Moreover, not many first-rate research directors were content to spend three or four years on a study, present it in colorless, statistical prose, and never express a personal view. As time went on, authors began to receive principal billing, with the committee report a useful appendage. For some studies no committees were appointed, or they served as merely advisory to the author.

Relief Abroad

Russell Sage Foundation involvement in the war had seemed slow, with for me initial frustrations. One of these particularly affected Publication Department. War restrictions were becoming general; gasoline, for example, was rationed at two gallons a week. And then came paper rationing for all publishers. The January, 1943, order was mild, restricting publishers to 90 percent of their 1942 tonnage. Unhappily 1942 was a year in which our departments had produced almost nothing, with our tonnage probably the lowest since 1907. We practically exhausted our allowance by mid-January, and had to cancel printing orders while appealing to Washington. I went about telling our now eager researchers that normal studies could be published on postcards, and extra long ones on double postcards. Finally we were allowed to average the last three years as a base; tight, but possible.

As the war progressed, relief and rehabilitation abroad became a major Foundation concern. Charity Organization Department began a series of Occasional Papers, making available earlier practices in administering relief. Programs covered included Near East relief, the Red Cross in World War I, postwar aid to Germany, relief programs in France, Russia, and during a Chinese famine, and the early World War II operations in France of the American Friends Service Committee. Such lessons from experience were noted as the need to put a representative on top of each freight car of food, to complain vigorously if that car were shunted onto a siding or otherwise "mislaid."

We were facing, said Shelby M. Harrison, "the largest task in mass relief and far-flung reconstruction the world has yet seen. This is the long mile beyond Berlin that the United States must travel without faltering, or all the miles to Berlin may prove an empty victory."[6]

Charity Organization Department, chiefly in the person of Donald S. Howard, also assisted in preparing materials for the early courses to train military and naval officers for civil administration in occupied territories. But in October, 1943, Howard joined the Office of Foreign Relief and Rehabilitation Operations, at first on loan and then on leave of absence. Soon he transferred to United Nations Relief and Rehabilitation Administration (UNRRA), becoming chiefly responsible for welfare research and planning and assisting in drafting UNRRA's welfare policies. He had periods of service in London during the V-bomb barrage; with Supreme Headquarters in Paris on welfare aspects of the military-UNRRA program for displaced nationals; and in 1945 was transferred to China where he became deputy director of UNRRA's China office, until March, 1946.

Rolf Nugent, whose earlier war services have been noted, also joined UNRRA in February, 1944. Working chiefly on problems of supply, he had assignments in Washington, London, Australia, New Zealand, Yugoslavia, and Italy. The war over, his final UNRRA assignment was to China and the Philippines. On his return journey via Japan, in July, 1946, he went swimming with a

---

[6] "Some Wartime Social Gains," address before the New York Academy of Public Education, 19 November 1942.

friend from the beach at Kamakura. The tide was strong, and they were having trouble reaching shore. Mr. Nugent did not make it, though apparently he died of a heart attack rather than drowning.

We were close friends. I received the crushing news in Vermont, where I was then working on my section of the Foundation *History,* and had tentatively indicated reopening of his department upon his return to the Foundation. After his death the Department of Consumer Credit Studies was not continued.

Other Foundations and the War

During the later war years I was gathering material for a book on foundations, described in Chapter 8. Early in 1945 we sent out a questionnaire asking information about 1944 program (which turned out to be the last full year of war), with this specific item: *Important war-induced changes in our program included the following:* . . . The replies provide an unusually full picture of foundation activities related to World War II.

With executives typically in the higher age groups, foundations were not seriously affected by Selective Service, but contributed much of their highly trained research personnel to wartime agencies on a voluntary basis. Long-term projects of importance were continued where possible, but usually with reduced staff and under special difficulties. Said The Rockefeller Foundation, "Fundamental research is in fact today a mere trickle compared with the mighty stream it formerly was." Where cooperation with scholars abroad was important, difficulties often became insuperable.

Requests for aid from ordinary sources decreased. However, a number of foundations, contrary to standing policy against "relief" giving, made special contributions to wartime agencies such as American National Red Cross, the National War Fund, and United China Relief. Scholarships, fellowships, and loan funds were largely dormant, for, as one fund in this field reported, "the war has eliminated almost entirely the need for loans going to young men." Foreign scholarships and fellowships practically disappeared. Many foundations accumulated the resources ordinarily used for scholarships to meet the extra demands expected at the close of the war.

The most significant change of all, however, was the swinging of research projects and personnel into direct wartime service. The Maurice and Laura Falk Foundation foresightedly authorized in 1938 a study on wartime control of prices. Milbank Memorial Fund reported "research work, particularly in nutrition and population, has been widely expanded." Phelps-Stokes Fund aided in "organizing and financing a Committee on Negro Americans in Defense Industries." The Commonwealth Fund redirected its program of medical research to emphasize aviation medicine, control of infectious diseases, and shock. The John and Mary R. Markle Foundation reported six appropriations in support of teaching tropical medicine. A small research appropriation of The Rockefeller Foundation in 1936 grew under combat pressures into the war's vast penicillin projects. Practically every foundation reported efforts in its field of special competence directed toward needs of the armed services or the home front.

By 1944, programs were centering on postwar planning. Efforts in this field of Twentieth Century Fund and Russell Sage Foundation have already been detailed. Carnegie Endowment for International Peace emphasized public education "on postwar problems and reconstruction, including necessity of international organization," and The Woodrow Wilson Foundation expressed similar aims. The George Robert White Fund voted establishment of a war memorial and recreation center in the city of Boston as its postwar project. The Falk Foundation reported that "the majority of the economic research studies now being financed deal primarily with problems of demobilization and economic reconstruction after the war."

It was satisfying to find that, during the feverish war years when most men and agencies spared little time or thought for needs beyond the pressing present, the foundations characteristically took the longer view and performed a large share of the vital planning for the years ahead.

A Note from My Diary

It is now a few minutes past 8 o'clock, the evening of 14 August 1945. Since early morning there have been wild rumors of Japanese acceptance of the peace terms. With the family away and no food in the house, I went to New York for breakfast, and found sizeable crowds in Times Square, watching the electric news bulletins on the Times Building, throwing paper sporadically from windows, blowing horns.

By mid-afternoon the report came that the Japanese note was really only a complaint against the use of atomic bombs.

I left for dinner on this sour note. Needing to shop for groceries, I had dinner in Englewood, and was near a radio another patron turned on. At about 6:30 special bulletins began coming—the Swiss attaché had delivered a message . . . Secretary Byrnes was hastening to the White House . . . finally, the press services announced an important message "might" come from the White House about 7 o'clock.

I debated waiting it out at the restaurant, but the disappointments day after day since Saturday, and the thought that if it was the real thing I would find stores closed tonight and tomorrow, hurried me out. I finished buying the groceries and by luck made a running connection with a bus. As we approached Oak Street, I looked at my watch—three minutes to seven.

I went down Oak Street at a rapid clip, dropped the groceries and milk on the nearest chair, flipped on the radio to WJZ. Four words of a conventional program and then a sudden pause.

"We interrupt our program for an important announcement . . ." The speaker's voice was trembling. "The war is over!"

For an hour I have been listening to the official and unofficial jubilation. And now finally one word for myself. I have hated this war, and all it means and has done to us. I must not forget. Most people will, and speedily. But if any time, any year, there is a clear way open to me to do something that matters to prevent a future war, that shall be done at whatever cost.

CHAPTER 7

About Family Allowances

THREE persons made me think about children and families in America. Frederick Wynne, an electrical engineer, and his wife, when I first knew them, had a boy of ten. They think the one-child system is a bad one, and would gladly have had more children—but there had been the Depression. For three years Fred was nothing but a radio repairman on odd jobs. Since then he has never felt secure, and the Wynnes have not had another child.

Dr. Bernard Duel is the nationally known head of a great educational institution. I have not used his real name since he might not relish my identifying him with some personal advice he gave me a few weeks before I was married. Talking about giving children proper opportunities in the light of salary levels in the "educational" field (but I knew he meant mine), Dr. Duel said, "We spaced our children so that only one would be in college at a time." Dr. Duel and his wife have had two children.

Joe Corrigan drove a coal truck. I got to know him quite well one summer when I substituted for the vacationing weighmaster in Father's coal yard. One day Joe asked for time to make his regular monthly visit to the relief office. I knew he was our best-paid driver, and I demanded of Father justification of a wage policy that made his best workman a relief suppliant.

"Joe's a good worker," Father acknowledged, "and I pay him every cent the job's worth. But it is scarcely my fault that Joe has eleven children."

Four adults, foresighted, prudent, desirous of giving their children the best in environment and education, have a total of three children. Two adults, living in cramped and unhealthful quarters and unable even to feed their brood without the aid of "relief," have a total of eleven children.

What Price Children?

At Russell Sage Foundation I had adequate research tools at hand, and began looking into what was happening to the American family. It was obvious that recent changes had shattered its economic base. Several generations ago, when most people lived on farms, the family was a going concern. "For every mouth, two hands are born" was a comforting adage in those days, when from the age of six or eight children were doing substantial chores and more than made their modest keep. Rearing children was frequently a profitable business.

It seldom is now. This is not because today's John is less strong than yesterday's Jake, or Shirley less willing than Susie; they have less chance. Most modern Johns and Shirleys live in cities, where productive chores are fewer; they go to school longer each year, and for more years. One old-fashioned form of family security—child labor—has quite properly been legislated out of existence. Meanwhile the costs of rearing and educating a child have skyrocketed.

I did some estimates on the costs of raising children (by this time we had three of our own) and came up with a formula that holds reasonably well even for families at different income levels and under today's price changes. A child costs about as much as the house that family occupies. The parallel runs farther. Children are on a sort of FHA plan: a substantial down payment, then monthly installments for a period of about twenty years. If you have two, three, or more children, you are contracting for the cost equivalent of two, three, or more houses, with most payments running simultaneously! But payments on a house are saving rent, building a permanent value, and at worst can be abandoned after a few payments. A child merely adds to rent. He cannot handily be abandoned, whatever the shift in your circumstances. At the close of the twenty-year payment period, he is suddenly not yours at all, but belongs to himself—or, if we continue involvements like Vietnam, to his country.

Fortunately, few of us who are fathers and mothers take only the economic view of our families. Children mean so very much in love, fulfillment, and downright fun. But because children have ceased to be partners in a going concern and have become a heavy burden financially, the American family is on dangerous footing.

Family Allowances

My readings disclosed that almost all other countries were meeting this problem by a system variously called children's allowances, or family allowances. These are cash grants, unaccompanied by a means test, to families (often paid to the mother) toward maintenance, care, training, education, and advancement of children. Before World War II family allowance systems were in effect in twenty-eight countries.

In the United States Paul H. Douglas had advocated such a system in his *Wages and the Family* published in 1925. Eleanor F. Rathbone, British pioneer in the movement, declared: "Whatever the amount that can be afforded for the total remuneration of any group of workers, that amount will go farther in producing real well-being if part of it is spent on children's allowances." John M. Keynes, noted British economist, said: "Family allowances must come to the front. For the burden of the rising cost of living depends very largely on the size of a man's family."

In the United States, the idea of family allowances still strikes most people as a complete novelty. Yet we have long been using this principle, but in disjointed programs with many gaps and inequities.

Public schools are a subsidy to children which the bachelor landowner helps to pay. Free milk and free dental service in some schools, playgrounds for children, half fare on conveyances, and reduced amusement prices, are other minor subsidies. The Social Security Act took a long step in this direction. In 1966 its cash benefits for children amounted to $1.5 billion. But in many states for the mother to receive aid for children the father must either die, desert, or be put in jail. Up in Vermont I knew a father who sometimes did generously get himself jailed; his family of fourteen was then much better off than on any wage he could earn.

Our queerest subsidy for children, as it works out in practice, is the income-tax law. Because the $750 exemption for a dependent child is in effect applied to the highest rate paid, in 1972 the relatively few married taxpayers with a taxable income of more than $200,000 received a handsome "rebate" of $525 for each dependent child. But the millions of taxpayers who reported incomes of $4,000 or less received a maximum of $127.50 per child, or nothing at all if their income was too small to be taxable.

A further advantage of family allowances is its contribution toward solving the "equal pay for equal work" dilemma. Salaries tend to be low in any profession or occupation where the large majority of workers can be recruited from persons without dependents. Examples are teachers, social workers, librarians, nurses, messengers, army privates. It may even be necessary that this be so. Our total wage and salary income could not support our 88 million employed persons at a salary adequate to maintain the commonly accepted standard of living for the wage earner with a wife and two children.[1]

So, what happens? Take teaching, for example. Salaries have greatly improved, but school boards even in wealthy communities are not apt to pay the single "schoolmarm," however good she is, a salary on which she could comfortably support a house, a nonexistent husband, and two children with college in prospect. Men who are apt to have such dependents stay out of occupations like teaching, or they are given administrative posts at better salary levels, whether they merit them or not. This is not good for the profession, nor fair to the women teachers—some of whom do have dependents. If family allowances were in effect —and some school systems have independently set them up—a reasonable salary level could be established without discrimination, and supplements would take care of dependency needs where in fact they exist.

A War Measure?

Then came the war. In time of peace, so sweeping a proposal might well await the long research it deserved into problems of administration, sectional differences, alternative possibilities such as payment "in kind" (school meals, shoes, and so on, instead of cash), and ultimate effects on population. Now we should have to have "family allowances" in any event for servicemen's families, and if made general, they might help solve some of the severest inflation problems of the war economy.

So I began to speak out. First was an address at the National

[1] In 1965, perhaps a typical year before the severe gyrations of recent inflation, the labor force was 78 million, wages and salaries $392 billion—almost exactly $5,000 per wage earner, assuming nobody, corporation president, doctor, lawyer, merchant chief, got a penny more. Then in 1967 the Bureau of Labor Statistics reported the annual cost for a four-person family to maintain a "moderate" living standard was averaging $9,191 in urban areas, $10,195 in the New York area.

Conference of Social Work on "Family Allowances for America?" at New Orleans on 14 May 1942. "I am not ready to take a stand today for or against family allowances as a permanent American policy," I said, "but I do think that they might offer a desirable and workable solution to an emergency problem the war has brought us."

As the deepening war brought severer problems of commodity control, finance, and price inflation, I became more convinced of the worth of the proposal, particularly for the war period. In November, 1943, *The Atlantic Monthly* published my "What Price Children?" which discussed the subject very broadly, but with particular war applications:

> We all know that the money we are free to spend must soon be reduced to the amount of goods—outside of tanks, airplanes, and other war supplies—we are still able to make. That is common sense and orthodox economics. Spare money in people's pockets is the floodwater of inflation which will break through any dam of price control or rationing we attempt to set up. . . .

> The fact is that nearly all our measures to meet the special problems of war finance run afoul of this single problem of family needs varying with family size, and we have drifted into a morass of complicated adjustments and half-measures instead of meeting that single problem directly and positively.

> I propose, primarily as a fiscal war measure and secondarily as an aid to family life, the prompt adoption of a system of children's allowances in the United States.[2]

Considerable newspaper publicity and correspondence followed publication of this proposal. A most appreciated letter came from Paul H. Douglas, already noted as one of the earliest proposers of such allowances. Marine Captain Douglas, as he then was, took part of his 1943 Christmas Day to write me from a Pacific isle that "it still seems to me to be a correct policy—its one weakness, perhaps, being to diminish the initiative of fathers in providing for their children, a consideration which seems more important to me now than it did a score of years ago."

Sir William Beveridge, who in Britain's Beveridge Plan had proposed children's allowances as the first of three assumptions underlying his whole plan for "social security from birth to death for everyone," came to America and lectured warmly in favor of such a program, both in Britain and in the United States. Such

2 "What Price Children?" in *Atlantic Monthly*, November, 1943, pp. 97, 98.

allowances were finally put into effect in Great Britain in 1945 substantially in accordance with Sir William's proposal. Canada adopted them even earlier, in the Family Allowances Act of 1944.

In the United States we were forced into widespread family allowances for service families. Near the war's end family allowance checks for all the armed services reached a monthly total of $250 million, this sum including both the government contribution (about 65 percent) and the deduction from the serviceman's pay. A general bill was introduced into Congress, but made little progress. Public school systems, some colleges, and a few industrial concerns adopted allowance plans. But spotty adoption in any field had its hazards: persons with large families gravitated toward school systems or companies with such benefits, and conversely such employers were suspected of discriminating against employment of persons with many dependents.

For some years I continued trying to promote the idea, along with others.[3] But after the war's end the immediate emergency faded, interest slackened, and I had to regard my considerable efforts as time wasted on a lost cause. Other concerns, where there seemed at least some hope of progress, demanded my time.

Now, in the 1970s, I have time to look back on these efforts of more than two decades ago. Was the idea sound, could it still be useful?

Substantially all the arguments originally advanced for family allowances are still valid, and some of them increasingly strong. Violence in our cities has many causes, but chief among them is poverty. The severest factor in poverty is family size, as it always has been since we changed from the farm to an urban society. We pass, or at least argue, in the Congress and in the states, a wide variety of relief measures, going so far as a serious proposal for a negative income tax. To halt runaway inflation we have adopted wage and price controls.

Let us look for a moment at a single case of price inflation. Milk goes up 2 cents a quart. John is a bachelor, Joe a married man with four children, and each of these individuals consumes a quart of milk a day. The price increase costs John some 60 cents a month, and he demands a wage increase. But it costs Joe

---

[3] My subsequent writings in the field included "How About Family Allowances?" *Parents' Magazine*, June 1944; "Should You Be Paid for Your Children?" *Family Circle*, 18 May 1945; "Family Allowances for Social Workers?" *Social Work Journal*, January 1949. A proposal to Russell Sage Foundation for a study of the subject was not acted upon.

$3.60. If the wage is adjusted to John's new needs, it is wholly inadequate for Joe; if it meets Joe's actual additional costs, it gives John spare cash to force other prices upward. If we add free milk for needy families to our myriad of special programs, we will require added administrators (at handsome salaries) to manage the new program and see that only needy families benefit. And so "demands" for relief in this country mount and mount.

I have not been happy in these later years with the growth of big government, and particularly with the crazy-quilt of relief programs—a quilt of many patches that still does not cover the shivering subject.

A major advantage of the negative income tax is that it does not discourage—as do nearly all relief programs—the will to work and thereby improve one's lot. Similarly, a family allowance system should have no needs test, and would remove entirely from relief rolls many families with marginal income. I continue to believe, with Eleanor Rathbone, that amounts so spent will go farther "in producing well-being," and in restoring many families to self respect and individual effort, than any other program now on the horizon.

After long silence, a few voices are being raised proposing family allowances in the United States. Daniel P. Moynihan, special assistant to the President, made a proposal in 1967.[4] Senator George S. McGovern, then chairman of the Select Senate Committee on Nutrition and Human Needs, in a major address in January 1970, proposed a federal allowance of $50 to $65 a month for each child in an attempt to abolish poverty. This allowance would go to every child regardlesss of family income, but the (then) $600 deduction for children would be abolished and for wealthier families a substantial part of the allowance would return in taxes.[5]

New careful surveys of costs, methods, and possible side effects are required, and now will be done by others. But I remain convinced that a family allowance system would be a wise policy for the United States.

[4] Moynihan, Daniel P., "The Case for a Family Allowance," *The New York Times Magazine*, 5 February 1967, p. 13 ff.
[5] *The New York Times*, 21 January 1970, p. 1 ff.

CHAPTER 8

Focus on Foundations

THE Russell Sage Foundation Library had collected information about foundations from its earliest days. In 1915 it published what is in effect the first directory of foundations, presented as a "bibliography" concerning just 27 foundations. The entries include brief descriptions of the foundations and a list of reports, books, pamphlets, and articles "indicative of the work of the various foundations."[1] Further "bibliographies," all under the same title, were issued in 1920 (54 foundations), in 1922 a "Supplementary List" (10 additional foundations), in 1924 (127 foundations), and in 1926 (179 foundations).

For the 1930 edition the title was changed to *American Foundations for Social Welfare*, and it was no longer in the Library bibliography series but the first (L1) in a new pamphlet series; it described 185 foundations, of which 33 were community trusts. I took a lively interest, being now on staff, in these growing records of foundations, and worked closely with Mrs. Bertha F. Hulseman, the librarian, in preparation and promotion of the next revision, issued in 1938 with 188 foundations.

American Foundations and Their Fields

Meanwhile another series of directories was starting. As already noted, Twentieth Century Fund made a survey of foundations in order to find for its own operations a neglected field. This survey was issued in 1928 for the trustees only as a folding chart, but reissued in 1931 with accompanying analytic text as a

[1] *American Foundations.* Bulletin of the Russell Sage Foundation Library. No. 11, June 1915, 10 pp.

pamphlet, *American Foundations and Their Fields*, edited by Evans Clark (122 foundations). A revised edition "Covering Activities of the Year 1931" appeared in 1932 (129 foundations), and in 1935 a third pamphlet covering grants in 1934 (123 foundations), all edited by Evans Clark, director of the Fund.

Raymond Rich Associates, a public relations firm, had been handling publications for Twentieth Century Fund, and the succeeding issues in 1939 and 1942[2] were issued under their imprint, permission having been granted for this continuation after the break with the Fund in 1939. Data collected for the directories represented an important business asset for a firm serving clients needing to raise funds.

A New Proposal

The Rich Associates editions *IV* and *V* were cloth-bound volumes of substantial size. Though these were prepared by a commercial firm, Russell Sage Foundation saw no reason to extend its own series so long as the need was met with reasonable adequacy from any source. But as the war progressed Raymond Rich Associates, becoming involved in emergency campaigns, indicated that it would not be able to issue another directory, at least in the foreseeable future.

At this point I sent a memorandum to Mr. Harrison. Our directory had not been revised since 1938. It was important that information on foundations be kept reasonably current, and Raymond Rich Associates were presently out of the field. I proposed that we undertake a new directory, but this time much more than a directory. In addition to listing and describing foundations, this publication should discuss in brief form something of their history, organization, resources, fields of activity, and general trends. Almost nothing of this sort was presently available to foundation executives and boards, and it might interest the general public. The staff could prepare the directory section; he, out of his long experience, should write the book.

We had long discussions. Administrative responsibilities, particularly in these war years, made heavy demands on his time.

2 *American Foundations and Their Fields*, IV, Compiled by Geneva Seybold. (243 foundations) Raymond Rich Associates, New York, 1939, 218 pp. *American Foundations and Their Fields*, V, Compiled by Geneva Seybold. (314 foundations) Raymond Rich Associates, New York, 1942, 274 pp.

But I was an experienced writer, he pointed out, and now also had more than a decade of experience in this field. Would I share in the writing? It would be published under dual authorship.

So it was agreed. Work began late in 1943, and for the next two years most of my writing time was spent on my first foundation book. Usually I worked at home mornings on manuscript; spent the afternoons at the Foundation directing the publication program, but also collecting data for the next day's writing. As time went on it became obvious that most of the actual writing would have to be done by me; but Mr. Harrison's long experience was very useful in consultations and in revision of manuscript.

Writing Proceeds

Mr. Harrison and I had no substantial disagreements on the text. Our opinions did somewhat vary on the matter of perpetuities. He was strongly in favor of rigid provisions whereby a donor could pass on to all future generations the fruits of his skills and his labors. I agreed that in the present economic setting perpetuity for foundations did not present a problem and should be permitted; but I also saw some dangers in obsolescence, creeping inflation, and possible future great growth in institutional investment holdings. Both views were presented, with a note of

> a trend in recent years . . . in the direction of allowing at least discretionary liquidation, but it is too early to think of this as pointing toward an established or necessarily desirable general policy.[3]

In the 1940s the then Bureau of Internal Revenue had not taken a stand against accumulation by foundations. Some donors, bemused by the apparent possibilities of compound interest, were setting up funds with provisions requiring the accumulation of all or most of the income for long periods of years. Both Mr. Harrison and I believed foundations should spend at least their investment income. In an effort to demonstrate that compound interest over long periods is an economic impossibility, I presented a statistical example that has proved useful since.

Caesar invaded Britain in 55 B.C. Assume he invested the

---

[3] Harrison, Shelby M., and F. Emerson Andrews, *American Foundations for Social Welfare*. Russell Sage Foundation, New York, 1946, p. 70.

equivalent of a single American dollar in a splendid British bank which compounded interest annually at 5 percent. Ten years later, about the time of his death, his investment would have become a modest $1.63. In 100 years it would have grown to only $131.50. But in 500 years it would have been more than $39 billion. And in 2,000 years (about the time I was then writing) the original dollar would have grown to a worth expressible only by 43 digits. It should be obvious that compound interest on any long-term fund would exceed the whole world's worth, and long before that point was reached, society would find some way of limiting or liquidating it.

The Directory Section

Much of the writing, particularly such sections as "Fields of Activity," had to await research done mainly for the directory section, which presented its own problems.

In the 1940s Internal Revenue did not open its records to public inspection. Past directories offered meager lists; there were only 314 foundations in the 1942 Rich directory. New information had to be obtained from the reports of the few foundations regularly issuing such documents, or from newspaper clippings, correspondence, visits, and other special efforts. Believing that an adequate descriptive directory was both in the public interest and a desirable control measure for foundations themselves, we began intensive labors.

A master list was first compiled, based on all previous directories, extensive correspondence in Russell Sage Foundation files, newspaper clippings, the Lindeman foundation study, Central Hanover Bank and Trust Company's department of philanthropic information, files of other foundations such as Carnegie Corporation of New York, Twentieth Century Fund, The New York Community Trust, mailing lists of fund-collecting agencies such as John Price Jones and Tamblyn and Brown, and miscellaneous smaller lists volunteered from various sources.

Some 5,000 presumptive foundations were thus discovered. Many did not meet our definition (including two companies that manufactured "foundation" garments and a construction firm). In this first screening we also eliminated foundations known to be now defunct, those with capital assets below $50,000 unless they had been recently formed and were expected to grow, ecclesiastical and educational foundations not functioning independently. The final master file included 908 names.

A questionnaire was prepared, limited to two pages as a compromise between the detailed information we would have preferred and the replies it was reasonable to expect in a busy war year. It was sent out with a careful letter on 10 January 1945 to a list now reduced to 811 foundations. On 15 February a second letter was sent to the 385 foundations which had not yet replied, accompanied by a card requesting the date when a reply might be expected.

A heavy correspondence on specific problems was concurrently conducted by Mr. Harrison and myself, and by Margaret B. Hodges who had been borrowed from the Social Work Year Book Department for special assistance on the directory. Personal visits were made to a number of foundation offices to clear up points of special difficulty and to effect a random sampling of reasons for nonreply.

Finally, on 16 April a third letter went out under registered mail so that we might have a record of its receipt. For it was our determined policy to include in the directory every foundation known to exist and believed to fit within our definition; in the absence of descriptive data it would be listed as "Information declined," or "No reply to requests for information," as the case might be.

Of the original list of 811, 250 were disqualified on receipt of further information and 56 for bad addresses. The remaining 505 appear in the directory. Descriptions are included for 364 of them; the remaining 141 (28 percent) would not cooperate, 49 refusing information and 92 never replying to repeated requests.

Some Foundation Dimensions

In any research project it is exciting when the replies come flooding in and can be added up to answers, sometimes unexpected, to questions in the field. We knew better than anyone else the serious remaining gaps in our information, but soon we did have a better picture of the foundation field than had ever before been available.

By making conservative financial estimates for the foundations which refused information we arrived at capital assets of $1.8 billion for all known foundations for the base year 1944, with grants of $52.4 million. This is not large in comparison with present figures of $25.2 billion in assets and $1,513 million in grants,[4] and we were careful to point out that it was no vast sum in terms of the then-current economy.

Total foundation expenditures ($72 million) appeared to be about 3 percent of the estimated budget of private philanthropy. The total capital of all the foundations, if requisitioned for war purposes, "would have kept the United States war effort going less than eight days." Compared with certain consumer expenditures, one year's tobacco bill "much more than equals the endowment of all existing foundations," and a year's alcohol bill "would finance all foundation expenditures, at the 1944 rate, for seventy-two years."

The lists of ten largest American foundations in 1944 and in the current (1971) *Foundation Directory* show such marked differences it may be worth bringing them together:

ASSETS OF TEN LARGEST FOUNDATIONS

1944	Millions	1969	Millions
Rockefeller Foundation	$190	Ford Foundation	$2,902
Carnegie Corporation of New York	167	Lilly Endowment	778
Ford Foundation	109	Rockefeller Foundation	757
Board of Directors, City Trusts		Duke Endowment	510
of Philadelphia	88	Kresge Foundation	433
Hayden (Charles) Foundation	50	Kellogg (W.K.) Foundation	393
Kresge Foundation	48	Mott (Charles Stewart)	
Kellogg (W.K.) Foundation	47	Foundation	371
Carnegie Institution of Washington	44	Pew Memorial Trust	367
Commonwealth Fund	43	Sloan (Alfred P.) Foundation	303
Mayo Properties Association	28	Carnegie Corporation of New York	283
Total	$814		$7,097

The changes in rankings are interesting, and the difference in totals startling. However, this is not quite an accurate comparison. We knew in 1944 that there existed at least seven other foundations with assets above $10 million, and three of them—The Duke Endowment, James Foundation of New York, and The Surdna Foundation—should probably have been among the top ten. But they declined financial data and we had then no means

[4] *The Foundation Directory, Edition 4.* Edited by Marianna O. Lewis. The Foundation Library Center. Distributed by Columbia University Press, New York, 1971, p. xi.

of obtaining this information from other sources. But similarly the 1969 listing fails to include The Robert Wood Johnson Foundation, in process of becoming second only to Ford in size.

Only five foundations in the 1944 list were still among the top ten by 1969—Rockefeller, Carnegie, Ford, Kresge, and Kellogg. All these had grown in assets, The Ford Foundation by nearly 29 times. Carnegie Corporation of New York did not quite double its assets, and dropped from second position to tenth. Total assets for the top ten leaped from $814 million to a little over $7 billion.

The Ford Foundation

As we were working on the book we heard rumors of vast new potentials for The Ford Foundation. It had started in 1936 with an endowment of $25,000, a modest figure often quoted. Almost immediately it began to get substantial sums both from the Ford family and from Ford Motor Company, but these figures were not then disclosed. Later records indicate that through the base year for our statistics, 1944, The Ford Foundation had received in cash from the Ford family $1,816,450, and from Ford Motor Company $11,215,000. (This was before Ford Motor Company set up its own company-sponsored foundation, Ford Motor Company Fund, incorporated in 1949.) Moreover, in 1937 Henry Ford and Edsel Ford had each given the Foundation 125,000 shares of Ford Motor Company stock, and in 1944 Henry Ford gave it an additional 1,400,000 shares. Meanwhile, Edsel Ford died in May, 1943, and the press indicated that the major portion of his estate was going to the Foundation in company stock. (It turned out to be 1,153,809 shares valued at the estate settlement in 1947 at $135 a share.)

Our questionnaire to The Ford Foundation was returned with exemplary promptness, on 16 January 1945, but without a scrap of financial information. We could scarcely go to press with so little about this new giant. When schedule permitted, I took a train to Detroit (one did not fly in the war years) and on 21 March 1945 bumped out to Dearborn in a bus. Excerpts that follow are from my memorandum written on the train that evening, in ink until the pen ran dry, and then in pencil:

> The Ford Foundation is in the old Ford Motor Company building, a drab gray four-story structure on Schaefer Road, Dearborn,

with the hundred smoking chimneys of the Ford River Rouge plants for backdrop. The Foundation actually has no office, no paid executives, no established policies. Its tremendous wealth—which is at least as large as the reports—came in the midst of war, and no one has had time to give it any but the most desultory attention. Henry Ford II (aged 28) is titular head, and reported genuinely interested, but is not in uniform by specific government request to press war production, and his subordinates keep from him all possible Foundation matters.

The person in active charge is Fred Thomson, assistant secretary of Ford Motor Company. His chief function is the Ford Company's real estate, and he and one secretary, in two offices merely glassed off from rows of identical offices, handle as a side-line the affairs of what is clearly the largest foundation—in resources—in the world.

He greeted my telephone confirmation of the appointment with no enthusiasm, saying yes, he would see me, as agreed by letter, but couldn't imagine what we'd have to talk about. When I arrived in his office—after considerable delay at the reception desk in spite of appointment—he indicated he could spare about ten minutes, but had no information to give out. But at his later request, I stayed for nearly two hours, was sent back to the station in a special car, and with a request for memoranda on points we could not finish because I had to leave for my Chicago train.

Finances: Expect to have an income of "from twelve to fifteen million a year." Total capitalization not actually known, since the Foundation, which receives 95 percent of Edsel Ford's estate, will receive this only after the inheritance taxes on the heirs' 5 percent have been paid, which latter is not yet determined since the value of Ford Motor stock is not fixed. *But* about [this figure was given in confidence, but was very large] in mere tax on the 5 percent has already been paid—estimate for yourself what the 95 percent may reach!

The Ford Foundation will substantially own Ford Motor Company. [The memorandum might have noted what is the fact: all the shares were Class A nonvoting stock, so that "ownership" was not control.] They already recognize the problems this presents, and the need to separate very carefully the operations of the two—which is why, for example, "Mr. and Mrs. Ford" sponsor certain portions of the Ford Hour on the radio involving Greenfield Choir, etc., which the Foundation otherwise supports.

Activities: Admittedly the past program has been improvisation. Greenfield Village and Museum have been supported. Antioch College received a grant "because Edsel always liked it, and we used to have some Antioch boys in the plant." But this was a bad idea, for since then a steady parade of presidents of small Ohio colleges have been coming. (It hadn't occurred to them that this might happen!)

The Foundation owns a good bit of land near Dearborn, and is trying to sell it off in building lots. I mentioned Forest Hills and the advantages—financial as well as social—of city planning, and this, too, was a brand new idea. But most current expenditures are sufficiently indicated by mentioning a gift of $100,000 to American Red Cross, lesser gifts to local Catholic and Protestant hospitals, the Edison Institute, community chests.

I told him something of the Rockefeller history and the Senate investigation, and he wishes further references on this. He recognizes the desirability and importance of full public reports, and promises so to do as soon as program is fixed and capitalization known. He seems personally impressed with the genuine desire of the Fords to put their money to public use, and told me a few personal stories about them. . . .

In the book we listed The Ford Foundation with "*Capital Assets*: Approximately $109,000,000. *Expenditures*: Not stated."

Publication

American Foundations for Social Welfare was published on 13 May 1946. Press coverage was wide, and the reviewers generous in their comments. "Invaluable for anyone working in the foundation or allied fields, and of great general interest," said *The World in Books*. Sales were good, with over 3,000 the first half-month, a reprint needed by August, and a second reprint two years later. While many of these copies went to fund-raisers, requests for advice and information from the foundation field also rose sharply. Since Mr. Harrison was planning retirement in about a year, many of these requests began coming to me.

Publication of the book resulted also in many invitations for speeches, magazine articles, encyclopedia pieces. One of these gave me a welcome opportunity to develop one emerging interest of foundations that had been little noted:

Some twenty-one centuries ago a well-heeled Roman by the name of Gaius Maecenas decided to back a few of the literary dark horses of his time. Two of his lads, Quintus Horatius Flaccus and Publius Vergilius Maro, turned out rather well. Because he helped this brace of farm boys, one of them the son of a slave, his memory survives, and he has given a name to a practice still important in publishing and other hazardous arts.

In the twentieth century Maecenas is usually incorporated, and more often than not he is a foundation. . . .[5]

The Foundation History

Even before the foundations book was quite finished, I became committed, reluctantly and almost disastrously, to another large writing task in the foundation field.

As this chapter has indicated, Russell Sage Foundation from its beginnings recognized the desirability of wide knowledge about foundations, and evidenced this concern in its careful recordings of all known foundations in bibliographies and directories. As largely an operating agency, it was publishing four or five books and usually more pamphlets each year, presenting in detail large segments of its own program; but in the earlier years it did not issue annual reports. In 1917 the Foundation had in type a ten-year report, but World War I scattered nearly all the staff to emergency duties, and when the war was over the material was old and was never printed.

Mr. Harrison and I, however, were quite firm on the importance of reporting:

> One of the most effective forms of control has been public opinion. Serious abuses of power seem unlikely so long as the actions of boards of trustees and foundation executives are open to public review and comment. Many foundations are careful to publish full reports of their actions; unfortunately another large group, including many of the newer family foundations, fail to do so. It is probable that increased pressure will be brought upon all foundations enjoying tax exemption to furnish full reports on both finances and activities. Unless informed public opinion is available as an effective control throughout the foundation field, renewed demands for rigid governmental controls may arise, and foundations may lose one of their most useful present assets, their freedom for independent and pioneering action.[6]

At this point the Foundation had not yet issued an annual report, but a comprehensive forty-year summary was in preparation to cover 1907 to 1946, and annual reports for subsequent years were planned.

With our stern admonition to other foundations in mind, I

[5] "Foundations—a Modern Maecenas," in *Publishers' Weekly*, 8 March 1947, pp. 1464-1468.

[6] Harrison and Andrews, *American Foundations for Social Welfare*, published in 1946 by the Foundation, pp. 98-99.

looked into the state of our own *History* and became alarmed. John M. Glenn, retired director and the Foundation's chief architect, was most appropriately general editor, but in 1946 was in his eighty-eighth year. Miss Lilian Brandt had been added to staff to do most of the actual writing. Foresightedly, work had been commenced in 1942, but in view of the meticulous care appropriate for this permanent record, it had proceeded slowly. The final third, beginning with the Depression 1930s, was not even started, and it would be three or four years, at best, before it could be completed.

At a conference, as manager of publications I expressed concern over this scheduling. Surely a forty-year report should be published somewhere near the fortieth year; and there was our own reputation for reporting in jeopardy. Could not something be done?

They came up with a suggestion that was almost a command, and in my consternation over its nature, I do not remember whether it was Mr. Glenn or Mr. Harrison who made it. Since I had been with the Foundation for precisely this unfinished time span, and moreover as editor of *The R S F Bulletin* had been constantly reviewing and writing up the programs of all departments, would not I undertake this task while Miss Brandt and Mr. Glenn were completing the other sections?

At the time of the conference the foundations book was not yet off press, and my writing chore there had been heavier than originally contemplated. I was in need of a rest. But it was true that no one else on staff had as complete a view of all the work as I necessarily acquired as director of publications. Also, I had a deep affection for Mr. Glenn, and hoped that this record of "his" foundation might be finished in time for him to enjoy it. On 23 February 1946 I agreed to become the third author of the *History*.

It was almost disastrous, from the health viewpoint. That summer I went indeed to our summer home in Vermont, but laden with typewriter and documents. I had twelve fact-packed chapters to write, to clear with department directors, and to put in final form by the self-set copy deadline of December. It was done, but my diary says: "Most of the year has been spent in a writing treadmill. I am tired, tired."

Russell Sage Foundation: 1907-1946, by John M. Glenn, Lilian Brandt, and F. Emerson Andrews, is a two-volume history of 746 pages. A section from it, dealing with establishment of the Foundation, was preprinted in pamphlet form and distributed on the actual fortieth anniversary date, 11 April 1947; the massive boxed *History* was officially published on 24 November. We placed in Mr. Glenn's hands a special copy with signatures of all present and past staff members who were still living and could be found.

In retrospect, I am glad to have had a share in producing this long overdue record of the Foundation which has been so large a part of my life. Because Russell Sage Foundation had a major role in the shaping of social work as a profession, and in many of the early experiments in welfare methods, it is an important record, and is carefully done.

I am less convinced that the history of an institution is best produced by staff. The advantages of superior access to records and intimate personal knowledge must be balanced against a tendency, which is even the more dangerous if it is unconscious, to magnify successes and overlook or omit failures. (This is a danger, the reader is warned, that also besets autobiography, including this one.)

The Ways and Means Committee

A few days after the *History* was published I was called to Mr. Harrison's office, right after lunch. Had I been reading in the papers about the current Hearings in the House of Representatives?

Yes. The Ways and Means Committee was looking into the great numbers of commercial businesses that were reorganizing under the tax umbrella of all sorts of exempt organizations—colleges particularly, but also some foundations—and thereby avoiding the federal corporation tax. The most celebrated case concerned New York University and the C. F. Mueller Company, makers of spaghetti.

Precisely. Well, the Ways and Means Committee had now asked Russell Sage Foundation to testify, presumably because of our recent survey of foundations and our reputation as knowing a great deal about the whole field. The Committee's telegram had arrived only that morning, with our testimony scheduled for tomorrow morning. Neither Mr. Morris Hadley, our president, nor he was in a position to go. Would I undertake this testimony? The time was tomorrow morning.

So I telephoned Mrs. Andrews to meet me for dinner with

razor, toothbrush, and a clean shirt, and took the subway down to the Wall Street office of Morris Hadley. Then and since, Mr. Hadley has seemed to me the ideal foundation trustee, informed, wise, farseeing, considerate of others. We discussed the nature of my testimony, and then he, realizing this would be my first appearance before a Congressional committee, offered some sage counsel.

"The Committee members are likely to ask you some perfectly silly questions," he said among other things, "but I suggest you treat such a question, no matter how silly, as if this was about the most important subject you had considered in a long time, and answer slowly and carefully. Remember, too, we have nothing to hide; you can be perfectly candid."

The next morning, 12 December 1947, I entered the hearing chamber in the New House Office Building well before the opening time of 10 o'clock, and had time to look about. The members of the Ways and Means Committee, chaired that year by Harold Knutson of Minnesota, were ranging themselves on a raised semicircular dais. In the pit were a table and a chair for the witness; off to the side, a table for a stenotypist and a sort of jury box for reporters. Beyond the railing sat the audience, and this Hearing was going to be well attended—my own routine testimony was to be immediately preceded by New York University!

First, as the schedule further intimated, there were statements from representatives of three hospital associations. They pointed to their noble works and the need that their exempt status be left untouched. Committee questions were few, polite, and brief. Then I had a ringside seat at the celebrated New York University case which may have had most to do with a sharp change in the Internal Revenue Code.

Chancellor Harry Woodburn Chase expressed in a letter his apologies for not being able to attend; he would be represented by John Gerdes, lawyer, alumnus of New York University, and former president of its Alumni Federation. The letter cited the 50,000 enrollment of the University and declared "that tax-exemption privileges for institutions of higher education should be maintained as one of the great bulwarks of democratic opportunity in this country."

Mr. Gerdes then made the point that New York University had not taken over any commercial businesses. The firms at issue were each owned by separate alumni "foundations" with all profits ultimately consigned to the University.

The Committee dug for facts. In addition to the spaghetti company, there were three others—Ramsey Corporation, makers of piston rings; American Limoges, China, Inc.; and Howes Leather Company, Inc. Under prodding, Mr. Gerdes admitted a considerable number of other similar arrangements were under consideration, but none had been completed in view of the unexpected furor over the Mueller Company matter.

Warm interchanges took place over whether these arrangements permitted unfair competition, with the exempt companies able to set better prices because of no liability for taxes. And what guarantee was there that the profits, or even the forgiven taxes, would go at any near date to education? None, Mr. Gerdes admitted, but he proposed an amendment requiring that at least the amount representing forgiven taxes be paid over promptly, and in fact this had been done by the N.Y.U.-associated companies.

What about payments from the remainder of profits? It turned out that usually nobody had put up any original money; banks loaned the alumni groups the full amount of purchase price, and it was presumed that bank interest and amortization would come out of profits—which, the Committee pointed out, meant probably a long delay before education got any funds beyond the amounts lost in taxes.

At one point Representative Walter A. Lynch of New York commented, "The action taken is so extraordinary and so revolutionary . . . that it occurs to me probably the whole system of tax exemption for educational and charitable organizations might seriously be threatened if this precedent is allowed to spread."

Suddenly the testimony was ended. It may be pertinent to add here that the Revenue Act of 1950 sharply changed the previous ruling, under which the end purpose of profits determined exempt status. In the new Act exempt organizations, except religious, are required to pay ordinary corporation taxes on taxable income of any business not substantially related to the exempt purposes of the organization itself.

A Bit of Testimony

When I was ushered to the witness chair as Mr. Gerdes left, I wondered whether the heat of the previous discussion had created a dangerous climate. So I began carefully, with a brief word about Russell Sage Foundation itself and then the chief facts about all foundations, in effect a résumé of our findings in *American Foundations for Social Welfare*, a copy of which we presented to the Committee. Since we had not had time to prepare a written statement, I asked permission to enter in the printed record a brief article Mr. Harrison and I had written (actually for the *Social Work Year Book*) which summarized these findings. Mr. Knutson asked about length. "There are six and one half pages." It was ordered printed.

There were a few questions, particularly about duplication of efforts by foundations. At one point I spoke for myself rather than the Foundation:

> Speaking now not as an official representative of the board of trustees of Russell Sage Foundation but simply as an employe of the foundation which has made a study of the foundations, I will say that we are deeply concerned by some of the foundations which have arisen recently, as I believe this Committee has been. We think there are serious problems which may endanger the good work of the foundations which have followed to the best of their abilities the public welfare and social welfare.

> In Mr. Harrison's and my book, we have made certain recommendations in this field. . . .[7]

Our recommendations concerned better reporting and spending at least total income and are printed in the *Hearings*, where they reached a very few readers. In a subsequent paper for *The New York Times* I expanded them to three:

> (1) That foundations enjoying tax exemption publish full reports on both activities and finances (nearly all the larger ones already do);

> (2) That exemption be denied those foundations which over a period of years fail to spend their approximate income;

> (3) That foundations pay taxes upon business enterprises which they wholly own and conduct for profit.[8]

These proposals were certainly not new, and may have had no effect on the tax-writing committees. But all three were substantially embodied in the 1950 legislation.

[7] *Revenue Revisions, 1947-48.* Hearings before the Committee on Ways and Means, House of Representatives, Eightieth Congress, First Session, Part V. December 2,3,4,5,8,9,10,11, and 12, 1947. Government Printing Office, Washington, 1948, p. 3544.

[8] Andrews, F. Emerson, "New Challenges for Our Foundations," *The New York Times Magazine*, 3 April 1949.

CHAPTER 9

Philanthropic Giving

Wᴵᴛʜ the retirement of Shelby M. Harrison on 30 June 1947, change was the order of the day at Russell Sage Foundation. The new general director was already announced as Dr. Donald R. Young, executive director of Social Science Research Council, but he would not be able to assume office until July, 1948. However, under the acting general director Ralph G. Hurlin rapid strides were made toward the new program, involving three principal policy changes.

It was announced that for the present applications for grants would not be considered, and still-active grants were terminated with usually a final appropriation of two-and-one-half times the amount of the previous annual award.

The operating program was changed in structure. Old departments, some of which had been in existence for decades, were abolished in favor of a smaller, coordinated staff, with temporary personnel engaged for specific projects.

The third decision, announced as the most fundamental of all, was to designate for primary attention "a closer and more effective relationship between social welfare practice and the social sciences." The Foundation would seek to build bridges between ivory-towered scientists and practitioners, with the latter needing to understand the theories in order to put them to use, or sometimes to disprove them.

Uproar over the first two changes was somewhat milder than might have been expected. Continuing grantees—some of them had been on the list for as long as forty years—were dismayed at the barren future prospect, but it was hard to be bitter in the same letter that acknowledged a grant two and a half times the normal size. Distress in the staff was severe, though it happened that three department directors were in any event just at retirement age. They were retired—one of them vainly volunteering to stay a few more years to complete several projects—and their departments were closed. Other directors resigned, not always with conspicuous eagerness, to accept positions elsewhere. An effort was made to retain and reassign as much of the clerical staff as possible.

The old building was sold in favor of smaller and more economical quarters at 505 Park Avenue. My sentiments were expressed in a letter[1] written from the old quarters to Mrs. Andrews, up in Vermont with the children:

> Tonight we close down the Foundation officially at 130 East 22nd and reopen Monday at 505 Park. It gives me a queer feeling. After 21 years I had a feeling of helping own this building; now we go out to be squatters in an alien land. . . . It's time to close up shop now, and take home the plans for the new office, which I must mark out in chalk on the bare floors, come Monday.

Even the fine library was abandoned, partly the victim of its own success. From a small collection taken over in 1911 from the Charity Organization Society and State Charities Aid Association, chiefly for use of the Foundation staff and the associated agencies, it had grown to a collection of some 50,000 books, nearly 200,000 unbound items, and 40,000 patrons a year. Costs steadily mounted, absorbing an ever larger portion of the Foundation income. With the impending move, space was not available. So the finest specialized library in its field was given up, and its collections dispersed. The New York School of Social Work had first choice; duplicates, and items not desired by the School, went to the library of the City College of New York.

Before these distributions were made I was permitted to remove a segment relating to foundations and philanthropy. This was in view of the special services I was rendering as a consultant on foundation matters, increasing ever since publication of our book on this subject. But I had also a dream that was growing.

I began to suspect that I knew something about philanthropy, having for twenty years been in a key position to meet its principal leaders, read its literature, and observe its recent changes. No really comprehensive study of the subject had ever been pub-

[1] Letter dated 22 July 1949.

lished. Why should I not try? As a first step, I had prepared a paper stressing recent developments.[2]

A Proposal

The sweeping changes within the Foundation affected Publication Department only marginally. My assistant who had been hired to enlarge the public relations aspects of our activities had to be released. It was acutely painful to bid farewell to so many of my associates in the former departments. But first Dr. Hurlin and then Dr. Young indicated that the publishing operation would be necessary in the new program.

The first special assignment from Dr. Young was to make a survey of the publishing operation of Social Science Research Council for his successor there, Pendleton Herring. I submitted my *Memorandum on Social Science Research Council Publishing Program* in August, 1948, suspecting my astute new boss would himself review it with some care as an appraisal of one of the few executives being carried over.

Several months later Dr. Young called me to his office. The change in program would be resulting in almost no publications in its initial stage. Even at my present half time, I had perhaps some leeway. What would I think of using this time to do a general survey of nonprofit publishing?

I agreed on the spare time and the desire to put it to profitable use. But I had a different and somewhat vaster proposal to suggest. I presented the study of philanthropy idea, bolstered by the published *Atlantic* article which I just happened to have handy. Dr. Young listened, read the article, and suggested that I prepare quickly a memorandum for the trustee meeting to be held in a few days. So I presented this proposal on 1 December 1948:

Subject: HANDBOOK ON GIVING

The Problem. Private giving is a big business—between $2 and $3 billion annually. These sums are important to recipients, and possibly even more important to the givers in terms of stimulating their understanding of, and participation in, major human problems. But givers are honestly confused. The rules have changed drastically, some of them within the past few years. Whole large groups (the

[2] Published as "The New Era in Giving," *Atlantic Monthly*, November, 1946, pp. 114-118.

blind, the needy aged, etc.) who used to be a first charge upon charitable purses are now covered under the Social Security Act. Critical analysis of the results of some giving, designed to make giving more effective, has left many people more aware of the difficulties than of the fresh opportunities in this new era in giving.

The Proposal. I suggest preparation of a Handbook on Giving, which would present clearly, simply, and as interestingly as possible the present situation.

It should include just enough history for perspective, and to suggest broad trends. It should provide a minimum of statistics, but enough to lend proportion to a field notorious for its lack of basic data. Positions would not be taken on controversial issues, nor in favor of particular fields or channels of giving, but the objective data would illumine these questions.

Content: Sections should probably be included on: A Glance at History. The Role of Government. Giving Abroad, Private and Public. Who Gives, and How Much? Corporation Giving. Contributions from Labor. Avoiding Charity Rackets. Federated Giving. Foundations. Community Trusts. Voluntary Agencies, National. Local Agencies. Religious Giving. Colleges and Schools. Scholarships and Student Loans. Health Agencies. The Arts. Financing Research. Taxation Factors. Endowments and Interest Rates. Trusts and Bequests.

In working on our book on Foundations I have already done much of the needed research and established channels to the needed information. The project could be completed rather quickly and economically, with merely expansion of my own working time and some legal assistance.

Purposes Served. Primary users of this Handbook on Giving would be prospective givers, and the lawyers and bankers who are their advisers. Executives of welfare agencies, board members, and fund collectors would be the second group.

Through its means Russell Sage Foundation might considerably expand its present important services in guiding philanthropy. It could presumably stimulate some new gifts, and turn toward effective work funds, now perhaps uselessly employed, much vaster than any direct monetary contributions we could ourselves make.

A few days later I was again summoned to Dr. Young's office. The trustees had approved, and I could begin at once. As I had suggested, I would now go on eight tenths foundation time, still needing to reserve one tenth for writing interests and one tenth for my Twentieth Century Fund commitment. I had estimated that with reduced publishing at present, half my Russell Sage time could be spent on the writing project. But Dr. Young made it clear that I was a free agent and could do my writing at home, in the office, or wherever and whenever I pleased. I would be responsible only for the best possible manuscript, hopefully delivered in the predicted two years.

That was the beginning of a delightful relationship. Donald Young is a hearty, solidly built Pennsylvania Dutchman, born in Macungie, Pa. He makes up his own mind on a given subject, and is quite willing to express his views, sometimes brusquely. There are those who consider him severe, even brutal, in the way he cuts through what he regards as error, or the pussyfooting of do-gooders unwilling to face scientific fact. But toward those who win his confidence he shows deep personal consideration, generosity, and a lively wit. Publicly and privately, I have acknowledged him as the best boss I ever had, giving me support and counsel when needed, and that absolute freedom which is for me the first condition for good work.

"This morning," gloats my diary for 16 December 1948, "I begin work on the new project." As it progressed and it became evident that it was going to be much more than a "handbook," the title changed to *Philanthropic Giving*.

It was no small undertaking. Though I had already done much of the basic research—for the *Foundations* book, for instance, I had digested the 122 books and articles appearing in its bibliography, and quite a few others—gaps remained, requiring more reading, field trips, interviews, and serving on a variety of committees where pertinent information could be picked up. In all, preparation of the book involved consulting more than eight thousand references, ranging from books in several volumes through pamphlets, magazines, newspaper clippings, and memoranda on conferences.

I should have welcomed some of the modern retrieval techniques, but in the 1940s only beginnings had been made in this field. I did use at Yale the Human Relations Area Files, started by George P. Murdock as the Cross Cultural Survey. From published and unpublished materials, facts on behavior in each society are organized under 79 major topics, plus subcategories. As in all such endeavors, classification was the problem. "Charity," "Giving," and "Philanthropy" might seem key words to me, but did not inevitably suggest themselves to the cataloguers. But I did find useful references for my historical section without the need for going through whole hefty tomes on history, anthropology, and the like.

Fortunately, most of the literature central to the field I had already reviewed, and have the kind of locater mind that often remembers the position on the page of a desired quotation. As the references accumulated into the thousands, I developed a filing system. Each chapter or main subject within a chapter had a separate folder. I never took home any of that deluge of references except for the section on which I was immediately working. So I did not drown in that documentary flood, and sanity was saved.

One chapter, "Foundations and Community Trusts," was easy. I could simply condense the material already published in our foundation book, bringing up to date a few of the statistics. This time we listed The Ford Foundation assets at $238 million. Other chapters involved considerable new research, and sometimes plunged me into the middle of controversies.

Federated Giving

I was thus catapulted into the center of the most serious of the welfare wars in 1949, when I was writing the chapter on "Fund-Raising." It necessarily dealt with both individual agency solicitations and federated campaigns, such as community chests and the new "United Funds."

Chests themselves were not new. A Federation of Charities and Philanthropy was organized in Cleveland in 1913. During World War I the multiplication of appeals, including those for relief of sufferers in Europe, induced some four hundred communities to organize war chests for joint solicitation of funds. Many were disbanded at the end of the war emergency, but not all. In 1918 the surviving chests formed a national association. In 1919 thirty-two cities still had joint fund-raising organizations, under a wide variety of names, and in Rochester, New York, Harry P. Wareham appears to have coined the name "community chest."

The central idea is eminently sound. In essence, a community chest is a citizen-and-agency-controlled organization which has the principal duties of acquiring and spreading information on welfare needs; coordinating the work and reviewing the budgets of the participating agencies; campaigning to meet the chest's accepted share of these budgets; and disbursing these funds to the agencies. It promises to the individual contributor immunity from appeals for funds by the included agencies, except in the case of a capital drive or special situation.

Through the first quarter century chests grew steadily but not spectacularly. For chest year 1925,[3] 240 campaigns raised $58 million; for chest year 1950, 1,318 campaigns raised $193 million. But although in the latter year the many more chests covered a much larger proportion of the population, the gifts as a percentage of national income had risen not at all—they were still an insignificant 8 cents out of each $100 of national income, precisely the percentage raised by the mere 240 chests in 1925. To bring these figures closer to date, for chest year 1970, 2,107 community chests and united funds raised $787 million, or about 10 cents on each $100 of the national income of $796 billion.

Despite the annual ballyhoo which leaves a public impression of great and increasing success, this is a miserable record. The reason is not obscure. Federated giving can be outstandingly successful only if contributors generally give substantial amounts to the chest or united fund, recognizing that this is not "just another drive," but a combined drive to which their contribution should be many times their usual gift for a single cause. But many individuals give according to the fatness of their purses at the moment, rather than the nature of the drive. They may even give less to a federated drive, where the heart appeal of individual agencies is obscured by multiplicity, than to a single agency with a fine emotional appeal. Some years later I supervised a pilot study on givers' attitudes, and while the sample was too small for generalization, it is illustrative:

> What do our interview schedules show as to dollar amounts? . . . We found 41 replies which itemized contributions both to chests and to other agencies. In nine of these cases the community chest contribution was in fact larger than that to any separate agency. In five others it was exactly the same as the contribution to at least one other favored agency, usually American National Red Cross. In all others it was actually less than the contribution to at least one favored individual agency. . . .

> Total chest contributions of these 41 donors were $515.25, or an average of $12.57 each. The median gift was $5.00. The gifts of these same persons to welfare agencies exclusive of chests amounted to $5,732, or roughly eleven times their chest contributions.[4]

[3] Year in which funds are to be expended. Usually the campaign was conducted the previous fall, but collections may continue into the chest year.

[4] Andrews, F. Emerson, *Attitudes Toward Giving*. Russell Sage Foundation, New York, 1953, pp. 82, 83.

In recognition of this problem chest executives in the late 1940s began emphasizing business contributions and solicitation of employes in plants. For both of these purposes, federated giving is nearly ideal. The corporation, desiring to discharge its obligation as a "corporate citizen" in the communities where it has employes, can determine its appropriate share for a combined campaign more easily than for a wide variety of individual appeals. And since in-plant solicitations were becoming common for an increasing number of agencies, it saved important top staff and worker time if these could all be combined into one annual plant drive. Most companies were willing to take the further important step of permitting annual pledges, to be deducted weekly or monthly from pay checks. This neatly solved the twin problems of the individual contributor to the chest—he no longer was limited to the spare cash on hand, and the collection problem on a longer-term pledge was handled by his employer.

Some private agencies, and notably the "big five"—cancer, crippled children, polio, Red Cross, and tuberculosis—opposed federation, and tried to keep their local chapters from joining chests. With their prestigeful names, appealing causes, and ability to recruit unpaid solicitors for massive drives, they were able to collect more dollars (for polio, dimes in those days) by their own efforts than chests could apportion them.

Detroit became a storm center. Industry, led by Henry Ford II and other industrialists, with the support of the labor unions, decided that the losses in time and the heavy costs of numerous individual solicitations in plants were no longer to be endured. They helped organize in Detroit a drive limited to industrial and plant solicitation under the name United Foundation of Detroit, which "invited" all national fund-collecting agencies to join, with notice that no other plant solicitation would be permitted.

It campaigned for $893,500 in February and March, 1949, and I made a flying trip to Detroit on 25 March. At lunch I listened to the presentation of Walter C. Laidlaw, energetic leader of the drive. That evening I had dinner with a local executive of the National Foundation for Infantile Paralysis and heard his equally impassioned opposite arguments. Polio refused to accept any money from this drive, so a payment of $30,294 was finally made to the Sister Kenny Foundation. Red Cross, too, insisted on a separate campaign; in the Ford plant the subscription card for the drive as a whole included an added line, printed in red, permitting separate subscription for the Red Cross. The hastily organized campaign did not reach its full goal, but raised $750,000. In the fall of 1949 the United Foundation took the next step by including the local agencies of the Detroit community chest ("143 campaigns in one!") in its Torch Drive for $8.55 million; it went over the top, raising $9.2 million.

The United Fund idea, with heavy industrial support, spread from city to city, and now in most large communities there is an autumn "united fund" drive combining many local agencies and some, but not all, of the national appeals. The welfare war is not ended. The federated drives increase their dollar totals from year to year, but barely keep up with inflation and growth in national income.

Our contributions, both through the federated and the individual drives, fall pitifully short of the actual needs in both health and welfare. And so the money we refuse to give voluntarily we now contribute through our other pocket, federal taxation. Several years ago[5] I estimated total charitable giving, excluding religion, for an average American family at $66 for the given year. This covered all nonsectarian charities—the community chest, Red Cross, schools, health agencies, the library, police fund, and others. But the same family, without knowing it and with no chance to dictate selection, paid out that same year, in the portion of its taxes that went to the Department of Health, Education, and Welfare, $357 for medical research, hospital construction, school aid, scholarships, public assistance, and the many other "philanthropic" purposes that fall within the budget of merely that federal department.

My present views on federated giving have not much altered from those expressed in the book I was preparing in 1949. The multiplying of individual appeals is a burden which must somehow be lightened. Chests and united funds are in theory an admirable solution. In practice, they remain ideal as a channel for the giving of corporations and have much to recommend them in plant solicitations, though here giving begins to resemble impersonal taxation. As a channel for the giver in his own home, results have been dismal.

Some device needs to be found to stimulate our interest, and if possible our personal involvement, in one or several of the particular causes now lost in chest appeals covering anywhere from a dozen to over four hundred agencies. Possibly a formula could

[5] In "The Fifth Freedom," Appendix I, pp. 283-291.

be worked out permitting the donor to designate one or several agencies of particular interest to receive half his total contribution, with these agencies thus stimulated to keep in close touch with such donors. This might give efficient agencies with appealing causes a slight advantage (and keep them in the united fund), but the undesignated other half and the undesignated corporate gifts should permit total distribution in close accordance with informed over-all planning.

Federated financing will succeed to the extent that it is oriented, not to agencies and their desires, but to givers, their habits, their preferences, and their deep needs. If philanthropy is to flourish, givers must be made understanding partners.

Charity Rackets

Charity rackets had to be covered, if only to put them in perspective in contrast with the tremendous overemphasis common in the press.

The best example of donor gullibility I picked up was the case of Robert E. Hurst, in Memphis, Tennessee, who circulated a paper asking contributions to "the Fund for the Widow of the Unknown Soldier." He promptly collected $11, which he later returned, explaining that it was going to be hard to find the *unknown* soldier's widow.

One afternoon Mrs. Andrews helped in a P.T.A. survey to find out how many preschool children were in our section of the town. One lady saw her coming up the walk, reached the door first, and handed her two dollars.

With givers so careless, it is not surprising that some racketeers turn to charity, with their own profit paramount, and the cash receipts of the high-sounding cause negligible or nothing. Statistics in this field are unreliable, since only discovered frauds can be tabulated. The best evidence I could uncover suggested that the total take in outright rackets was not proportionately large, perhaps from 2 to 3 percent of the philanthropic dollar. But the racketeer steals twice—both our dollars and our willingness to give. I took some pains to describe the various information agencies, maintained in most cities by the Better Business Bureau, Chamber of Commerce, or Council of Social Agencies, and for national funds, the National Information Bureau in New York.

In terms of money wasted, there is a problem more serious than actual rackets—the vastly greater sums that go every year to honest, well-intentioned organizations which can pass any financial audit, but achieve little social benefit from the funds they receive. The very purpose of the organization may be outmoded. There may be unnecessary duplication. Management may be wasteful. Costs of solicitation may be too heavy, or some of the methods objectionable, the size of the budget excessive in comparison with other more pressing community needs. So I said:

> The contributor who examines his charitable list with care, seeks information on any doubtful items, and takes an intelligent and continuing interest in the organizations he does assist is giving more than money. He is helping raise standards in the field.[6]

The Tompkins-Rabin Hearings

A few years later a New York State joint legislative committee announced hearings in New York City on charity rackets, to begin on 14 December 1953. The committee was headed by State Senator Bernard Tompkins as chairman and Assemblyman Samuel Rabin as vice-chairman.

The committee had been operating since July. It had found that there was no New York State law regulating or supervising charities or any public agencies (there were private ones, as already noted) where a contributor could have access to information on fund-seeking organizations. A questionnaire was sent out, and the replies analyzed by committee staff, with inspection of the organization's books where the information furnished seemed dubious or inadequate. The committee "soon discovered that New York State, partly because of the absence of any statutes, was considered a 'happy hunting ground' by a number of National groups which were barred from soliciting elsewhere."[7]

Local welfare agencies acknowledged the seriousness of the problem, applauded efforts at correction, but were tremendously distressed over the prospect that news stories, which would inevitably emphasize the bizarre and the fraudulent, would reduce their own receipts, particularly as the hearings were scheduled for December, the highest "giving" month of the year. The com-

---

[6] *Philanthropic Giving*, p. 171.
[7] *Report of the Joint Legislative Committee on Charitable and Philanthropic Agencies and Organizations*. Legislative Document No. 26. Albany, 1954, p. 10.

mittee was sympathetic, but determined to go on with the hearings. After some negotiation it was arranged that I should be the first witness, in the hope that testimony on the whole field of philanthropy would bring rackets into perspective and result in saner press coverage.

Before daybreak on 14 December I woke to the sound of driving rain. Two large, unwieldy charts had to be taken from my office to the downtown New York County Court House, and this was no morning to stand on a street corner trying to hail an improbable taxi. So we got the children up, fed, and to school long before their usual time and drove our own station wagon to New York through flooding rain to transport the precious exhibits.

With the aid of the charts dutifully held up by court attendants, I indicated that of the $4 billion total charitable contributions of 1950, about 18.5 percent ($750 million) came from New York State, and of this perhaps 3 percent, or between $20 and $25 million, may have gone into outright charity rackets. "These figures," said the Committee *Report*, "were substantiated by other experts in the field." My further testimony was based on a series of questions prearranged with the Committee's attorney, with added queries from Senator Tompkins and others, definitely not prearranged. However, by this time I was an experienced hearings witness, and I hoped that the testimony contributed some general perspective to the rackets problem.

Several other general witnesses were heard, and then for the rest of Monday and three more days we listened to testimony on rackets themselves, occasionally startling. One witness was George Bieler, a professional "boiler room" operator:

> He specialized in telephone solicitation using twelve to fifteen assistant solicitors. Although the telephone lines and other incidentals were supplied free of cost to him by the charity his "cut" was usually 40 percent "off the top." His most valuable assistants brought their own "sucker list." . . . No one showed hesitancy in assuming whatever character or name would be most effective in obtaining contributions, and Bieler himself admitted to masquerading in various enterprises as a judge, a doctor, a colonel and a bishop.[8]

The Disabled American Veterans, Inc., and its fund-raising arm, the D.A.V. Service Foundation, also received major attention. The committee disclosed that, based on reports of the D.A.V. auditors, the organizations had raised from 1950 to 1953,

[8] *Report*, p. 23.

primarily through unordered fountain pens, license-plate tags, and puzzle contests, a total of approximately $21,480,000. Of this, fund-raising costs ate up $14,529,000 (68 percent), administration $2,401,000 (11 percent). Welfare disbursements totaled $3,837,000 (18 percent), and a balance remained of $713,000 (3 percent).[9]

As a result of these hearings the New York legislature in 1954 added three chapters to its Social Welfare Law. Chapter 418 requires registration of "every charitable organization [except religious, and certain other groups under particular circumstances] which intends to solicit contributions from persons in this state by any means whatsoever," with annual reports which are open to public inspection. Chapter 419 requires registration and bonding of professional fund raisers and solicitors. Chapter 420 requires the written consent of any person whose name is used in soliciting contributions. Many other states now have similar laws.

Religious Giving

To return to the book: aside from charity rackets, the most difficult field for gathering statistics proved to be religion. This was critical, for all our data suggest that in recent years approximately half of all philanthropic dollars go to religion, with this term including charitable and educational agencies under church control as well as direct church support.

Solid figures were hard to come by. The Church of Christ, Scientist, would not even supply figures on membership, its manual forbidding "the numbering of people and the reporting of such statistics for publication." For Jewish data, there proved to be no central tabulation of giving for congregational purposes in the three bodies, Reform, Conservative, and Orthodox. Moreover, for this group with religious traditions pervading so much of their living, it was exceedingly difficult to distinguish between giving for religious or for secular causes, and matters were further confused just then by the new creation of the State of Israel, with extremely generous contributions to such organizations as the United Jewish Appeal.

For Roman Catholic giving, there were the difficulties of more than a hundred dioceses in the United States, each a separate financial unit apparently reporting only to Rome; special contri-

[9] *Report*, p. 20 and Fig. 4.

butions to Catholic Charities and to the religious orders; educational contributions for parochial schools and the Catholic colleges; the international Church. I tried to find my way through this maze, proceeding from parish priest to Cardinal, and was usually received courteously but told that information either did not exist or could not be made available. Finally from a source that shall be unnamed I did obtain data for a single diocese, and in very guarded language made a general tentative estimate. But on the value of invested funds I could not even hazard a guess.

The Protestant picture presented an opposite difficulty. Some 222 Protestant denominations were in existence in 1949, many of them supplying financial data, but with such wide differences in program and reporting methods that summations were difficult. A helpful series covering 15 of the larger bodies was being maintained by Harry S. Myers, of the United Stewardship Council, whom I visited in his Michigan home. His pioneering work, continued and amplified by what is now the Section on Stewardship and Benevolence of the National Council of the Churches of Christ in the U.S.A., is a bright spot in a smog area.

Through the years, often under compulsion of federal, state, or local law, organizations enjoying the privileges of tax exemption have been required to make increasing disclosure of their finances. This is a reasonable requirement, and I have supported its extension. Full disclosure of both finances and program seems the safest method of preventing abuse, while avoiding the dangers of governmental controls. But religious agencies have been exempted from such legislation, and attempts at their inclusion they resist with such mighty organized pressure that legislators retreat without a battle.

This is a grave mistake. I am well aware of the Biblical injunction, "When thou doest thine alms, let not thy left hand know what thy right hand doeth," and have always declined to permit my name to be used on a patron list. But this reticence should not extend to corporations, religious or other, with respect to what they do with the monies they receive or already have.

However, even individual church boards still practice this secrecy. I have recorded my early and continuing interest in The Riverside Church, first under Harry Emerson Fosdick. This Church is governed by two boards, the trustees who are concerned primarily with the finances of the church, and the deacons responsible for spiritual matters and program. I have served in many capacities in this church, including ten years on the board of deacons, with two of them as chairman. But once I was asked to serve as chairman of the Budget Committee, and at the same time was refused access to the church audit, which was not available to the membership, or even the officers other than trustees. Without access to this basic budget information, I found it necessary to decline.

Here and elsewhere arguments against disclosure are advanced vehemently and sincerely. Givers of large endowments, it is said, might be embarrassed. (But many of them have endowed foundations, where every penny of endowment and expenditure is open to public inspection.) News of large sums might discourage the small giver. Possibly; but also lack of factual knowledge may often result in inflated rumors, and there is another Biblical injunction that "Ye shall know the truth, and the truth shall make you free."

I am happy to report that in November, 1969, The Riverside Church altered its policy and mailed to the full membership a summary of assets, liabilities, and fund balances, including endowment at both book and market values. One hopes that this example will be widely followed and that religious leaders generally will insist upon full disclosure for themselves, as for all other segments of the philanthropy field. If this does not occur legislation may soon require it, but meanwhile scoundrels will increasingly use religion as their last safe refuge.

In New York State where a few people may band themselves together under a pious name, call themselves a religious organization, and avoid the charity laws, one such organization was discovered to be renting out nuns' habits at $2.50 a day, the "nun" thereafter soliciting alms in bars, restaurants, subways, and railway stations in the name of the organization, and keeping for herself everything above the $2.50 rental charge.

Religion receives far too large a part of total philanthropy to sail any longer through a fog of secrecy. In *Philanthropic Giving*, after acknowledging the inadequacies of the supporting data, I estimated 1949 contributions to religious bodies at $1.9 billion, probably an underestimate. But lest this not inconsiderable sum seem a matter for prideful satisfaction, I called attention to the $6 billion Christmas expenditures for that year:

> Christmas, it has been widely forgotten, is a religious holiday. To celebrate the birth of the founder of Christianity we give in presents

to one another three times as much as we give to all religious causes during the whole year.[10]

John M. Glenn

John M. Glenn, first general director of Russell Sage Foundation, was no longer well. One day early in 1950 I visited him in his apartment, to bring him news of what we were now doing and hoping to express some of the appreciation of us all for the organization of which he had been the first and chief architect. He was still intellectually keen, interested in the latest news of everyone he had known, and up to exchanging quips with the pretty waitress as we lunched. He had one sad comment as we parted:

"When you are as old as I am, spring never comes any more."

He died in his ninety-second year, a few weeks later, on 20 April 1950. Manuscript of my book, nearly completed, took on one addition, a dedication:

To the Memory of
JOHN M. GLENN
A WISE COUNSELOR AND FRIEND
TO ALL WHO WORKED WITH HIM
FOR "THE IMPROVEMENT OF SOCIAL
AND LIVING CONDITIONS"

A Book Is Published

As the summer of 1950 approached, the manuscript was done. It had been a vast task. I was weary, weary.

Our boys were now fifteen, twelve, and eleven. It was time they saw the America over which I had tramped and driven and flown; indeed for some years we had half promised that we might be '49ers, going to California just a century after the original big migration. But in the summer of 1949 I was too deeply involved in the book for any but the briefest vacation. Now, however, the manuscript could be sent to the printer, and I could read some proof en route.

So we took six weeks for our long-planned trek west. It proved high in altitudes, latitudes, and just plain fun. We gave the boys

[10] *Philanthropic Giving,* p. 187.

their first "ocean" voyage across Lake Michigan, found an August day in the Salt Lake Desert so chilly we had to turn on the car heater, climbed volcanic Mount Lassen, waded in the chilly Pacific, spent a night in a Redwood forest. We climbed a Rocky Mountain whenever we needed a stroll, and were in summer snow or in sight of it every day for a month.

On the way back we finally reached Jasper, that finest of all America's mountain parks. In a week's rest there the tight springs uncoiled at last, and the diary reports "For the first time in more than a year I feel really rested, relaxed, at peace with the world, ready for another year."

When I returned there were still a few updatings, page proof, and index, but I had energy back, and the end was in sight. On the morning of 11 November 1950 five advance copies were ranged on my desk. It was in an unusual sense "my" book—original idea, research, writing, and as publication director of the Foundation, choice of type, layout, page design, all details of manufacture. Publication date was set for 20 November, just within the two years promised to Dr. Young.

As publication approached, it became evident that news media were interested. So I broke my usual rule of not bothering about news releases until reaching the office, and bought a *Times* early Monday morning, the 20th. There it was, two columns on page one, with a long overrun, second story, chart, and described as "the most comprehensive survey of philanthropy ever undertaken in this country."

Advice to Givers

The *Times'* second story was devoted to suggestions to givers with which I had closed the book, and it is possible that they are worth repeating here, in the abbreviated form I later adopted for speeches.

1. Give adequately for the need, but not lavishly; give in ways that will stimulate giving from others.

2. Give toward rehabilitation rather than relief; toward cure rather than treatments; still better, give toward prevention.

3. Give toward research and discovery, and especially toward discovery of the conditions of health and well-being.

4. Give in such ways that the gift will not sap effort or confirm a

feeling of inadequacy, but will stimulate the recipient toward renewed activity to help himself.

5. Give to your own community, where you know about needs and services; but also to poorer communities, which have greater needs and fewer to help.

6. Give nationally and internationally, for we need to be one world.

7. Finally, in all your giving, give thought. For with thoughtful giving even small sums may accomplish great purposes.

CHAPTER 10

Corporations as Donors

Eᴠᴇɴ before bound copies of *Philanthropic Giving* were in, Dr. Young was asking me what I wanted to do next. I said the big gaps in the field that we might attack were studies of (a) corporation giving, (b) the motivations and attitudes of individual givers, and (c) a more comprehensive survey of foundations. The last could wait, in view of our 1946 book. As to attitudes, the techniques of social research were scarcely yet adequate for valid scientific findings, but the subject was important and should be explored. The most urgent need was for a good study of corporation giving; the practice was expanding very rapidly in dollars given, but with little guidance and few facts.

Some preliminary exploring in the fall of 1950 found corporations eager for such a study and willing to cooperate. With trustee approval, I began intensive work early in 1951.

The Situation

The beginnings of substantial corporation giving date from World War I and it was recognized in the federal tax structure in 1935 under Depression urgencies. When my new study was commencing, the reported amounts had increased from a level of about $30 million a year in the late 1930s to a wartime peak, sparked by an excess-profits tax, of $266 million in 1945. Totals fell from that peak with the expiration of that tax, but remained above $200 million in each of the succeeding years. As a further measure of size, the corporate contribution had closely paralleled the total collections of community chests in every recent year, and of course about one third of these chest amounts were coming from the corporations.

But while the chest movement had its national body with mountains of statistics, guidance manuals, and careful surveys, corporate giving was a wasteland. Back in 1930 the National Bureau of Economic Research had published a study, based chiefly on information from community chests. National Industrial Conference Board was periodically conducting surveys of practices of its own members, chiefly large manufacturing companies, and these had restricted circulation. Beardsley Ruml and Theodore Geiger were preparing a pamphlet, *The Five Percent*, which exhorted corporations to give up to the full deductible 5 percent (published 1951). Other bits and pieces existed, but no one had gathered them together, and they were not enough for any clear pattern.

Early in my interviews, which were off the record and often quite frank, I found three main attitudes toward corporate philanthropy. Quite a few corporate executives were completely negative, and gave nothing, an attitude that still persists.

"Give money to charity?" sputtered one president. "Why, that's nonsense. Any money we would give must be taken either from profits, which belong to stockholders, or from wages of employes, or show up in higher prices to our customers. We have no right to do any of those three things."

Others saw such giving as a civic duty, particularly in the new economic setting of the postwar period. Henry Ford II stressed this view in a statement made when Ford Motor Company Fund was being set up in 1949:

> Traditional sources of financial support of private institutions operating in these fields are tending to disappear. We do not like the consequences inherent in the alternative facing such private institutions—that of having to turn to government for much-needed financial aid. In our opinion, this situation places an increasing responsibility upon American businesses in their role of industrial citizens.

Still others see enlightened selfishness as both the necessary legal basis and the proper business attitude toward corporation giving. Said the executive in charge of company donations for one of the largest corporations in America:

"Don't use my name, or some folks would think I was pinko. But I think American corporations must go much farther in giving. Let's say all welfare services make a circle of 360 degrees. If a corporation sets up operations in a backward community in Brazil, it occupies the whole 360 degrees. It builds the church, the roads, constructs hospitals and schools, pays the doctors, brings in the teachers, finances all the welfare services there are —not because it's a philanthropist at heart, but because it can't make a good profit, and perhaps can't operate at all, in a community that doesn't have those services. In the United States, corporations now take in about 45 degrees of that welfare circle. We don't need to go the whole 360, but we ought to get to about 180 degrees."

Gathering the Facts

Our research staff consisted of one secretary and myself, and I still needed to handle publications for Russell Sage Foundation, to act as consultant to Twentieth Century Fund, and to fit in some free-lance writing. It was a busy time.

A chief resource was the Bureau of Internal Revenue. Beginning in 1936, its annually published *Statistics of Income* for corporations included an item "gifts and contributions" helpfully reported by type of corporation, by asset size, and (in the manuscript *Source Book* which I was able to consult in Washington) geographical and other useful breakdowns. These figures required some qualifications, but they made the broad trends clear.

Corporate contributions had grown from a level of a mere $30 million a year in the late 1930s to a plateau of about a quarter billion in 1949, the latest year reported in time for our study.[1] The popular view that the big corporations were the most generous proved entirely wrong. In 1948, for example, the very numerous corporations with assets below $1 million gave at a rate of 1.3 percent of net profit; those with assets between $1 million and $100 million, at a rate of 0.8 percent; the 601 giant corporations with assets of $100 million or more, at a rate of 0.3 percent of net profit.

Of course, as I was careful to point out in the full study, these broad averages are subject to qualification. They are a bit like the case of the railway porter who was asked by an inexperienced traveler what the average tip was. The porter declared it was two dollars. When she paid this sum he was profuse in his thanks, adding, "You're the first that has come up to the average." Similarly, the "average" for the very small corporations is sub-

[1] For more recent data and further statistical refinement, see Nelson, Ralph L., *Economic Factors in the Growth of Corporation Giving*. Russell Sage Foundation, New York, 1970, 116 p.

stantially inflated by inclusion of the statistics of the many corporations in this group which have negative income. Example: Two corporations have an income of $100,000 each and contribute $1,000 each, at a rate of 1 percent. A third corporation has a loss of $100,000 and makes no contribution. All three corporations have a combined income of only $100,000, but made $2,000 in contributions, at a rate of 2 percent—twice as much as the actual rate for any of them. But even after correction is made for this factor, the giving rate still descends, though less spectacularly, with increase in corporation size. This was true in all years studied, and remains the situation.

Moreover, in many small closely held corporations some of the "family giving" is discharged by the corporation, achieving the corporation tax deduction and avoiding transfer as personal income.

The rate of giving varied widely among different types of corporations. Trade and service companies are usually small and close to their customers; they are subjected to heavy pressures —"customer blackmail," one company president called it—and see at first hand the advantages of giving in their own communities, and the penalties for not giving. Their giving rates are high and help explain the record of the smaller corporations.

Dollarwise the greatest contribution comes from the manufacturing industries, which in most years have more than half the total profits of all corporations. In sample year 1948 manufacturing had $18 billion in net profit, 52 percent of total corporate net profits; this group contributed $119 million, almost exactly 50 percent of that year's $239 million total reported contributions.

Geographically, the Bureau had no data later than 1941, and this only in the manuscript *Source Book*. Again, the findings were not those anticipated. Regionally, the South and Middle West had the highest rates. The Mountain States and the East were predominantly low, with such industrial states as New York, Pennsylvania, New Jersey, and Michigan all in the lowest category; less than 0.3 percent. This is radically different from the ratios in personal giving, where high rates, I had reported in *Philanthropic Giving*, were "confined to the industrial East and a few southern states." The geographical difference in corporate giving may be due less to regional influences than to the already noted fact that big corporations give at lower rates than smaller ones, bringing down the rate for nearly all the highly industrialized states.

The Bureau of Internal Revenue was most helpful, both in its published statistics and in granting access to its nonconfidential files. For our mass statistics only the government had the power to compel returns from all corporations and the facilities for tabulating information from the more than 600,000 returns. But these returns did not report on the individual giving of even one corporation, its amount, or the fields supported; it said nothing about motivation; and at that time no series had yet been run indicating what proportion of corporations reported any gifts.

Later, for 1958, the Treasury did run a special series showing the number of corporations which reported any contributions. The record is startling. For that year, the report covered 990,381 corporations. Only 273,909 (27.7 percent) reported contributions. The very large corporations, with assets of $100 million or more, usually did have giving programs, 801 out of 1,203, or almost exactly two thirds. Of intermediate corporations, 60.8 percent contributed. But of corporations with assets below $1 million, only 25.5 percent reported contributions—one in four. This means, of course, that with the "average" including so many noncontributors, those which do contribute are much more generous than the average suggests. But the total picture of only slightly more than a quarter of all corporations in the contribution picture even by 1958 is not widely known, and was disturbing.

The Questionnaire Survey

For more detailed study of corporation giving we used a questionnaire and personal interviews. The questionnaire was sent in March, 1951. It was a two-page document on which the corporation was identified only by a code number, and the replies were guaranteed confidential, "to be used only in nonidentifiable summaries, unless released by special arrangement." It was sent in March, 1951, to a random sample of 1,200 corporations of all types from Poor's *Register of Directors and Executives*. Questions covered type of business, assets, number of employes, net income (for 1950), deducted contributions, additional sums to similar organizations given as a business expense, analysis of contributions by fields, procedures for processing requests for gifts, employe solicitation policies, and a "confidential down-to-earth statement on factors you give most weight in deciding on a contribution."

Our first mailing, explaining the survey and urging a full response, brought in promptly some 240 adequate replies. Later mailings, supplemented by visits and telephone calls, produced a final 326 complete returns, or 27 percent, which is relatively good for a voluntary study asking intimate questions in a difficult year. There were 43 other returns not complete enough for tabulation, but helpful; 44 flat refusals; 787 failures to reply.

Among the nonrespondents was a prominent newspaper corporation, which later asked for early release of the findings, which would be of much interest to its readers. I took great pleasure in informing that editor that our survey was less complete than it should have been because of failure of certain corporations to respond; example, his. But we had more sympathy with Corporation No. 1979, which could not complete the questionnaire because "our Statistical Department is so busy now making out reports for the Federal Government that it takes about all of their time to do this."

The picture that emerged, while it cannot with safety be blown up for all corporations, is the best available picture of corporation giving in 1950. It showed 44 percent of corporate contributions going to welfare agencies, nearly five sixths of this amount being given directly to community chests and united funds. About 27 percent went to health agencies, with hospitals the chief beneficiaries. (The claim of local hospitals serving corporation employes is obvious.) Educational agencies received 21 percent, but not all of this went to colleges and schools; about one fifth of the total was given to a wide variety of "American way" organizations, few of which were college-related. Religious agencies received 4 percent; this is a field in which corporations find contributions difficult, with directors and employes in many sects. A remaining 4 percent was too miscellaneous for classification.

Our request for frank answers on motivation brought replies from 248 corporations, naming from one to five factors given "most weight in deciding on a contribution." The following percentages therefore add to more than 100 since one corporation might cite two or more factors. Thirty percent of replying corporations frankly acknowledged benefit to the company as a chief factor in their giving; and this percentage rose to more than half for the largest corporations. Nine percent cited benefit to employes; 28 percent "public relations or customer pressure." These three factors, all of which involve direct or indirect business benefits, are collectively quite influential in guiding and motivating contributions.

A still larger group, 42 percent, cited "duty to the community." Thirty-one percent declared themselves influenced by the worthiness of the cause; 16 percent by a sense of moral obligation or corporate good citizenship. In this large group of answers self-interest is not explicit. Because these are the "noble" motives, some overreporting is not unlikely.

Finally, 8 percent were influenced by a desire to limit expansion of government into welfare fields; 7 percent by their profit position and tax considerations; and 5 percent by the example of other companies.

Individual replies were sometimes more revealing than the group summaries into which they had to be fitted. "Union pressure" said one company. Another, a brewery, specified "public reaction if we do not contribute." We found also the opposite situation. A distillery reported refusal of gifts by certain religious and youth organizations.

How Is Giving Done?

Both the questionnaire replies and the interviews present a disturbing picture of office procedures. With honorable exceptions, corporations in 1950 had not yet efficiently organized their giving operations. In most companies the fault was not delegation to the office boy of this chore, involving usually less than one tenth of 1 percent of company expenditure; most companies fell into the opposite error of letting all its detail go clear to the top, where there is neither time nor specialized knowledge for efficient handling.

In a stunning 89 percent of the sampled companies requests for contributions went directly to a single top executive, usually the president himself. Three percent, usually large companies, had contribution committees. The whole board of directors functioned in 2 percent of the cases. The rest scattered—finance committees, local or district managers, a company-sponsored foundation. Less than a third of the corporations set up contributions as a budget item.

What usually happened when perhaps hundreds of appeals a year dropped on the busy president's desk? Judging from the replies, he gave in to the squeezes when they began to hurt. For the rest, he took refuge in the "safe" causes he's heard about year after year. Eighteen percent of the sampled companies gave all their contributions to annually recurring drives, and 91 percent gave at least half their 1950 contributions to such drives. Most of these agencies need support, but to give only to them is to miss opportunities to fit the company's gifts to particular needs of its community and its own special knowledge and resources. This is not so much giving as giving up.

Company-Sponsored Foundations

Among the "honorable exceptions" were nine of the sampled corporations which had set up company-sponsored foundations to process most of their gifts. That this was to be a spectacular development in company giving became obvious as the study was in progress. In the single month of January, 1952, I received 162 letters from corporation executives, or legal firms representing them, asking about setting up such foundations.

There were reasons for this beyond regularizing corporation giving and acquiring trained staff. That was the period of the Korean War, and by 1952 tax rates for corporations in the excess-profit bracket had risen to 82 percent. They could siphon off into a foundation up to 5 percent of net profits at the bargain rate of only 18 cents on the dollar in cost to stockholders, hold these assets in this new kind of philanthropic bank against years of low or absent profits, and then pay them out; or perhaps retain them as almost costless assets, the income from which would discharge a substantial part of philanthropic obligations for many future years.

I devoted a chapter to this foundation development, sensing its importance. We had then no count on such foundations, but now know that of all the 1,472 company-sponsored foundations large enough to be included in the 1967 *Foundation Directory*, 620 (42 percent of the total) were set up in the four years 1950 through 1953, and these foundations held 49 percent of the assets of all listed company-sponsored foundations.

Now that the Internal Revenue Code has introduced liberal carry-over provisions on contribution deductions for corporations, the short-term "hills and valleys" feature is a less important factor. But most of the other advantages remain. One of the severe dangers in all corporate giving is the possible effect of a major depression. With few or no profits for several years, it is probable that most corporations would reduce or cease their welfare contributions, just when their help was most needed. With a cushion in the company foundation this would not be necessary.

Administrative advantages are also important. Requests for contributions are channeled to the foundation, relieving business executives of the chores of acknowledging and handling, and reducing the heat put upon them by personal solicitors. Such requests can be effectively checked in an office set up for that purpose, under an executive who devotes much or all of his time to such tasks. Budgeting is a simpler matter when all recurring drives and most emergency causes can be provided for with one annual appropriation and it is not necessary that this sum be wholly used within a single calendar year.

Personnel is another advantage. Intelligent philanthropy is a complicated business, more nearly an art. It cannot be well performed in a few minutes of spare time by a busy executive, however outstanding he is in making motorcars or toothpaste. It cannot safely be relegated to a superannuated employe, who needs three or four more years to build up his pension—a situation we too often found. It should be the primary responsibility of a person or committee with expertise in the kinds of philanthropy the corporation wishes to support, and continuity in this task to ensure sound judgment on persons and organizations supported, and to develop fresh forms of creative giving. This is possible under special appointments or contribution committees, but it is more probable under the regularized staffing of a foundation.

Over the years I have come to know, and applaud for their abilities, several dozen men, and one woman, in charge of the giving programs of large corporations. Many of them have not come up through the corporation, but have been specially selected for this assignment. Most of them are the executive heads of company-sponsored foundations.

Technically, such foundations are governed by their boards of trustees, though in practice the recommendations of the foundation executive, who may or may not be one of the trustees, usually prevail. Typically, company foundations have as trustees only members and officers of the sponsoring company. The corporation probably could not legally contribute to an uncontrolled foundation. But I have recommended that such foundations include among their trustees one or more persons not connected with the company, but offering a broader view, perhaps particularly in a field the corporation wishes to support, and inspiring public confidence. A few such foundations have done so, but the practice is not yet general.

Creative Giving

One day during the study the Bulova Watch Company sent a car to take me out to the Joseph Bulova School of Watchmaking in Woodside, Long Island. This is one of the few companies that had been giving substantially its full 5 percent for many years, chiefly through its Bulova Watch Company Foundation, set up in 1944. I found the handsomely appointed school full of disabled veterans, whom it trains free as watch repairers. Most were paraplegics—wheel-chair cases—and the school has its own wheel-chair basketball team. These men, trained to high skill in one of the few occupations a legless person can readily perform, go out to well-paid jobs, usually in retail jewelry stores. In its first five years, the school director told me, they had graduated 346 men, 95 percent of whom were now gainfully employed. The company received its tax deduction for expenditures in building and operating the school—and to keep this line clear, does not itself hire any of the men. The government "loses" the unpaid taxes, but a large group of veterans, who might have had to be supported wholly by government subsidy the rest of their lives, are now gainfully employed, paying personal income tax. More important, men who have given much to their country are restored to self-respect and an interest in living. And this is a philanthropy which, because of the technical know-how involved, could have been set up by only two or three companies in the United States.

That half day at the School lifted my spirits and supplied a fine example of creative corporate giving—the sort of thoughtful giving by which a corporation, capitalizing on its own special knowledge and technical facilities, multiplies the value of its giving. In our study we came across a few other examples, but they stood out as rarities in a wasteland of the commonplace.

The Rich Foundation in Atlanta, chiefly supported by the department store of that name but with also some family contributions, concerned itself with special local needs: a building to house Emory University School of Business Administration; a radio station for the city and surrounding area, owned and operated by joint boards of education; an outpatient clinic for a local hospital.

Mrs. Andrews and I drove through Corning, New York, and there visited the new Corning Museum of Glass, which preserves glass of scientific and historic importance and encourages the study of glass and glassmaking. This Museum has obvious values for the Corning Glass Works, but is also a distinguished public service.

When the Southern Railway System went to whistling diesels and scrapped its steam locomotives, it had a lot of engine bells left over. Now 64 belfries in as many white and Negro churches summon the devout to worship, but also ring out the praise of a corporation executive who, by thoughtfulness, turned a waste product into a useful gift.

One of the projects of The Sears-Roebuck Foundation, supported entirely by Sears, Roebuck and Company, was the "Cow-Hog-Hen" program which gave purebred livestock to clubs of farm youngsters to improve and diversify livestock in their communities. And who will complain if better herds and flocks put more cash in farm pocketbooks, with which to buy more from mail-order catalogues?

A few other examples brightened the record, but for the field as a whole we had to make the judgment, "disorderly and chaotic." Where the giving was not merely traditional, it was sometimes dangerously self-serving.

One corporation tried to have a major executive on the board of every agency, college, or other institution to which it made substantial contributions. Where this is done as a matter of service, as for instance in heading up fund drives or supplying accounting or other technical aid, it can be a valuable form of non-monetary contribution. In this case the purpose was admittedly to be in a position to suggest activities of direct interest and concern to the corporation. While most agencies seem to feel that only one taint attaches to money—'t ain't enough—contributions coupled with efforts at control have sometimes been refused.

The Law

At the time of our study the right of a corporation to give away stockholders' money was still moot. We retained as legal consultant Ray Garrett, then chairman of the Committee on Corporate Laws of the American Bar Association. I leaned heavily upon him in drafting the legal and tax chapters of the book, and he supplied an appendix which attempted to summarize all cases in the United States that bore significantly on corporation giving.

The federal statute granting deductibility had been on the books since 1935. By 1952, 29 states and the Territory of Hawaii had passed permissive legislation of some sort, and the covered states included all the industrialized area from which corporate contributions were substantial. The permissions were in some states restricted, but newer legislation often embodied the "model law" proposed by Mr. Garrett's committee, which provided broad power "to make donations for the public welfare or for charitable, scientific or educational purposes." In the light of these developments, we concluded:

> The bugaboo of illegality has been largely laid. Corporations which in the past used to frighten off undesired solicitors are sometimes finding it difficult to rid themselves of the doubts they induced, but in the light of recent developments their fears seem nearly or quite groundless. Corporations can give to philanthropic causes if at least some direct relation to their own interests can be demonstrated.[2]

The A. P. Smith Case

But the legal battle was not quite over. We had warned in the book that "some responsible legal opinion supports the immutable contract doctrine"—that a corporation's charter is a contract that cannot be altered or broadened by legislation passed subsequently.

In our study we had become aware of increased interest in support of liberal arts colleges. There were problems: if a grant was made to one, "the other 1,199 come around mad as hornets." Also, support for technical courses in a corporation's field were easily defensible, but what about mere general support in a liberal arts college? Nevertheless a group of prominent corporation executives, including Frank W. Abrams of Standard Oil Company of New Jersey, Irving S. Olds of United States Steel Corporation, and Alfred P. Sloan, Jr., of General Motors Corporation wrote and spoke widely in favor of such contributions. "Capitalism and free enterprise," declared Mr. Olds, "owe their survival in no small degree to the existence of our private, independent universities."

[2] *Corporation Giving*, p. 240-241.

At this time, according to my grapevine, lawyers for Standard Oil Company went to Mr. Abrams, pointed out his own eloquent addresses in favor of contributions to private colleges, and said that in their view Standard Oil could not contribute one penny, for it was a New Jersey corporation; although New Jersey had passed a permissive law, their charter antedated the law, and could not be changed.

If my grapevine was not true, then the following historic events constitute a most remarkable coincidence. A South Orange, New Jersey, housewife named Ruth F. Barlow entered a stockholder complaint over a contribution of a mere $1,500 to Princeton University for general purposes. The contribution had not been made by a corporation of national prominence, but by the A. P. Smith Manufacturing Company, a small New Jersey corporation that, among other things, makes fire plugs. Out of nowhere appeared eminent legal counsel for both sides. (The aggrieved lady was never seen.) I began to be invited to special luncheons at the Princeton Inn by President Harold W. Dodds; my luncheon companions would usually include the president, eminent lawyers, Mr. Abrams, Mr. Olds—all of us tremendously concerned over that $1,500 gift.

In the devious ways of the law, the A. P. Smith Manufacturing Company became plaintiff, asking for a favorable declaratory judgment on its contribution, against Ruth F. Barlow and other stockholders.

The case began in Newark on the stormy morning of 11 December 1952, before Superior Court Judge J.S.C. Stein. The witnesses included Frank W. Abrams, Irving S. Olds, President Dodds, and other persons of extraordinary prominence for so minuscule a case. I was there as an expert witness (my study had been published three months earlier). The skilled lawyers carefully raised every possible argument for and against corporate giving in its broader aspects. But the opposing lawyer tried to exclude all testimony relating generally to corporation giving, and to limit testimony to this one particular gift.

My diary record is gloomy on my own part. "A most useless day. . . . A weary Court by the time I reached the stand decided not to admit at all general testimony on corporation giving." Months later in the printed decision I learned that a copy of *Corporation Giving* had somehow got through, at least to the New Jersey Supreme Court, where it was cited. Judge Stein's resounding decision is worth quoting in part:

Such giving may be called an incidental power, but when it is considered in its essential character, it may well be regarded as a major, though unwritten, corporate power. It is even more than that. In the court's view of the case it amounts to a solemn duty.[3]

To leave no stone unturned the case was finally appealed clear up to the Supreme Court of the United States, which in effect affirmed it by finding in it no "substantial federal question."[4] This key case removed any lingering doubt of the legal validity of corporate giving if even the slightest relation can be found to corporate interests.

Corporation Giving Published

The book was published on 8 September 1952. It was not the once-in-a-lifetime affair that publication of *Philanthropic Giving* turned out to be, but because this new giant in giving was important to colleges and other seekers of funds, a flood of requests came in for speeches and special articles. I accepted as many as my schedule permitted, for research is useful only to the extent that it can be brought to persons who need its facts. Besides, it was sometimes fun.

In Cleveland, I was to give the keynote speech at the National Conference on Solicitations. A delegate with a New York badge sat down beside me in a hallway, awaiting the opening session.

"I see you're also from New York," he said. "I don't usually come to these things, but this guy Andrews is going to speak, and I ought to hear him once."

"That's a coincidence," I remarked, "that's just why I'm here. I have to hear that fellow, too."

We met at a cocktail party later and have been good friends since.

Six months after publication a rough listing from office memoranda indicated I had already undertaken at least twenty-five speeches or special articles on the subject. The addresses ranged from the American Council on Education, the National Conference of Social Work, and the National Council of Churches to local efforts such as the Financial Secretaries of New York and the Allentown (Pennsylvania) Kiwanis Club. Major

---

[3] Superior Court of New Jersey, Chancery Division, Essex County, Docket No. C-1274-51, the A. P. Smith Manufacturing Company, Plaintiff, *v.* Ruth F. Barlow, *et al.*, Defendants. Opinion (May 19, 1953), p. 13.

[4] Supreme Court of the United States. No. 383. October Term, 1953.

articles included "New Giant in Giving: Big Business," in *The New York Times Magazine*, "Will Corporate Giving Solve College Deficits?" guest editorial in *College and University Business*, and "This Business of Giving," in *Atlantic Monthly*, the last reprinted in the April, 1953, *Reader's Digest*.

The family was by this time a trifle weary of the subject of corporation giving. When one evening I announced that the *Atlantic* article was about to be reprinted in *Reader's Digest* with its 17,000,000 circulation, son Peter had the crushing answer:

"Now you're all washed up, Daddy; you can't give that speech any more."

Afterthoughts

Nevertheless my interest in the subject remains keen. Shortly after our own study was completed, I served as special consultant to The Committee on Corporate Giving in Canada, which conducted a study closely modeled upon our own.[5] On a visit to London in 1966 I discussed British corporation giving with officials of P.E.P. (Political and Economic Planning). They reported mounting interest, several existing pamphlets, and a proposed study of their own on "social responsibilities of company directors." A government bill was before Parliament, which would require reporting of all donations above £25.

Of course I have followed more closely developments in the United States. After the sharp increase at the time of the Korean War, certainly induced in part by the stratospheric level of excess-profit taxes, annual amounts dropped from the 1953 peak of $495 million to a plateau of around $400 million. Then they began to rise again. The most recent year for which we have final figures is 1968, with $1,005 million. Preliminary estimates suggest that for 1971 the total may be in the neighborhood of $925 million, registering recent reduced corporate profits.

This is still not a large part of total philanthropic giving, nor a big item in the corporate budget. But it is an important part of the budgets of many health and welfare agencies, and of education, to which a larger share of corporate gifts have recently been assigned.

Business statesmanship needs to consider what its share should

[5] Shea, Albert A., Editor. *Corporate Giving in Canada.* Published for the Committee on Corporate Giving in Canada. Clarke, Irwin & Company Limited, Canada, 1953.

be in supporting existing free enterprises in health, welfare, education, and research, and possibly in initiating fresh ventures in these areas. Such support is not a necessity. Private individuals can and do bear much of this burden, and government will take over any essential services which fail of private support—and add them to the tax bill. Giving is less a duty than an opportunity.

As it grows in size and experience, corporation giving can fill a unique place in the scheme of philanthropy. It can take special care of the needs of the local community, with which it is intimately acquainted. This hardheaded giver can require and study financial statements of all soliciting agencies, and help bring sense, order, and honesty into a disorderly field in which good intent has sometimes resulted in little practical accomplishment. With better staffs, corporations can become creative givers, using the special knowledge and resources of their particular industry toward the common welfare in ways not possible for other donors.

True, this giver will be guided by self-interest. But we are coming to learn that the highest self-interest is often scarcely to be distinguished from the thing we used to call altruism.

So long as I was an official in research organizations dealing with the field, a proper objectivity required that I not be associated with any corporation. Upon retirement in 1967 I was asked to join the board of directors of Shell Companies Foundation. This is one of the few company-sponsored foundations that ever since its establishment had included a "public" member, not associated with the company. I had long and favorably known its chief staff officer, Walter M. Upchurch, Jr., recently retired. I accepted the Shell invitation, remaining on the Board until March, 1973.

CHAPTER 11

Congress and Foundations in the 1950s

In the early 1950s a strange malady which has been likened to the witchcraft hysteria in colonial Salem was sweeping America. This time the Soviet Union was vigorously endeavoring to infiltrate organizations and convert persons to its doctrines, and Communism was the terror. The feared witches were any persons who had fallen under that spell, or were even suspected of having any contacts with the Soviet.

Witch-hunts proceeded all over America, and a mere accusation without proof was good for headlines. Some of the informers and witch-hunters were sincere persons attempting to act in the public interest. Others, often politicians, found witch-hunts a swift road to publicity and high public office. There were no hangings (there had been nineteen in Salem, and one man was pressed to death), but hysteria swept the land and the careers of innocent men were ruined by false charges, or mere suspicions.

Senator Joseph R. McCarthy was so notorious a leader in this evil era that it has become known as "the McCarthy period." In the early 1950s he was at the height of his influence, charging that the State Department was riddled with "Communists and homosexuals." His 205 Reds in the Department were later changed to 81; exhaustive hearings developing more than two million words failed to substantiate any accusation. Mr. McCarthy continued his charges, involving even General George C. Marshall, but was careful to make all his statements within the Senate, where Congressional immunity protected him from libel suits.

Foundations became aware in 1951 that they were not to escape this wave of hysteria. The attack came, however, not from

McCarthy but in the House of Representatives, from fiery E. Eugene Cox of Georgia. There were those who believed that Mr. Cox had Senatorial ambitions, and Communist-baiting seemed an easy road to wide publicity.

Foundations are uniquely vulnerable to political attack. They have no alumni, no patients, and no parishioners, ready to wreak voting vengeance upon any politician rash enough to attack them. They have few voting friends. Foundations have an average of about six trustees apiece. Grantees are little help, for enemy-making refusals outnumber acceptances by about ten to one. Even grant recipients may be resentful over receiving less than they hoped, or because of an accompanying condition. The better known foundations have names that usually connote great wealth, inviting attack, and the better-run of them are apt to be involved in exploratory and often controversial projects, well in advance of popular understanding or approval.

An Investigation Is Demanded

In 1951, in several flaming speeches, Representative Cox proposed an investigation of foundations. He made many unsupported charges, such as:

> Our boys are now suffering and dying in Korea, in part, because Rockefeller money encouraged trends in the Chinese colleges and schools which swung China's intelligentsia to communism. [These instances are] only a few examples, among many, of the tragic misuse of foundation money. . . . The resolution is deserving of the serious consideration of those who fear for the safety of our country.[1]

He proposed creation of a select committee to be composed of seven members of the House of Representatives which would be:

> —authorized and directed to conduct a full and complete investigation and study of educational and philanthropic foundations and other comparable organizations which are exempt from Federal income taxation to determine which such foundations and organizations are using their resources for purposes other than the purposes for which they were established, and especially to determine which such foundations and organizations are using their resources for un-American and subversive activities or for purposes not in the interest or tradition of the United States.[2]

[1] *Congressional Record*, 81st Congress, 1st Session, Vol. 97, Part 14, p. A4833.
[2] House Resolution 561, 82nd Congress, 2d Session.

The concluding phrases made it clear that a new witch-hunt was on. Calmer heads pointed out some of the dangers of such an investigation. "What member of the proposed committee," asked Representative Johnson of California, "could say with certainty what our traditions are? Who is there that by investigation can develop the mold to which all of us must conform in order to be in harmony with American traditions?"

But the resolution was passed on 4 April 1952, and on 2 July an appropriation of $75,000 was given this committee, with orders to complete its report by the first of January, 1953. Every foundation knew the fat was in the fire, and very soon indeed they would be feeling the heat.

The committee early made one prime decision. Instead of employing a professional Red-baiter as its general counsel, as Mr. Cox had proposed, it offered this key position to Harold M. Keele, Chicago lawyer. Mr. Keele is a short, solidly built, dark-complexioned man, able and articulate and full of energy. Later, when I had grown to know him well, he told me that in response to the committee's invitation he had expressed certain convictions which amounted to an ultimatum.

In his view Congressional investigations should be conducted with dignity, and with as little fanfare of publicity as possible. They should proceed, not in the spirit of a prosecuting attorney as had been the case in many recent Congressional hearings, but in the temper of a British royal investigating commission, seeking to look at all the facts and to arrive at a balanced judgment. If the committee desired an investigation of that type, and only then, would he be willing to serve.

Mr. Keele was appointed.

The Foundations Prepare

One of Mr. Keele's early actions was to sit down at lunch with the heads of most of the large foundations in an attempt to secure their cooperation. He told them he planned a thorough investigation—his college-trained staff included several men with FBI or Central Intelligence Agency experience—but it would be conducted fairly; and if it was to be completed within the brief time allowed, he must have the cooperation of the foundations. A questionnaire would be coming to them shortly.

At a subsequent meeting of foundations, which I attended, it was agreed that replies would be made to the specific inquiries of the committee. However, led by the lawyer element, the group showed no enthusiasm for "prejudging" the investigation by undertaking other forms of requested cooperation, such as general advice, comments on the questionnaire draft, or letters expressing approval of the announced purposes of the investigation.

Dr. Donald Young and I felt that a more constructive and cooperative attitude should have been taken. Indeed, Dr. Young pointed out that he had already offered my assistance, as a student of the field. It was agreed that this was proper as representing the aid of a research specialist rather than that of a particular foundation or the foundation group. Beginning the very next morning, 17 September 1952, I began to have meetings with Mr. Keele and his staff.

Whatever may have been the doubts of some of the foundations and their lawyers, all but one did fill out the "voluntary" questionnaire when it came. It proved to be a lengthy and complicated document. In the longer form submitted to all foundations known to have assets of $10 million or more, the nine sections included ninety questions, many of these multiple; sometimes a single question required tremendous documentation, as for example:

> C-7. List those institutions, operating agencies, publications, specific projects, and individuals, which have received aid from your organization and the amounts and years and nature of such aid since 1935.

Questions D-14 and D-15 required full data on funds of any sort granted or paid to any individual or organization "criticized or cited by the Un-American Activities Committee of the United States House of Representatives or the Subcommittee on Internal Security of the Judiciary Committee of the United States Senate." The search through the millions of words of the hearings of these committees was an almost endless task, involving many thousands of names, often supplied by the McCarthy type of informer, of persons who may have merely attended a dinner sponsored by an organization later suspected of infiltration by Communists.

For the larger foundations replies grew to book size (Henry Allen Moe's response for John Simon Guggenheim Memorial Foundation ran to 329 pages), and the expenditure of many thousands of dollars in staff work. For a month or more top foundation executives in New York were practically unapproachable.

They did not even see each other, for one of the questions they had to answer was this:

I-2. State whether you have consulted with the representatives of other foundations with reference to this questionnaire and the answers thereto after receipt of this questionnaire.

The Hearings Begin

On the morning of 18 November 1952, the hearings chamber in the New House Office Building was crowded. An overflow of reporters were invited to occupy end seats on the raised dais, usually reserved for committee members. With the first words of Chairman Cox it became evident that the policy of cooperation had been wise. Instead of his earlier searing denunciation of foundations and repetition of charges from irresponsible sources, Mr. Cox now said:

> I should like to make it perfectly clear that the committee will strive to conduct the hearings in a fair and judicial manner, and if possible do nothing that will afford an excuse for the accusation that it is likely to become a smear or a whitewash. . . . there is not a member of this committee who is hostile to the foundations or the idea of philanthropic giving. There is not one who wishes to injure the foundations or impair their proper functions.[3]

Mr. Keele had agreed that the hearings would begin, not with fireworks on controversial aspects of foundation programs, but with general testimony on the place of foundations in the American scene. Ernest V. Hollis, of the United States Office of Education who had done some writing on the early history of foundations, was to open with this aspect. I was to follow with about an hour's testimony on present position. The Treasury would describe the provisions for tax exemption. A group of distinguished witnesses from the various sciences and education would speak to the worth of foundation contributions in their respective fields.

I listened restively to Dr. Hollis, who had been out of touch with foundations for many years and was mentioning such matters as the macaroni factory without noting that legislation had

---

[3] *Hearings Before the Select (Cox) Committee to Investigate Tax-Exempt Foundations and Comparable Organizations*, U. S. House, 82nd Congress, 2d Session. Government Printing Office, Washington, 1953, p. 2.

stopped that tax loophole, and spouting vast figures on numbers and assets, which he later modified by acknowledging his definition included colleges, hospitals, scientific societies, or other charitable bodies with a principal fund.

But chiefly my restlessness sprang from a strange thing that happened to me on the way to this particular forum. As I was crossing the Capitol grounds Mr. Keele caught up with me.

"Mr. Andrews, I have news for you."

"Oh. Your schedule is so full you want me to cut back to half an hour?"

"Not quite. Norman Sugarman, the Treasury man, collapsed at his desk last night, and will not be able to go on today. After Hollis finishes this morning, you are on for the rest of the day."

So, I was indeed restless, listening with one ear to Dr. Hollis and trying to think what on earth I would say on this national sounding board for nearly a whole day.

Shortly after 11:00 I was called to the stand. Mr. Keele made generous reference to my philanthropic studies. I introduced our tighter definition of foundations, and indicated that by this definition we found, not 35,000, but 1,007 foundations with assets of $50,000 or more, and total assets currently of $2.6 billion. My prepared material lasted comfortably to lunch adjournment.

At lunch, I started to eat, and found myself suddenly perspiring heavily. That could mean a major digestive upset, so I stopped, bought the first chewing gum in twenty years, and lay down on a stone bench facing the Capitol. By 1:30 when we reconvened I was feeling fit again.

Things went well, I think. Mr. Keele and the committee asked many questions, and since I really did know a great deal on this subject, words, illustrations, even occasional humor, came easily. On the constructive side, I had an opportunity to introduce our own questionnaire answers to items G-4 through G-7, concerning public "interest" in tax-exempt foundations and possible government regulation:

> Governmental regulation is undesirable except insofar as necessary to achieve the degree of accountability suggested above. . . . A program to ensure accountability for all foundations might include:
>
> 1. A registry of all foundations and charitable trusts, presumably through uniform legislation in all the States, under the laws of which such organizations are usually originated. The registry should be public, segregated, and kept current.

2. Compulsory annual reporting, including a full financial statement and a description of activities. These reports should be open to the public. To some extent this purpose is already accomplished on the federal level through compulsory filing of Form 990-A.

3. Provision for regular review of such reports by a public authority possessing power to correct abuses. Presumably such power resides in the States which were the constituting authorities, and would be exercised through the office of the respective attorneys general.

These measures do not envisage control of program, which is regarded as unwarranted and dangerous. The mere existence of power to divert such funds into only such channels as might receive wide public support at a given moment would both discourage new gifts of thoughtful donors and threaten the essential ingredient in the success of the foundation movement—freedom to experiment.[4]

The afternoon did not seem long, and I had the feeling that the testimony was well received. Representative Angier L. Goodwin of Massachusetts called it "a very masterly presentation," and presiding chairman Brooks Hays of Arkansas said as he adjourned the session, "Dr. Andrews,[5] we are very grateful for your helpful testimony. It is an extremely valuable contribution." The next day I went to Mr. Cox's office to make typographical corrections in the transcript (which ran 85 typed pages!) and he was equally complimentary. One discounts heavily for Congressional courtesy.

The next day I was recalled briefly, but for the rest of the long hearings was mostly a fascinated listener. One of the effective early witnesses was Vannevar Bush, president of Carnegie Institution of Washington. On the question of federal expansion versus private initiative he was outspoken:

DR. BUSH: I believe very strongly indeed in the system of private initiative which has made this country great. I believe in the type of philanthropy which has made the foundations possible, and I would much prefer, if it were possible, to see the entire burden carried by private benefactions and by private action, because I believe that the nearer we come to having the Federal Government grow indefinitely, controlling everything, supporting everything, the nearer we come to a socialistic state, which I would much deplore.[6]

[4] *Answers to Questionnaire*, Russell Sage Foundation, 1952, pp. 23-24.
[5] I received an honorary L.H.D. from Franklin and Marshall College in 1952, but instruct staff and request friends not to use it. "Doctor" is better reserved for the medical profession.
[6] *Hearings*, p. 153.

The Foundations Testify

The excitement would begin, it had been predicted, with the questioning of individual foundations. The Ford Foundation was the first called, and its testimony lasted for two days. Ford executives, trustees, and lawyers, most of them nationally prominent, occupied nearly two rows in the hearings chamber. The public had its first long look at the world's largest private philanthropy.

Henry Ford II, a plumpish young man in his middle thirties and then board chairman and president of Ford Motor Company, was one of the witnesses. He testified that The Ford Foundation had begun in 1936 as chiefly a channel for the personal benefactions of his father and grandfather. But upon their deaths and the settlement of their estates it became obvious that vast sums would be at the disposal of the Foundation. A committee was appointed to study the possible future program. Mr. Ford wrote to H. Rowan Gaither, Jr., hired to direct this study:

> We want the best thinking available in the United States as to how this foundation can most effectively and intelligently put its resources to work for the public welfare.[7]

Meanwhile, the family divested itself of majority control by appointing new trustees, because, said Mr. Ford, "We felt that this trust was so large that the family should not have control of it."

Probably to his amazement, the investigating committee demurred.

"In the public mind," said Chairman Cox, "is there not a great deal lost from the foundation standpoint in Mr. Ford's severing his connection completely with the foundation?"

They were mollified only upon being assured that young Mr. Ford remained chairman of the Foundation's board, and in one recent year spent "42 full working days" on foundation affairs.

The committee asked Mr. Ford to comment on the opinion, often expressed, "that the whole scheme and plan of the Ford Foundation was a method whereby the Ford family could retain control of the Ford Motor Company."

Mr. Ford testified that he was in prep school when the Foundation was first started, had not heard direct comments from his father or grandfather, but was certain one of their purposes was "to carry on their obligations to charity, as they saw them," but

[7] *Hearings*, p. 199. Introduced in the testimony of Mr. Gaither.

that "there may have been some other reasons [such as] the possibility that they could still maintain a certain relationship between their stock and the operations of the company."

Chief testimony on general policies of the Foundation was given by Paul G. Hoffman, then its president and director. He referred briefly to the five goals, "the goal of peace and the goal of trying to strengthen democratic institutions, strengthen the domestic economy and advance education and pioneer in the field of behavioral sciences," and talked at length on Ford activities abroad, particularly India, Pakistan, and the Free University in Berlin. The Ford Foundation had appropriated some $72 million in the past two years; of this, $35 million went to education, but their educational applications had exceeded $300 million. Mr. Hoffman was lyrical about "what we have here in America."

How the wind was beginning to blow in the committee was evident in Mr. Cox's comments at the close of the Hoffman testimony:

> THE CHAIRMAN: You preach a fine doctrine and it is something which ought to be carried to the firesides and the homes of people. . . . You have made a very fine case for the Ford Foundation. As a matter of fact, you have made a fine case for all the foundations.[8]

Similar and growing friendliness to the foundations became evident on the part of other members of the committee as the testimony of the major foundations unfolded.

The hearings continued from 18 November through 30 December, with of course Thanksgiving and Christmas recesses, and occasional other intervals when the committee did not meet. I sat through nearly all the sessions, with a few necessary business interruptions (including testimony in the A. P. Smith case mentioned in the preceding chapter).

Communist Charges

The hearings had been set up especially to determine which foundations were promoting "un-American and subversive activities," and this phase was by no means neglected. As far as some of the press was concerned, it was the only aspect substantially reported. One day I shared a cafeteria table with the reporter for a large Eastern daily. He told me his special assignment for

[8] *Hearings*, pp. 259, 262.

the year was stories on Communist infiltration, and he had been sent to these hearings merely to report on that subject.

When Mr. Keele had shown me the list of foundations "invited" to testify, I asked him why he was going to grill so many of the best-known and probably innocent foundations and omitting certain dubious ones, for example, the Robert Marshall Foundation which had even had its tax exemption recently revoked. He replied wryly that here the Congress had outsmarted itself; that foundation had refused to answer the questionnaire, declined to testify, and on threat of subpoena had pointed out, quite correctly, that his committee had authority only to examine "tax-exempt" organizations, which they no longer were.

However, questions on subversives were raised with each of the testifying foundations. But Mr. Cox's advance charges against The Rockefeller Foundation, Carnegie Corporation, John Simon Guggenheim Memorial Foundation, and several others dissolved in the light of the testimony. In the case of The Rockefeller Foundation, a total of 28,753 grants had been made; questions could be raised with respect to two organizations and 23 individuals out of that total, or fewer than one in a thousand. In many of these cases the grant was made long before the person became subversive, or his doubtful affiliations could be known, and in no case—with this or any other foundation which appeared before the committee—was any grant made with evident subversive intent.

Fireworks were expected in the questioning of Carnegie Endowment for International Peace, whose president in 1947 and 1948 had been Mr. Alger Hiss, recently found guilty of perjury in connection with the famed "pumpkin papers" of Whittaker Chambers, a confessed Communist. The testimony was clear, brief, and quite unexciting. John W. Davis, formerly candidate for President and a trustee of the Endowment, testified that Mr. Hiss had been recommended to the nominating committee by John Foster Dulles, Secretary of State, and his whole past career carefully reviewed by several persons before his election. As to his service while president, both Mr. Davis and Joseph E. Johnson, the current president, testified that his activities had concentrated on support of the Marshall Plan and the United Nations, without the slightest "bias in favor of the Soviet Government or of the satellites of the Soviet Government."

On Communist infiltration, the committee questioned not only the foundations but a number of former Communists and informers. These witnesses were sworn, and other precautions taken in an effort to keep this portion of the hearings to the high level of the rest; but the gross inaccuracy, to use the politest phrase, of some of these witnesses and the press handling of their testimony made this the committee's most dubious venture.

Some information was turned up on Moscow's program to infiltrate cultural and educational groups, including foundations. But that program had suffered failure so far as getting Communists or Communist sympathizers into responsible positions in any of the larger foundations.

The informers named again many of the persons the foundations had already listed as receiving grants which in retrospect were mistakes or at least dubious; and they added other names, sometimes with deplorable results.

In an extreme example one Maurice Malkin, "consultant" with the Immigration and Naturalization Service, U. S. Department of Justice, testified that Michael W. Straight, president of William C. Whitney Foundation, "has been in every Communist front practically—most important Communist fronts since its inception." Mr. Straight pointed out that at the time alleged he was an undergraduate at Cambridge University, England, and not even in the United States. Mr. Malkin replied in a letter, after the hearings were over, that he had made a mistake, confusing Mr. Straight with "a Robert Strong or Michael Strong," and now wished to correct the record "and eliminate and repair any harm to a man of whom I know nothing about."

The charges appeared in headlines; the correction in an appendix to the hearings[9] which few will ever see. One can only hope that future Congressional committees will not call as witnesses unstable persons willing to call gossip truth, to garble names, and to do harm they can never repair to persons "of whom I know nothing about."

The hearings proper ended on 23 December, though there was an emergency session on 30 December for two professors who wished to clear themselves. The committee staff, required to finish its final report by 1 January, prepared to work through the Christmas holidays. On the evening of 22 December, Mr. Keele has told me, he showed a draft of the first half of the *Report* to Chairman Cox, then in hospital, who approved it. Two days

[9] *Hearings*, p. 782-783.

later, while taking a blood transfusion and discussing plans to be home for Christmas with his wife, Mr. Cox suddenly died.

I was asked to make myself available for factual consultations during the hectic following period, and was in Washington for two days, on one of them on duty from 9:00 A.M. until 1 A.M. the next morning. A secretary broke down completely, but Mr. Keele and his director of research, Joseph C. Kiger, worked on.

The Final Report

The committee submitted its Final Report on schedule, on 1 January 1953. It was a unanimous report, though Representative B. Carroll Reece of Tennessee added a paragraph pointing out the "insufficient time for the magnitude of its task" and suggested a further inquiry.

The Final Report did not hold foundations blameless. They had made mistakes, some of them were less cautious in their grants than the committee felt desirable in the present international situation, but

> So far as we can ascertain there is little basis for the belief expressed in some quarters that foundation funds are being diverted from their intended use. . . . That the Communists succeeded in obtaining from the foundations financial aid and assistance for numerous members and sympathizers seems conclusive to the committee. In the aggregate, the number of such grants and the amounts involved are alarming. Proportionately, when viewed in the light of the total grants made, they are surprisingly small.[10]

Mr. Keele himself, in a later address, summarized the major findings:

> The report of the Cox Committee noted that foundations "remain an important and vital force in American life"; that "their dominant and most significant function has been displayed in supplying the risk or venture capital in advancing the frontiers of knowledge"; that "they have rendered great and significant services in many fields" including medicine, public health, education, the natural and social sciences, government, race relations, economics, art and international relations; that "the present need for foundations is even

[10] *Final Report of the Select Committee to Investigate Foundations and Other Organizations,* House Report No. 2514, 82d Congress, 2d Session. Government Printing Office, Washington, 1953, pp. 6, 7.

greater than it has been in the past" and will increase in the future; that foundations are "a vital and essential factor in our progress."[11]

The committee agreed with the foundations that there should be no governmental control of program. Its positive recommendations were two: public accounting should be required of all foundations, and the Ways and Means Committee was urged to "re-examine pertinent tax laws, to the end that they may be so drawn as to encourage the free-enterprise system with its rewards from which private individuals may make gifts to these meritorious institutions."

So ended the Cox Committee Hearings. Too hurried and not without flaws, they have supplied a rich storehouse of information and opinion concerning foundations in the early 1950s, and set a pattern for fairness and objectivity that might better have been followed in the several more recent "Hearings" to which foundations have been subjected.

Operating Principles of Foundations

The Cox Hearings had several important sequels.

Some of us realized that only part of its collected wealth of information would become available to the public in the published hearings. The questionnaire material was a richer store, for in it every foundation of substantial size had answered ninety searching questions, revealing not only detail on its operations, grants, trustees, and possible subversive relationships, but making considered comments on such general questions as:

E-1, Should foundations . . . sponsor projects which may have as a direct result the influencing of public opinion in the fields of politics? Economics? Education? International relations? Religion? Government and Public Administration? Other Fields? Explain fully.

E-3 (h), In your opinion, what effect have educational and philanthropic foundations and comparable organizations had on education in the United States? In other countries?

G-1, What, in your opinion, is the function of tax-exempt philanthropic and educational foundations in society today? Are they supplying a vital need? If so, to what extent?

[11] Keele, Harold, "Government's Attitude Toward Foundations," in *Proceedings*, Conference of Michigan Foundations. James Foster Foundation, Ann Arbor, 1954, p. 27.

G-5, In your opinion, is some form of governmental regulation of foundations necessary or desirable?

I made diligent inquiries as to availability of this material, having in mind several projects of my own. Being developed by a Congressional committee, it would be open to public inspection, I was informed, but presumably in a special collection in the Library of Congress and only upon approval of the Clerk of the House. This meant almost nobody would ever see it. Inquiries made in 1967 reveal that it is now in the National Archives, again open to public use only with the permission of the Clerk of the House of Representatives.

We wrote letters to the fifty-four foundations which had answered the long questionnaire, pointing out Russell Sage Foundation's continuing concern with foundation materials and requesting from each a file copy of its questionnaire answer. We received eighteen such copies, though a few of them were found to have been "edited." They are now in the files of The Foundation Center in New York City, where they may still be examined.

During the hearings I had learned to know Mr. Keele's director of research, Joseph C. Kiger. Mr. Kiger earned a doctorate in history at Vanderbilt University, and before his employment with the Cox Committee had taught that subject at the University of Alabama and Washington University (St. Louis). His introduction to foundations began with his employment by the Cox Committee, a brief assignment, but perhaps unexampled in concentrated opportunity for study of foundation developments. I knew that a college professor whose job ended in January might be briefly at loose ends, and suspected Joe Kiger was by this time deeply interested in foundations and would like a chance to study further in that field. So, with Dr. Young's consent, after the hearings were concluded we asked Professor Kiger whether he would like to undertake, under auspices of Russell Sage Foundation, a survey of the present operation of the larger foundations, based principally on the material presented by the foundations themselves to the Select (Cox) Committee.

He accepted the challenge. His brief book was written during 1953 and published by the Foundation early the next year under the title, *Operating Principles of the Larger Foundations*. It affords convenient summaries of much of the information developed by the Cox Committee, together with many direct quotations from the questionnaire responses.

The Reece Committee

A second and less pleasant sequel was engineered by Representative B. Carroll Reece, of Tennessee. He was the member of the Cox Committee who, although finding time to attend only one of the many public sessions of that committee, complained at their close of "insufficient time" and suggested a new inquiry.

Speedily, on 23 April 1953, he submitted a Resolution to the House to set up a new committee to "conduct a full and complete investigation and study of tax-exempt foundations," with $125,000 expenses.

The House appeared to have little enthusiasm. However, by summer the Eisenhower Administration was becoming exceedingly eager to get its bill for excess-profits tax out of the Rules Committee, where it languished. According to political commentators, Mr. Reece, a member of the Rules Committee who had shown no enthusiasm for the tax measure, announced that he would be willing to back the Administration on excess profits. A few days later his own Resolution reached the House, and was approved 209 to 163 on 30 July. The budget was reduced to $50,000, and the appointed committee included Angier L. Goodwin, who had been a member of the Cox Committee, and two Congress members who had opposed the new inquiry, Wayne L. Hays of Ohio and Gracie Pfost of Idaho.

At Russell Sage Foundation we planned the same cordial cooperation that had been extended to Mr. Keele and his associates. Differences soon became apparent. René A. Wormser was appointed general counsel; he is a very able estate-tax lawyer, and I found him personally a pleasant gentleman, but so deeply, and probably sincerely, inoculated with the Communist hysteria of the period that it amounted almost to a phobia. Interviews with his chief research assistants, Norman Dodd, member of a New York investment firm, and Thomas McNiece, described as an economic analyst, were disquieting. It became apparent that this time the Hearings were to begin with presentations by the committee staff and certain persons selected by them known to be hostile to foundations. We made our publications and other sources of information available, but it soon became obvious that real cooperation was neither welcome nor possible.

The "hearings" of this Special (Reece) Committee to Investigate Foundations covered sixteen sessions between 10 May and 17 June 1954. Of the twelve witnesses, the eleven first heard were

Mr. Reece, three members of his paid staff with extensive reports, two Treasury Department officials on technical tax questions, and five general witnesses unconnected with foundations. The thesis supported by the staff testimony and the general witnesses appeared to be that great changes had occurred in America in the direction of socialism and collectivism, with one of the witnesses holding that even the federal income tax was a socialist plot to destroy the government; these changes were aided, it was alleged, through a "diabolical conspiracy" of foundations and certain educational and research organizations.

Constant bickering occurred between Mr. Hays of Ohio and counsel and witnesses. One day when Thomas McNiece, assistant research director for the Committee, was testifying, Mr. Hays read to him unidentified paragraphs "written some years ago, and not as of the present," describing the plight of the working man and what might be done about it. He asked Mr. McNiece to characterize these writings.

"All of these—I do not know your source—are closely comparable to Communist literature that I have read," declared Mr. McNiece.

Mr. Hays reported that they were from encyclicals of Pope Leo XIII and Pope Pius XI, and were "a very practical demonstration, Mr. McNiece, of the danger of lifting a sentence or paragraph out of context."[12]

During a final four hours and twenty minutes one rebuttal witness was heard, Pendleton Herring, but even he was not a foundation representative but president of Social Science Research Council, one of the accused research organizations. Then the stormy sessions were suddenly ended by a strictly party vote. The foundations were permitted to reply only through written statements, which were long afterward published as an Appendix to the main hearings, and soon permitted to go out of print.

The committee meanwhile issued 943 pages of its one-sided *Hearings* and a 416-page "majority" report, signed by three of the five members of the committee, but one of them, Representative Goodwin, quite negated his signature by submittng a statement which quoted at length many of the opposite conclusions of the Cox Committee and concluded with the remark, "Nothing has transpired in the proceedings of the present committee to

[12] *Hearings Before the Special* (Reece) *Committee to Investigate Tax-Exempt Foundations and Comparable Organizations,* U. S. House, 83d Congress, 2d Session. Government Printing Office, Washington, 1954, p. 607.

cause me to alter or modify the views I expressed in the Cox Committee report. I take this opportunity to again re-affirm them."

Mr. Reece reported that this statement reached his office just too late to be included in the printed report. It is therefore a rare document, unknown to many persons reading the Reece presentation. However, he was required to print the 12-page *Minority Views* signed by Representatives Wayne L. Hays and Gracie Pfost, which did not mince words:

> The minority does not agree with the report submitted by the majority. It not only disagrees with that report but earnestly believes that it should never be published.
>
> Each step of the proceedings of this committee placed an ugly stain on the majestic record of the United States House of Representatives and the great tradition of the American people. . . .
>
> This was not an investigation in which the purpose was to gather facts, to evaluate them, and then to arrive at fair conclusions on the basis of those facts. Instead, we are presented with an inquiry in which facts have played no part. The committee's activities were in single purpose directed at justifying conclusions arrived at even in advance of the enabling resolution of the House of Representatives.
>
> The minority cannot emphasize too strongly the abhorrence it holds for such a procedure and indeed the abhorrence which the House of Representatives and the American public will hold for the whole unfortunate transaction when the majority report is published. . . .
>
> In addition, the real mischief in these proceedings rests in the effect which they may have on the future conduct of the tax-exempt foundations. If, as a result of this inquiry, the foundations shall surrender to timidity, then the aim of those who would destroy the effectiveness of the foundations shall have been accomplished. Truly, the integrity of the foundations will hinge on the manner in which they meet this challenge.[13]

[13] "Minority Views" in *Report of the Special* (Reece) *Committee*, pp. 421, 428, 430.

CHAPTER 12

Philanthropic Foundations

B y this time, thanks to the hearings, the flood of foundation information that passed daily over my desk, my work with Mr. Kiger on his new study, and other matters, I was bursting with material on foundations which needed an outlet.

Professor Taylor's Book

The "other matters" included supervision of a book on a special aspect of foundations. In 1950 Eleanor K. Taylor, associate professor of social work in the State University of Iowa, had submitted to us for criticism her dissertation dealing with provisions in various states looking toward accountability for foundations and charitable trusts. This was in connection with her advanced studies at the School of Social Service Administration of the University of Chicago, which had been assisted by a grant from The Chicago Community Trust.

I took this manuscript to Dr. Young with a recommendation that we do much more than merely criticize it. My Introduction to the book carries the story:

> Publications of the Foundation had pointed out inadequacies in reporting by many foundations. Concern was expressed over growing instances of abuse; aside from the probably modest sums involved in those cases, the danger threatened that unless such abuses were cured, unduly restrictive legislation might be applied to all foundations. We therefore viewed Professor Taylor's manuscript with great interest, since it appeared to be the first comprehensive discussion of actual provisions in various states looking toward accountability for foundations and charitable trusts.

> After discussion, the Foundation commissioned Professor Taylor to revise her dissertation into a study primarily designed to serve

the interests and needs of government officials, foundation officers and trustees, lawyers, and legislators interested in discovering the present facts as to the accountability of foundations and charitable trusts and in working out a better future solution.[1]

Revision took some years, and visits back and forth. One wintry evening I stepped off the train in Ames, Iowa, and did not at first see Miss Taylor, who was to meet me. But there she was, far down the platform, vigorously beckoning. Soon I understood the problem; the University was engaged in a major basketball game, and it was necessary to remain close to the car radio. We drove to the door of Miss Taylor's apartment and sat in the car until the end of the half, when there would be time to dash indoors without missing a crucial basket.

The study was in manuscript by the time of the Cox Hearings, and we loaned a copy to that committee. It was published in September, 1953. It described provisions that exist in selected states and in federal legislation for recording, reporting, and reviewing the activities of foundations and trusts. It disclosed that in most states even the most rudimentary machinery for accountability does not function, and recommended measures for more adequate reporting and for review of such reports by an authority possessing power to correct abuses. A clear distinction was made between accountability and control, with emphasis on the need for continuing freedom to experiment.

A Project Begins

By the fall of 1953 the Taylor book was in the bindery, and my own study, *Attitudes Toward Giving*,[2] was in galley proof. I perhaps had time now to undertake a really definitive study of foundations. Proposed to the Russell Sage Foundation trustees, this was speedily approved.

Initially the project was called "Administration of Foundations," and visualized as being primarily of use to foundation trustees and executives. As I began assembling the vast materials already available in our files, conducting interviews, and organizing accumulations into appropriate chapter divisions it became obvious that a broader book was both possible and desirable. It should be useful not only to the foundation family, but to fund raisers, lawyers, bankers, legislators, and to some extent the gen-

[1] Taylor, Eleanor K., *Public Accountability of Foundations and Charitable Trusts*. Russell Sage Foundation, New York, 1953, p. 8.
[2] See p. 103.

eral public. The title was changed to *Philanthropic Foundations*. The old intensive writing schedule, which had been interrupted for only a few months, began again. I was at my typewriter in Tenafly almost every morning, went to New York at noon, and spent the afternoon being a publication director, consultant in philanthropy, and checking on the references I should need in the next day's writing. Many of the New York activities contributed directly to the growing manuscript, often by design but sometimes by accident.

The Davella Mills Foundation

One of the accidents was a news story I saw in *The New York Times* concerning The Davella Mills Foundation. I knew this Foundation well. It had been set up in 1935 by David and Ella Mills with initial endowment of $1.6 million, and followed the pattern of many family foundations. At the first meeting the trustees asked Mr. Mills for a record of his checks to charitable causes for the previous year, and for their initial program approved a duplication of that precise list. Soon the board, which included distinguished men, saw that it could not merely continue the charities of Mr. Mills. They hired an executive secretary and a stenographer, and began acting on requests which increasingly came to them. In a few instances the trustees themselves initiated projects. One of their special interests was scholarships, chiefly for foreign students studying in the United States. Their criteria included need and scholastic ability, but emphasized leadership potential and the desire of the student to turn his education to service.

After Mr. Mills' death in 1944, funds were substantially increased. But now the trustees chose larger present benefits as against perpetuity and began spending principal as well as income. By 1954 all was spent except for a small reserve to publish a history.

Then came the *Times* story of 1 October. It headlined the difficulty The Davella Mills Foundation had encountered in spending some $11 million over twenty years. Nearly a column reported its grants, with the proportion of refusals surprisingly small, probably because the Foundation never sought publicity and few people knew of its existence and substantial resources. But not a word about its closing out!

What had happened was only too obvious. The *Times* must

have been pressed for space, and the make-up man chopped off that final paragraph about closing. And did I know what was going to happen to those poor trustees after that unqualified story!

Arriving at the office, I called Paul H. Hudson, bank chairman and also head of The Davella Mills Foundation. His cautious secretary asked whether it was something about the Mills Foundation, so obviously the deluge had begun. I said, Yes, but I was not seeking a grant, and thought I might be helpful to her boss. To him I explained that I was writing a book on foundations, knew precisely what was happening to him and would happen for several weeks, and while he would have to reject all applications with perhaps a form letter, if he wanted the proposals analyzed, I would be most happy to perform this chore. And so for several weeks I received all the Mills application mail.

Although the *Times* corrected its story six days later, within a few weeks 513 persons and agencies had rushed in by mail to help the trustees spend their nonexistent millions. Fewer than half of them specified a dollar amount, the remainder leaving that matter for later negotiation or the donor's generosity. But the 214 mentioning amounts requested a total of $52 million!

Requests fell into these broad categories: support of local institutions (hospitals, churches, schools, libraries), 128; fellowships, scholarships, travel, and training grants, 97; scientific research and teaching, 53; educational and cultural institutions, for projects or development, 44; personal aid to individuals, 52; youth services, 33; charitable agencies and programs, 25; publication of manuscripts, 25; studies and activities in creative arts, 23; cures, remedies, and inventions, 7; conferences and meetings, 5; purchase or disposal of real estate, 3; miscellaneous, 18. Among the stranger requests received was one for $25,000 to produce a new soft drink; a mere "$50,000 to $100,000" to write books on religious themes; $10,000 toward a badly needed divorce; $288 to pay a 1952 income-tax assessment.

This example was an excellent case study of the volume and variety of applications foundations receive. I used it as such in Chapter 7, "Applications for Grants."

National Science Foundation

National Science Foundation was set up a few years earlier, in 1950. By 1954 it was deep in its task of compiling nationwide data on support of scientific research. Russell Sage Foundation was asked to conduct that portion of the survey which dealt with support of science by philanthropic foundations.

We agreed, with the understanding that results of the survey could also be published in my own volume. So I became a frequent visitor to its then makeshift quarters in the old Cosmos Club in Washington. I sent out the schedules in the fall of 1954, asking data for 1953 and two earlier base years, 1946 and 1939.

It was a fruitful cooperation. We provided the know-how for the foundation field, and conducted the survey without charge. National Science Foundation supplied their well-considered definitions of the sciences, and undoubtedly reluctant foundations were more apt to reply to this study with governmental backing. We found[3] that as of 1953, foundations were appropriating about $33 million for scientific research, an amount almost negligible in proportion to the national estimate of $5 billion for that year. But a large part of the national figure is "gadget" and war-related research—applied and developmental rather than pure research; the modest foundation amount is sometimes crucial in terms of new knowledge and human welfare, though in all recent years the percentage has been small.

The growth of National Science Foundation itself lends a startling perspective to research financing. It is of course not a private foundation, nor by most definitions a foundation at all; it has no endowment, and receives its funds from current appropriations of tax monies. But in its grants and administrative procedures, it is very similar indeed, supporting many projects that formerly relied chiefly or wholly on private foundations.

In 1953, the year of our study, its appropriation was still modest, a little less than $5 million. Over a longer term, this is the record:[4]

Fiscal Year	Budget Requests	Appropriations
1951	$ 475,000	$ 225,000
1953	15,000,000	4,750,000
1960	160,300,000	152,773,000
1967	525,000,000	479,999,000

This single national "foundation" is able to spend for science alone each recent year nearly half as much as all the private foundations together can spend on all fields.

[3] Reported both in Andrews, F. Emerson, *Scientific Research Expenditures by the Larger Private Foundations*, National Science Foundation, Government Printing Office, Washington, 1956, and in Chapter 10, "Scientific Research," of my *Philanthropic Foundations*.

[4] *Congressional Record*, 12 April 1967, p. H3978.

National Science Foundation conducted its own periodic later surveys of foundations, with my service as consultant, a relationship which continued until 1969. From that and other sources I have kept in close touch with the remarkable changes that have taken place in such support, particularly the swings among the fields of science. If a belief remains that foundations are monoliths with unchanging programs, this record supplies contrary evidence.

Take, for example, support for the physical sciences. In prewar 1939 the reporting foundations awarded less than 9 percent of their scientific grants to the physical sciences, as against more than 40 percent for social sciences and 51 percent for life sciences—which include the usually popular medical research. In directly postwar 1946 physical sciences had climbed to over 22 percent, the social sciences dropping to 25 percent, life sciences creeping up to nearly 53 percent. In our special study year, 1953, physical sciences were back at 8 percent and both social and life sciences at 46 percent of the science total.

Then came the realization that the Soviet Union might be outdistancing us in the physical sciences, a fear that was confirmed by Sputnik on 4 October 1957. Foundation support for the physical sciences climbed from $2.4 million to $10.4 million between 1953 and 1957, and in the latter year stood at 31 percent of total science support, ahead of the social sciences. By 1962 physical sciences stood at over $18 million, 40 percent of all science expenditure, and now ahead of both social and life sciences. Various factors undoubtedly influenced this climb, but it can scarcely be doubted that the international situation was prominently among them.

By 1966 support for physical sciences by foundations had dropped to a startling low, less than $5 million, and only 7 percent of the science expenditures. By this time one suspects foundations thought their contributions no longer significant in view of the immense government programs through National Science Foundation, National Aeronautics and Space Administration, the Atomic Energy Commission, and others.

The Foundation Trustee

Members of the governing board of a foundation bear a variety of titles, of which *trustees, directors, members of the corporation,* and *managers,* are the most common, but under any name theirs is the final legal authority for the organization. A chapter on trustees was essential, particularly as no study had been done since Lindeman's analysis as of 1930.[5]

We had a good start in the replies to the Cox Committee *Questionnaires*, which required listing of trustee names, addresses, terms of office, possible relationship to donor, and membership on other philanthropic boards. I chose twenty foundations, including all the very large ones and a sampling of those smaller or specialized. The total came to 202 trustees, a small proportion of the field, but because of the inclusion of the largest foundations, this group had ultimate control of a large part of total foundation assets. Information was obtained from the Cox Committee material, from *Who's Who in America* and other biographical references, and by direct correspondence with the foundations and sometimes the individuals.

Nearly all the trustees were men. Of the fourteen women, three were wives and five were daughters of the donors. Other donor-related trustees included six sons, three grandsons; two trustees were the donor himself. So the donor and his near relatives constituted just under 10 percent of the trustees.

Though I was polite about it, age was an obvious problem. Only three trustees were below thirty-five years of age, all of these direct descendants of the donor. Nearly half were above sixty years of age, and nine above eighty. I had reason to know that one of these gentlemen, an estimable man but completely deaf and nearly blind, was serving in his ninety-third year, for it was one of my duties as a then junior executive personally to escort him from board meetings to a railway station, where his much younger wife would be waiting to lead him home. For policy-making boards which need to be at the frontiers of present knowledge and peering into the future, a larger proportion of younger men would seem highly desirable.

Some foundations tried to meet this problem with election for short terms. This solved nothing. One foundation which limited term to a single year reported two trustees entering their thirty-third term. If a trustee is present when question of his re-election comes up and does not himself refuse further service, it is socially nearly impossible to retire him. A former foundation, Julius Rosenwald Fund, had provided for automatic retirement after a maximum of two three-year terms, with the possibility of reinstatement for another two terms after the lapse of a year.

[5] Lindeman, Eduard C., *Wealth & Culture.* Harcourt, Brace and Co., New York, 1936, pp. 32-46.

This permitted consideration of the true worth of the trustee during the year of his absence from the board. It is a procedure we later adopted, though in part for other reasons, when The Foundation Library Center was established.

Most (171) of the trustees had at least bachelors' diplomas, with 137 (68 percent of all the trustees) holding advanced or honorary degrees. There was a high concentration on Ivy League colleges: 32 Harvard, 30 Yale, 17 Princeton—a total of 46 percent of all the recorded undergraduate degrees from these three schools.

Religion showed a similar extraordinary concentration. Only 106 trustees reported religious affiliation. Of these, 95 (90 percent) were Protestant, a little more than 6 percent Jewish, and fewer than 4 percent Roman Catholic. Of the 95 Protestants, 35 were Protestant Episcopal, 26 Presbyterian, and 34 were spread among all the other denominations.

Occupationally, business (chiefly corporation officers, bankers, and financiers) accounted for 74 trustees, or 37 percent. Law came next with 38, 19 percent. Education and research were represented by 14 percent. Philanthropy followed with 9 percent, but these were in nearly all cases *ex officio* trustees as principal officers of their foundations. Remaining categories—publicists, government service, housewives, medicine, the arts, and religion —were negligibly represented, and in that order.

It is obvious that the trustee group for these larger foundations is not representative of American occupations as a whole, proportionally or in variety. The detailed biographies revealed only one farmer (tabulated under business), no wage laborer or union official, no clerical worker, only one salesman. Of the fourteen women, nine listed themselves as housewives.

College Trustee

Shortly after I had completed this study of foundation trustees I received a telegram from the president of my alma mater, Franklin and Marshall College, reporting that I had been elected a trustee at their meeting on 11 February 1956. "Hope we may count on your acceptance. Letter follows."

Because of special and often confidential relationship with foundations I have made it a rule to decline membership on boards or committees that seek foundation funds. This, however, was my alma mater, in which I have a deep interest quite beyond the financial. After an exchange of letters in which it was agreed that I should never be asked to serve in any relations between the college and foundations, I accepted.

College trusteeship presented, in a somewhat different setting, many of the same problems facing foundation trustees. Where is the proper dividing line between trustees and administrator? When a professor's expressed views anger alumni and business leaders in a local community, and also some members of the board itself, how defend academic freedom?

The problem of trustee age is also a serious one on college boards, including my own. We had a particularly unfortunate provision whereby after a certain age a trustee then serving became a life member of the board with full voting privileges. I battled for years against that provision, and as my own age advanced, could do so with ever better grace. The battle was at least partially won in a 1969 charter revision. Now at age seventy a trustee automatically becomes honorary, able to attend and speak at meetings and serve on committees, but without vote.

Foundation Reporting

Russell Sage Foundation had long been on record as to the desirability of full voluntary reporting by all the larger foundations. I therefore did a special chapter on this subject, after extensive research into the current situation.

A good example had been set by the Peabody Education Fund, organized in 1867 and perhaps the first American foundation in the modern sense of that term. Its trustees published pamphlet reports from their very first meeting, and soon uniformly bound volumes, so that "the fullest information on the subject should be within the ready reach of all who are interested in it."

Their example was not universally followed. In *Philanthropic Foundations* I published an analytic table of all the reporting foundations in our records. They numbered 107, with 61 represented by annual reports, 16 biennial, and 30 occasional, or single historical résumés. Of the 77 larger foundations identified for my National Science Foundation study only 28, or 36 percent, issued reports as often as biennially.

The reports varied radically in length, style, and adequacy. Nearly all were satisfactory with respect to personnel, including trustees, officers, and professional staff. Descriptions of projects supported varied from listing of projects (and not necessarily

all) to exhaustive discussions of each. Many were introduced by
a general statement on the purposes of the foundation and current program emphasis; some had an introductory essay on a
field of philanthropy.

Financial data were less satisfactory. Assets were often given
only at ledger value, which when compared with current income
was obviously far from actual worth. Administrative expenditures were sometimes a tender point, on which little or no information was supplied.

A particularly heated correspondence, and finally a visit to my
office, were initiated by the principal trustee of one of Royal Little's foundations, the Rhode Island Charities Trust. In the absence of financial data I proposed to publish significant provisions of the Trust's amended Charter. When the trustee objected
violently, I tried to make clear my position: I would be glad to
correct any error in the proposed statement, but if the facts were
in order the decision to publish must be mine. The book
appeared with this statement:

> The Rhode Island Charities Trust, established by Royal Little in
> 1937, was amended in September, 1945, when he resigned and his
> place was taken by three trustees. The amendment provided that the
> aggregate annual compensation for the three trustees should be 1%
> of the value of the corpus averaged throughout the year. All income
> from the Trust which is not distributed is added annually to the
> principal. . . . Payment to trustees, based on corpus, which recently
> had grown to $7.5 million, is substantial, and was apparently so set
> up to encourage the trustees to increase that corpus as rapidly as
> possible. They were relieved in the trust instrument from the restric-
> tions on most trustees as to relatively safe investments.[6]

Publication

Philanthropic Foundations was ready for press in the fall, after
every statement within it concerning a named foundation had
been checked with that organization. In a few cases objections
were raised, as in the Rhode Island Charities Trust instance, but
if the statement was not proved incorrect and was on public record, it went in. The book left no doubt as to my own position,
that full disclosure was in the public interest, and the best safeguard against undesirable governmental controls.

[6] Andrews, F. Emerson, *Philanthropic Foundations*. Russell Sage Foundation,
New York, 1956, p. 85.

Publication took place on my fifty-fourth birthday, 26 January 1956. It was a pleasant way to celebrate. Reviewers and correspondents were kind. Dean Rusk, then president of The Rockefeller Foundation, having borrowed an advance copy over the weekend, ordered thirty on publication date for trustees and staff. A Pittsburgh foundation head called it "a gold mine of reliable information and it is so well written that the reading of it is a joy." *The New York Times* did a long news story, and an editorial, "Spotlight on Foundations," which reported it "a challenging appraisal of their conduct and objectives."

CHAPTER 13

Stray Threads

Biography would be easier if all lives were like rivers, beginning from a primary source, picking up strength and direction from contributory brooks, and proceeding in a deepening stream to a determined destination. This life, at least, has not been like that. There have been diversions from the main stream, running a little way and perhaps drying up in a desert, but sometimes continuing. Some have been given paragraph treatment at the appropriate point in the time stream. Appendix B covers some literary diversions not related to philanthropy—an excursion into mathematics, books for children, attempts at novels.

A few others, related to philanthropy but not a part of the main stream, were not easily fitted into either of these procedures. "Stray Threads" is a chapter of miscellany, as diverse as lecturing to lawyers and serving as deacon in a church.

The Princeton Conference

On 1 December 1955 Dr. Young and I flew out to California to see if we could induce Pulitzer Prize winning historian Merle Curti to chair a two-day conference of historians to discuss the sad shortage of historical research on philanthropy. Professor Curti was then in residence in that fascinating hilltop think-tank, the Center for Advanced Study in Behaviorial Sciences, which The Ford Foundation had set up to give scholars a free year for work of their own choosing, mixing younger men with savants like Curti.

It was the first of my many meetings with this delightful gentleman, small and lean, keen of eye, witty, friendly, and a thoughtful observer of the American character. Although philanthropy had not previously been a special interest of his, he quickly agreed that voluntary giving is an almost unique characteristic of the Anglo-Saxon peoples, and more adequate study was important for a better understanding of our whole culture. He would accept.

The meeting was scheduled for 3 and 4 February 1956 at the Princeton Inn in Princeton, New Jersey. With Professor Curti's aid, we assembled a distinguished group of historians, representing a variety of special fields. They included Thomas C. Cochran, Henry Edward Guerlac, W. Stull Holt, Kenneth Scott Latourette, Richard B. Morris, Richard H. Shryock, and David Bicknell Truman. Observers for The Ford Foundation, which shared the conference costs, were Carl B. Spaeth and Mrs. Jackson Chance, who became executive director of Rosenberg Foundation. Dr. Young and I participated for Russell Sage Foundation, and I had the tasks of making arrangements and drafting the final report.[1]

The conference began in a terrific snowstorm. One attendant had to abandon his car in a snowdrift and come by other transportation. But come they all did, the Inn was comfortable, and the food delectable.

Under Merle Curti's skilled guidance, discussions were wide and stimulating, "with participants so interested," says my diary note, "that one had trouble getting a word in edgewise." The conferees decided that philanthropy needs to be examined "not only in terms of broad social changes, but as effects on the givers themselves, on recipients, and on government." There should be period studies, area studies, studies of institutions. We discussed many specific topics, such as relief and social welfare, the church, education, health services, the arts, charitable bequests (adequate historical studies were wholly lacking), foundations, corporations, labor, government, laws regulating philanthropy, its effects on the economy.

These materials, together with extensive lists of subjects proposed for study and a bibliography, were made available in the published report. But in my view one of the major accomplishments of the conference was stimulating the interest of Professor Curti in this field. He himself wrote several books, *American Philanthropy Abroad, A History* (1963) and, with Robert Nash,

---

[1] *Report of the Princeton Conference on the History of Philanthropy in the United States.* Russell Sage Foundation, New York, 1956, 84 pp.

Philanthropy in the Shaping of American Higher Education
(1965). He also obtained a substantial Ford grant for philanthropic studies at the University of Wisconsin, and under his direction and that of Professor Irvin G. Wyllie, numerous studies have been made, several of them resulting in substantial books.

A Ford in My Life

I have had many minor relationships with The Ford Foundation, and have known most of its principal officers through the years. The first proposed assignment—to serve on its original committee on policy and program—I declined, feeling that I did not have adequate background for the phase of the educational program for which I was proposed.

Later, after some of my philanthropic surveys had been completed, I accepted service on the special "Cambridge Committee" headed by Carl B. Spaeth, dean of Stanford University Law School, which met usually in Cambridge, Massachusetts, for the convenience of the several members who were on the Harvard Law School faculty. This committee proposed to work out a complete "taxonomy" (a gobbledygook word to which I objected) for philanthropy.

I resigned my Twentieth Century Fund consultantship and spent about two days a week on the Ford project, beginning in August, 1955. We looked at the whole field, defining philanthropy, estimating its volume, classifying philanthropic agencies by area of service, analyzing sources of funds, looking at the foundation segment with particular care, including some study of activity in controversial fields, and laying out suggestions for needed historical studies.

After the first committee sessions, my task was to put this material into a detailed memorandum, with statistical estimates, examples, and some open-ended questions. This I completed by December 1955, and my *Classifications in Philanthropy* was mimeographed for limited distribution.

Private Philanthropy and Public Institutions

In that same December The Ford Foundation made the largest single philanthropic gift ever recorded, $500 million. Of this total, $210 million went to accredited private colleges and universities in the United States in sums approximating their

1954-1955 payroll for instruction in the liberal arts and sciences, and $90 million to privately supported medical schools. (My *Philanthropic Foundations* was already running on press, but friends in The Ford Foundation, under pledge of absolute secrecy, tipped me off to holding up that press form so that we could include this major gift.)

It will be noted that these tremendous sums went to "privately supported" educational institutions. Of course the heads of tax-supported colleges and universities were immediately up in arms, and evidently got through to some members of the Ford board, with their pleas against what they regarded as unwarranted discrimination.

I was asked to do a series of interviews with leading thinkers, usually university presidents, on both sides, and submit a confidential memorandum presenting as objectively as possible the pertinent considerations. It had long been a subject of interest to me, particularly as over the years the distinctions between private and tax-supported institutions had been narrowing. So I undertook the task and began the interviews.

The gentlemen presented their views forcibly, and sometimes profanely. One state university president insisted that any restrictions imposed by legislatures were as nothing compared with the vested interests defended by private trustees; and whenever he heard of Mark Hopkins and his log he felt nauseated. Few interviewees would have insisted on my keeping their statements confidential, except for cleaning them up a bit; most of them regularly mounted soap boxes (college convocations and degree ceremonies) to promulgate them.

The Ford Foundation later permitted me to publish the chief contentions of both sides in unidentified form.[2] Condensed, the main arguments appeared to be these:

Favoring contributions chiefly to private agencies:

Compulsory contributions go to public institutions through tax payments—restore balance by contributing to private sector.

Dollars to a public agency may simply reduce tax appropriation and result in no added funds.

Tax exemption is a government policy intended to avoid governmental controls.

Private institutions are free from hampering political boundaries.

Only private agencies are free to investigate explosive issues.

[2] In "Private Philanthropy and Public Institutions," *The Educational Record,* American Council on Education, Vol. 37, No. 4, October, 1956, pp. 292-298.

More money is needed to match large salaries of public agencies, and hold able individuals where they have greater freedom.

The private agencies are more economical, avoiding red tape and civil service rigidities.

They provide greater variety and flexibility, the keys to progress.

In dealings with third parties gifts and services through private agencies are more acceptable than government largesse.

Performance standards can be set, valuable to both private and public agencies.

In view of the late violent swing toward public control of health, education, and welfare, all available funds are needed for the private sector if it is to survive.

Favoring contributions to tax-supported institutions:

Gifts should be based on need.

Gifts, being tax-deductible, should go in large part to public agencies where taxpayer benefit is most obvious.

Some institutions supported by state or local taxes are really national, and need broader support.

Needs are apt to vary inversely with taxpaying ability, so that poorer areas need private support.

Inadequacy in local tax support will result in federal subsidy, expanding bureaucracy and statism, unless private aid comes to the rescue.

In some specialties only public institutions are available, and these should receive support.

In some fields (example, agronomy) public institutions have a natural relation to other public agencies, but need added private support.

Matching contributions may stimulate legislative appropriations, doubling or more the private gift.

Voluntary agencies often represent duplications and sometimes outright rackets; conditions are safer under government supervision.

Public institutions are now doing most of the pioneering research and often have more adequate equipment.

Since public monies cannot be used in certain experimental ways, private funds are needed for rounded programs.

Gifts to public institutions go further for intended purposes since basic support is already supplied from tax funds.

Where the need is general and expenditures large, government will eventually take over; private support may merely prolong the inferior and delay the inevitable.

My own views on this question are reserved for the concluding chapter, "Afterthoughts."

British Philanthropy

The Ford Foundation, when it abandoned its own programs in the behavioral sciences, made substantial grants to Russell Sage Foundation to match Sage expenditures for social science personnel training projects and studies in philanthropy. In the latter field I inherited technical supervision of two projects in British philanthropy, initiated by Ford.

Dr. W. K. Jordan, then president of Radcliffe College and a professor of history at Harvard University, had made extensive studies of wills and other documents in Tudor and Stuart England under an original grant from The Ford Foundation and others. We undertook administration of the final stages of the grant, and publication of the several resultant books. "Kitch" Jordan is an extremely able researcher and writer, and work proceeded rapidly in spite of his other major responsibilities. I could do little for him but make general comments on his manuscript and applaud his industry and findings. We published the main summary volume, *Philanthropy in England, 1480-1660*, in 1959. It is a provocative look at the problems of poverty in the early modern world, the various measures taken by the Tudors and Stuarts in dealing with needs of the poor, and a survey of the beginnings of Britain's many thousands of charitable trusts.

The Foundation also administered the Ford grant for Professor David Owen's study, which carried the British history from 1660 down to 1960 and passage of the new Charities Bill, but Dr. Owen's book, *English Philanthropy, 1660-1960*, was published by Harvard University Press in 1964. This book had a long gestation while Dr. Owen was balancing his Harvard duties with authorship, and though I was by this time merely a consultant to Russell Sage Foundation, I followed this manuscript with considerable care.

It was from the late David Owen that I picked up what is in some respects my favorite British "charity." This is a trust established by one John Werk in 1453, the income of which, according to a later Parliamentary report, was to be used "to supply faggots for the burning of heretics."

When I was in London in 1966 and visited the new head of Britain's Charity Commission, the Honorable Tom Green, I mentioned Werk's Charity and asked if his voluminous records (at that time his office had registered 62,000 exempt charities under the new regulations, and the number was growing daily) could confirm it. Amused, he called for any supporting documents. Fifteen minutes later a secretary came up, bearing an immense and ancient volume which included a 20-line faded entry briefing a bequest by one John Werk in 1453 which specified certain ordinary uses and "certain superstitious uses," but with no mention of faggots. Perhaps some scholar will dig up the full will, and then we shall know whether the faggots may blaze away or must be extinguished.

Lawyers and Philanthropy

In the summer of 1958 The Ford Foundation sponsored a seminar on legal research in philanthropy, inviting professors of trust, estate, and tax law at principal law schools. The sessions were held at the University of Wisconsin, with Professor Richard W. Effland of that University's Law School in charge, and with participation in planning and in some of the sessions on the part of historians Merle Curti and Irvin G. Wyllie. For six weeks this group engaged in intensive research and discussion in various areas where the law affects philanthropy. During the last of those weeks I was special lecturer, asked to add to the bare bones of theory the flesh of experience.

It was a fascinating assignment. Normally I began my lectures at 9:30 and, except for a coffee break, continued until 1:00. The first day we discussed the recently created Foundation Library Center and its materials, the three recent Congressional investigations (everything off the record), and the similar Royal Little and Blatnik affairs. Tuesday we covered the history, present dimensions, sources, and destinations of philanthropy, with lively discussion of rackets. Wednesday was devoted to corporate giving and company-sponsored foundations. Thursday and Friday covered the whole record of foundations: history, management, tax exemption, accumulation, propaganda, and the like.

I tried to win respites by stimulating arguments among the lawyers, but apparently they had argued with each other for most of the previous five weeks and were now intent upon getting me to do the talking. One of the lengthiest items, and one in which everyone did participate, was a discussion of common-stock holdings of foundations and consequent voting responsibilities of trustees. It was acknowledged that trustees usually voted with management, although the Kress Foundation case and the voting of Rockefeller stock to oppose Stewart in Ohio were mentioned. One lawyer cited a case in which trustees were surcharged for damages because their failure to vote stock resulted in a corporation's inability to effect a needed change, with damage to its financial position.

Simultaneous cross-examination by skilled professors from seven different law schools was exhausting. Afternoons I usually collapsed into Lake Mendota for a swim, and evenings were apt to be social—with technical discussions continuing in lighter vein.

At various opportunities I tried to point out that estate lawyers, and to some degree others, often have opportunities to advise clients with respect to charitable dispositions. Therefore law students should at least know where to turn for reliable information on charitable causes and agencies, and have an acquaintance with the applicable law.

Two years later, as a direct result of suggestions growing out of this seminar, the *Virginia Law Review* published an issue devoted to "Law and Philanthropy." Three of the six articles in this symposium were written by persons attending the Wisconsin seminar, and I was invited to write the Foreword.[3]

American Association of Fund-Raising Counsel

The rise of professional fund raising has been noted in earlier chapters. The better firms subscribe to a code of approved practice, which includes standards of staff qualification for directors of campaigns and a prohibition against fees based on a percentage of collections. There are two national organizations of fundraising firms, the senior one being the American Association of Fund-Raising Counsel.

While I am sometimes distressed at the mechanics of superorganized campaigns—"kick-off" dinners with the food chosen to satisfy but not stupefy the attending solicitors, planned lack of seating so that waiters can drag in extras at the last minute making even a poor attendance look like an overflow meeting, "personal" letters which the signer has never seen before signing —the professional firms can point to their excellent records. They have raised vast and needed sums from a reluctant public, and at relatively low costs. Through the years I have come to know most of the leaders in this field, have sometimes spoken at

[3] *Virginia Law Review*, Vol. 46, No. 3, April 1960.

their special dinners and conventions, and have tried to help them be effective instruments in increasing private giving.

Late in 1954 Dr. Arnaud C. Marts, then president of the American Association of Fund-Raising Counsel, came to me for some special advice. I had known Dr. Marts for many years; for a substantial period he combined the presidency of Bucknell University with fund-raising activities, organizing Marts & Lundy which claims to have raised more than $1 billion, chiefly for colleges. Now the Association he headed was expanding its central office. In addition to usual trade-association services to the member firms, might it not also be of use to the general public? Would I make some suggestions?

My memorandum, submitted in December, pointed out that as of that time . . .

No center exists where accurate, current information on broad aspects of philanthropy can be obtained . . . certain agencies above-mentioned have conducted extensive studies and can give useful advice in particular fields, but none is staffed to keep general statistics up to date.

Inquiries in this area are often from the press or from other shapers of opinions and laws, and helpful answers will sometimes exert wide and constructive influence on American giving. My own office has important requests for data on philanthropy at least once a week . . . Such central compilation of philanthropic data, in addition to its helpfulness to the press and the public, would be of immense service to your member firms, many of whom now maintain partial files on these subjects, with heavy duplication of effort.

The proposed auspices of this service raise public relations questions, and may make certain functions inappropriate or impossible. The Association should not attempt to rate or compare educational and welfare organizations, nor advise donors on choice of agency. It can supply factual information on any agency about which specific inquiry is made, or direct inquirers to proper sources for such information. . . .

Its chief function for the public, however, will be to supply general information on voluntary giving, its sources, its volume, its directions. To the extent that the Association makes accurate information in this field readily available, its service office will be used and become widely known. Probably a part of the general public will remain suspicious of information emanating from "professional fund raisers," just as foundations never wholly escape charges of "tainted money." But by setting up a readily available source of accurate and disinterested information in this field, the Association may do more to build understanding and public confidence than by any other program within its present reach.[4]

The memorandum continued with specific suggestions for a program with initially four elements—a library, a clipping service, statistical analysis of pertinent data, and legal information. The degree of influence these recommendations had on the Association, which may already have had in mind some of these services, I am in no position to determine. An office was set up, and continues to operate. The Association publishes each year a much-used pamphlet, GIVING U S A: A Compilation of Facts Related to American Philanthropy, upon which my counsel has been annually sought.

The Riverside Church

My admiration for Harry Emerson Fosdick and association with The Riverside Church as soon as it was built for him "on the Hill" have been earlier recorded. But continuing participation in the program of this exciting church deserves further notice.

When we moved to New Jersey in 1935, shortly after the birth of our first son, the question of transferring church membership arose. There are obvious advantages in local church membership, where one is among neighbors, children can readily participate in local activities, and attendance is simple. But in the 1930s the experimental church school at Riverside seemed to us to offer advantages not then to be found elsewhere, and for us grownups, few places in America could approach the pulpit ministries of Dr. Fosdick and his successor, Robert J. McCracken. So we continued to commute to Riverside, at first by the 125th Street ferry, which was sometimes exciting when in winter the ferry had to break through fields of ice, and then by the George Washington Bridge after the ferry was discontinued.

I became involved in more church committees than I can remember—church survey, budget, communion committee, publications, chairman of Council I on public worship, structure and organization committee . . . Occasionally I sent notes to the ministers when in my job I came across a fact or anecdote they might find useful. One such, concerning inflation, was used by Dr. McCracken in a budget sermon. Said Dr. McCracken:

[4] Memorandum to Dr. Arnaud C. Marts from F. Emerson Andrews, dated December 1954.

I want to take a new line in today's Budget Sermon. For some years I have felt, though you may not have suspected it, that I should not press too strongly for increased giving. I no longer have such inhibited feelings. . . . For one thing, there is the bugbear of inflation. It is not a new problem. . . .

Dr. Emerson Andrews pointed out to me recently that there is an excellent illustration of the inflationary trend in successive translations of the parable of the Good Samaritan. In the Authorized Version issued in 1611 the innkeeper got twopence, in the Revised Version issued in 1898 one and fivepence, in Moffatt issued in 1913 two shillings, and in J. B. Phillips issued in 1952 ten shillings.[5]

Dr. McCracken also used, not in a sermon but at every-member-canvass dinners, my story of the Scotsman who summoned his minister to his deathbed and asked if he would be assured of salvation if he gave £10,000 to the Kirk. Aware of the life he had led, but anxious for the money, the minister replied, "It is an experiment well worth trying."

But I never heard of his citing a certain British trust which I sent him with tongue partly in cheek. It was a fund set up by Joan Smales, in the parish of Shoreditch, out of which those who listened to the sermon would be paid 20 shillings for their labor, while the preacher was given 10 shillings.

One day late in 1954 I was asked to stand for election to the Board of Deacons of Riverside for a five-year term. Nomination was tantamount to election, for we did not then have the "double slate" which has since become customary for that board. I protested that my religious views were unorthodox and I did not consider myself fitted for this task. That judgment, said the persuasive chairman, belonged to the nominating committee and the church; my decision was only on willingness to undertake a demanding task. And so I began the first of two five-year terms as a deacon of the Riverside Church.

During my second term I was elected chairman for 1963 and 1964. To be the lay program head of this church with so vast and varied a program was a complex task, even with the aid of a board of very competent people. Activities were numerous and varied, including beyond the central worship services a daytime nursery-kindergarten, arts and crafts, a radio station, a special Sunday service in Spanish for our Puerto Rican membership and neighbors, a Tower League for older folk, language tutoring, and

[5] "The Stub of an Old Checkbook," a sermon by Robert J. McCracken delivered at The Riverside Church, November 3, 1957. Issued by the Church.

much else. As in all organizations of substantial size, religious or commercial, there were personnel problems, sometimes severe.

Like most modern churches, Riversiders took great interest in social problems. The church is interdenominational and interracial, and did have on ministerial staff and in the governing boards blacks, Puerto Ricans, members of other races. Among its seven councils was one on Christian Social Relations, charged with keeping the membership informed on the social issues of the day. In so large a church, members represented all shades of opinion. Views of the John Birch Society, and persons well to the right of it, were not absent. Local pressure groups, recognizing a genuine need for a public school in the neighborhood and including many of our members, tried hard to get the church to vote to petition the city to devote park property for the erection of said school.

We had a position on controversial issues, which I tried to enforce. As a free church, our preaching minister, or any invited visiting preacher, was never to be told what he could or could not say. But neither minister nor any board or committee could commit the whole church to a position on a controversial issue. We thought also that it would prove divisive and inappropriate to vote on such nonreligious issues at a congregational meeting, where representation was inadequate and an organized minority might easily carry an election.

Then came the proposed civil rights legislation, and a long Congressional filibuster. Even on this question there was a minute opposing minority, but almost universal support. Without violating our rule for no official church position, we attempted to go so far as to get a recorded vote, pro and con, with respect to a resolution already passed by the board of deacons affirming its "support of all legitimate measures to eliminate from every aspect of American life discrimination against an individual or a group of individuals on account of race, color, or religious belief, and urges that the moral principles inherent in the foregoing should be implemented by affirmative action on the part of its members in support of the Civil Rights legislation now pending before the Congress of the United States."

Firebrands in the congregation were not happy with the precise wording, each wishing a particular change and regarding any other version as little less than treason, and of course not willing to have us send a factual record of the vote to the Congress, but to have a resolution passed committing the whole church to their particular version. The original plan finally won out, but it was the most difficult meeting over which I have ever had to preside. I was learning the truth of Voltaire's observation, that the righteous are more difficult than the wicked, for they are not limited by conscience.

The Tenafly Public Library

At the beginning of 1969 the mayor of Tenafly appointed me to the board of the Tenafly Public Library. As a long-time resident of Tenafly and a user of this facility, I accepted the appointment with pleasure, and expected my duties to be minor. At an early board meeting I learned that although library services of a sort began in Tenafly as early as 1891, it was in 1920 that the library became public—a book collection publicly supported, publicly controlled, and for general free public use. We were therefore on the doorstep of the fiftieth anniversary, and moreover Ruth G. Garomon, long-time librarian, was retiring. Would I, as the only writer on the board, undertake a history? Funds for printing were available.

It was an interesting assignment. I was at the time recovering from a severe operation and had sight of only one eye, but an efficient History Committee dug out the essential old records and rendered other aid. We found that the first librarian, during the private library period, received the not-extravagant salary of $40 a year. But in May 1910 the Association found itself quite solvent, thanks to membership dues, fines, and a charge of a penny a day on recent fiction, and voted Mrs. Callie York a 25 percent increase—from $40 to $50 a year.

The Depression brought a reduced budget but much greater use of the library, for the unemployed had more time to read. Each of the major wars resulted in special services, for soldiers in nearby camps and for civilians. Then there was the long struggle for a more adequate building. In this by accident I had a small part. Says the *History*:

> During this period Russell Sage Foundation's director of philanthropic research, a Tenafly resident, received a letter seeking advice on disposition of property for useful public purposes; it was postmarked Tenafly. Instead of a letter reply, he arranged a local conference.
>
> Suggestions were made in the field of the donor's professional interests, and the question explored as to whether he might also wish

to devote some funds to local projects. On an expression of interest, it was pointed out that the Tenafly Public Library was in dire need of a new building, but that project had for some years languished on dead center. A private gift, restricted to construction of a new library, might spur additional gifts from concerned citizens. With a substantial fund available and earmarked, the Borough might appropriate additional funds, if such were needed, to get the project promptly under way.

The suggestion was adopted. The donor in 1957 presented a gift in stock to Mayor Clifton S. Fleet to spur interest in a new library building; the donor was to remain anonymous, at least until his death. Since the present Library has a special McCandless Room, it can no longer be a secret that the late Charles W. McCandless was the generous donor.[6]

Both this earlier incident and current service on the library board are tastes of philanthropy at the level of a local agency that have been informing and pleasant.

The book was issued in 1970 in time for the anniversary celebration, with copies made available for all local citizens.

[6] Andrews, F. Emerson, *The Tenafly Public Library: A History, 1891-1970.* The Tenafly Public Library, Tenafly, N.J., pp. 37-38.

Part II

THE FOUNDATION CENTER

NOTE: The original corporate name was The Foundation Library Center. This name was legally shortened late in 1968 to The Foundation Center.

CHAPTER 14

The Foundation Library
Center

Eᴠᴇɴ before its 1956 publication, *Philanthropic Foundations* was setting in motion streams of events I did not then recognize. For instance, on 3 May 1955 I had a luncheon with James A. Perkins, vice-president of Carnegie Corporation of New York, to get his views on the then-completed nine chapters of the book, in which Carnegie Corporation was frequently cited. He was congratulatory on the project, cleared the direct quotes, and went on to express his concern over the tax-dodging and mismanagement of some foundations which brought the whole area into disrepute.

We discussed at some length the possibilities in self-regulation and more adequate reporting. Publication in that year of the Rich directory, *American Foundations and Their Fields, VII*, would supply useful information, but its entries were already dated and problems facing the organization made continuation of fact-finding unlikely on the scale and scope desirable. Moreover, adequate central collecting would involve questions almost amounting to accreditation which "would need to be handled with both courage and skill, backed by a group which could speak with authority and would be willing to withstand legal attack."[1]

A Prospectus Is Prepared

The currents grew stronger. Dr. Young and I were invited to a luncheon with Mr. Perkins and John W. Gardner, then president of Carnegie Corporation. They reported great concern

[1] FEA office memorandum on conversation, dated 3 May 1955.

among their trustees over deteriorating public opinion of foundations, stemming in part from the recent Reece fiasco, but also from a lack of accurate information readily available. Two possible steps had occurred to them, a book explaining about foundations and some sort of central information agency. Russell Sage Foundation had done most in this field; what were our views?

I referred to *Philanthropic Foundations*, of which Jim Perkins had already seen the opening chapters; it was agreed that this was a long step in the first direction. In the second area, we were answering the inquiries that came to us, but concentrated effort and a substantial staff would be needed to serve at all adequately the purposes they had in mind. I was asked to prepare a memorandum outlining these views.

On 25 May I sent over an eight-page memo titled "A Central Information Agency on Foundations." It reviewed the current unsatisfactory situation on foundation reporting. It saw as desirable "a foundation-financed central information agency," and suggested what it might initially do, and cost. It set up certain cautions, including a warning that in popular opinion foundations "are already financial colossi, and any organization that could be interpreted as an attempt to coordinate program would rouse grave fears. Care should therefore be taken that this organization remain at the information level and never attempt to speak for foundations as a group."

After further discussion I was asked in early July to prepare a definite prospectus which presumably could be presented to Carnegie trustees. John Gardner, Jim Perkins, and their lawyer, John E. F. Wood, a gentleman with wide experience in foundation matters, had their calendars clear for Thursday 7 July; could I be ready by then? I was a trifle busy with final chapters on the foundation book, commitments to the Ford group in Cambridge, and other matters, but the Fourth of July fell on a Monday, offering a long weekend.

On the agreed day we met, the three Carnegie officials with several pages of questions they wished to raise, I with my prospectus. We burst into laughter as we compared the two—my memorandum answered substantially all the questions, point by point. Of course there was further wide discussion, compromises, and questions held over. And the Carnegie trustees must make the final judgment.

A larger group held further meetings and made useful suggestions. A proposal that the organization be supported by foundation memberships, or even by grants from a large number of foundations, was rejected as savoring too much of a foundation-controlled trade association. One other foundation was approached with the suggestion that it share in initial financing; it declined.

A Decision

In the fall of 1955 Carnegie Corporation appropriated $100,000 for an initial year, with promise of further support if the organization was successful. A provisional board of trustees was appointed. Then for many months nothing appeared to be happening.

One day in early April, 1956, Dr. Young, one of the provisional trustees, called me to his office. He said that I was to be asked to serve on a temporary basis to get the organization started. He had discussed this matter with two members of his own board.

"The first thing both of them said was, 'Give Andrews as much time as is needed, but he must not go on Carnegie payroll.' So that's out."

I said I should need several days to think.

It was a tough decision. My position at Russell Sage Foundation was secure and offered growing opportunities under the best boss one could hope to have. Moreover, Dr. Young had indicated certain advancements at Russell Sage were impending—appointment as secretary and assistant treasurer, with salary increases.

The new organization would be an untried experiment. It would have financing for a first year, with a gentleman's agreement for further support if it happened to prove successful. Nothing like it had ever existed before; quarters would have to be found, staff hired, materials acquired, policies established, and then maybe nobody would really find it useful, or care. For several days I went about grumpily, lost in my own perplexities. It was 2 A.M. by the dim dial of the bedside clock when I woke Mrs. Andrews.

"I've decided. It's a gamble I must take—if they'll have me."

That afternoon I had an hour's talk with Don Young. I said we both ought to consider this proposition, not from the viewpoint of Russell Sage Foundation, Don Young, or that Andrews fellow, but what was best from a broader view. If it was true that this new organization would now be the strategic place for gathering and using knowledge about foundations, and if I could be braggy enough to believe I knew a little on the subject, then it might be the place I ought to be. I meant to find out just how much Carnegie was interested in doing the job, and then the decision would have to be mine. Dr. Young repeated, in a more resigned manner, his offer of advancement at Russell Sage.

Mr. Perkins assured me that no one else was being considered —though there were eager applicants—until it was found if I could be induced to take the job. I bargained for eight-tenths time, reserving one half day a week to supervise philanthropic studies at Russell Sage Foundation, and another half day for Ford and other commitments. And so it was agreed.

The Center Begins

In preliminary discussion the organization had been referred to under various names, including "Foundation Information Center." But at that period in American history, "information center" carried propaganda implications. "The Foundation Library Center" was the name officially adopted though it is far from being purely a library—possibly because support for libraries has long been a Carnegie tradition. Under that name it was incorporated on 25 May 1956 as an educational institution under authority of the Board of Regents of the University of the State of New York.

The original incorporators, serving as the first board of trustees, were Julian P. Boyd, professor of history and editor of *The Papers of Thomas Jefferson*, Princeton University; John A. Krout, vice president and provost of Columbia University; Emory W. Morris, president of W. K. Kellogg Foundation; Vernon Munroe, Jr., partner in the law firm of White and Case; James A. Perkins, vice president of Carnegie Corporation of New York; Robert L. Sutherland, director of the Hogg Foundation in the University of Texas; John D. Wilson, vice president of The Chase Manhattan Bank; John E. F. Wood, partner in the law firm of Dewey, Ballantine, Bushby, Palmer and Wood; and Donald Young, president of Russell Sage Foundation.

At the first meeting after incorporation, on 4 June 1956, I was made a trustee and confirmed as director (a title later changed to president). A December meeting added three more trustees: J. Kimball Johnson, director of The Cleveland Foundation; Robert J. McCracken, minister of The Riverside Church; and Walter

M. Upchurch, Jr., secretary of Shell Companies Foundation. In this first board exactly half of the trustees (not counting myself as *ex officio*) were nonfoundation people. This became an established policy, designed to ensure an independent board, not controlled by foundations but dedicated to the public interest. All have been distinguished people, many of national prominence, with whom it has been a delight to serve. Up to the present, only one person invited to be a trustee has declined to accept. A list of these trustees, with their terms of office, appears in Appendix D.[2]

I officially began work on Center payroll on 1 August 1956. The staff was my long-time secretary, Martha K. Branch, and myself, and though we had rented the seventh floor of the Christian Science Building at 588 Fifth Avenue, quarters would not be refinished for us until November. Russell Sage Foundation generously gave us space in the interim, and promised to let the Center have its whole collection on foundations and philanthropy, dating from 1915, "on depository loan." This was a proper safeguard in case the Center proved not viable. We still have the "loan."

We also purchased from American Foundations Information Service photographic transcripts of financial and other data on some 7,000 organizations of the foundation type. Mrs. Branch and I began organizing this material.

Having received our $100,000 check, we set up a checking account and rudimentary books. To help us in this operation, our treasurer, trustee John D. Wilson, sent us the auditor for The Chase Manhattan Bank, who also audits for the New York Stock Exchange. I had protested that our trifling account was not worth attention of such financial magnates, but on he came. After some preliminary talk and a glance at my small office he asked what accounting machines I had available, doubtless visualizing the rows of computers common in banks. Keeping my face very straight, I replied,

"I have an abacus."

I pulled open my desk drawer and showed it to him. For I did, and do, have an abacus, and enjoy using it to check simple computations.

Our first new employe was Ann D. Walton, who had foundation experience as executive secretary of the East European

---

[2] See pp. 305-306.

Fund. She was officially secretary to the board but also my first assistant, chief financial officer, personnel director, and an editor of several *Directories*, until her resignation due to family responsibilities (she had become Mrs. John A. Willis) in 1963.

As the day approached when we should begin to welcome the public to use our collections, we hired Miss Sara W. Dulles, niece of the Secretary of State, as librarian. She was the first of numerous Center librarians. They leave, not because of any dissatisfaction on either side, but almost invariably because, within a year or so, they either marry, or if already married, have a child. We have become resigned to these losses, and are practically able to guarantee one or the other of these events to any new aspirant for the library job. On a recent occasion when the charm faltered and a wanted child failed to arrive we lost the librarian anyway; she adopted one.

The Opening

Though the new quarters were not quite finished—it was a library without any bookcases or visible books for another month—the 12th of November was moving day for transferring thirty-five packing cases of books and files from Russell Sage Foundation.

That evening, after bedding the last of some seven thousand foundation records into shining new filing cabinets, I went forward to my own office with wide windows looking out on Fifth Avenue and dreamed awhile.

I might be muscle-tired tonight, but the future beckoned. Suddenly I had been given time, funds, and a staff to help folks build bridges between money and causes, between creative men and the time and tools they need. I would have a chance to make America's freest enterprise—philanthropy—even freer and more enterprising.

We had a preopening tea on 26 November, attended by the heads of nearly all the larger foundations. Included, among others, were H. Rowan Gaither of Ford, together with Quigg Newton then with Ford but later president of The Commonwealth Fund, Dean Rusk and Lindsley F. Kimball of Rockefeller, John W. Gardner and James A. Perkins of Carnegie, Maxwell Hahn of The Field Foundation, and Ralph Hayes of The New York Community Trust.

The doors were opened to the public on 10 December 1956.

The gathering and cataloguing of material were still far from complete, but a substantial collection was already available. *The New York Times* commented editorially on the opening as "an important event in the history of American philanthropy . . . it can and should do a great deal to forward the cause of 'full disclosure' in a field where it is needed."

At one of our earliest staff meetings I read the words Dr. Albert Schweitzer inscribed on the lamp which lighted patients to the quay for his hospital at Lambaréné:

> Here at whatever hour you come, you will find
> light and help and human kindness.

This might well be our own spirit. But I warned them also that the public might not care. We might have to rent a canary to keep us company.

We never rented that canary. The "customers" steadily increased, and both staff and space had to be progressively expanded. Special notices in newspapers and magazines sometimes brought a sudden crest of patronage. One of the farther out notices, promising far more than we could agree to deliver, appeared in *The Reporter*:

> Whether you are a writer, sculptor, lepidopterist, or student of pre-Columbian numismatics, you cannot do better than visit the Foundation Library Service [sic] at 588 Fifth Avenue, New York, where a staff of experts on benevolence will inquire into your desires and show you file material on every possible foundation functioning in your area.

But we did have a lepidopterist apply, and some of our stranger visitors are described in the next chapter.

Further Financing

Although we had been in actual operation only briefly, in January, 1957, Carnegie Corporation voted an additional appropriation of $400,000, payable in four annual installments, stating in its 1957 *Report*, "Having watched it through the organizational phase and during the early months of its activity, the Corporation is more convinced than ever that it will play an extremely useful role."

This took care of our regular budget for five years. But a minor emergency developed. One of our first tasks was preparation of a new directory of foundations, which in the same operation would update and increase our file materials on foundations. We had received permission from the Internal Revenue Service to visit their district offices and photograph the public portions of Form 990-A, had purchased equipment, trained an operator, and actually begun work in the New York Internal Revenue office. Then suddenly came an edict that no photographic equipment could be used in any Internal Revenue office.

So far as we could learn, this was an aftermath of the McCarthy period. A photograph of a return involving one of President Eisenhower's friends had been released to the press, and apparently the President felt that such a photographic reproduction was damaging publicity, more because of the form than content. So a Presidential Order had been issued that no tax-related materials could be photographed, even where the records were legally open to public inspection. At first Internal Revenue had assumed that returns of tax-exempt organizations such as foundations could be regarded as not tax related; but the Attorney General had just ruled otherwise.

Now we would have to hand-copy the records in the offices all over the United States, requiring expansion of field staff, high probability of error in spite of insistence on double checking, and greatly increased expense, well beyond our budget provision.

We explained these difficulties to The Ford Foundation, together with certain possible expansions of service, including depository libraries in other cities. In October, 1957, they announced a grant of $300,000 to The Foundation Library Center "for general support of its program over a period of approximately four years," matching the duration of the Carnegie grant and meeting our emergency. Funds were now adequate through 1960.

Early in 1958 Lindsley F. Kimball and I were sitting together at a conference, waiting to be called up for our speeches. We talked a bit about foundations in general, and then Mr. Kimball said suddenly,

"Andy, when is the Center going to come to Rockefeller Foundation for some money?"

I said we were financed through 1960, but our trustees were indeed beginning to think about the next period. We were delighted to hear that there might be a welcome mat at Rockefeller.

"This time," advised sagacious Mr. Kimball, "go for a ten-year period, and from several foundations. You're established now, and should take the longer view."

At the next meeting of our executive committee a Sustaining Fund for the 1960 decade was agreed upon, with budget set at $1,600,000. It was proposed to approach four foundations for $400,000 each. Carnegie Corporation's original grant had $150,000 left from balance in hand and a payment due in 1960, so that we asked, and quickly received, an additional $250,000. As The Ford Foundation existing grant also ran into the 1960 decade, we requested here also an additional $250,000 to complete their $400,000 for the new decade. This was approved, but not until near expiration of the older grant.

Since The Rockefeller Foundation had invited a submission, our chairman Vernon Munroe and I visited Dean Rusk[3] and Lindsley F. Kimball in December. The meeting ended with Mr. Rusk's remark that they had few conferences in which there was from the outset so much agreement. Their trustees voted the appropriation, and instead of paying it in annual installments, paid over the full amount, giving us the advantage of interest income.

One of our original trustees was Emory W. Morris, president of W. K. Kellogg Foundation. We had made it a principle not to ask for support from board members, whose unpaid services were already of great value to the Center. But Mr. Morris indicated that his trustees wanted to share in this Sustaining Fund, so a request was submitted. It was acted upon promptly, and a few days later I had another check for a full $400,000 to carry to the bank.

The estimates I had supplied for the 1960 decade included minor annual increases for expected expansions in service and monetary inflation. So far as the New York office is concerned, they proved remarkably accurate. When I retired in 1967 our expenditures for the New York office were almost precisely those budgeted for the period, and we had a surplus representing income from the prepaid installments.

Building the Collection

The Center endeavors to maintain in its New York office essentially complete material on every United States foundation, and

---

[3] Then president of The Rockefeller Foundation. When he became Secretary of State I sent him a congratulatory note. His amusing reply urged me to "keep the Foundation Library in good shape; some day I may be over there thumbing through opportunities for a job!"

in more recent years has been building up its foreign collection. It got off to a notable start with the Russell Sage and other materials already mentioned, and growth has continued over the years.

The collection is in three main categories. First are the reports of the foundations themselves. With their appreciated cooperation, the Center has nearly complete historical files, running back in one instance, Smithsonian Institution, to 1853. In 1957, after one year's operation, it had 1,640 reports from 222 organizations of the foundation type (these include agencies that call themselves foundations, but do not meet the Center's careful definitions). Ten years later such published reports numbered 3,461.

The collection on general philanthropy with emphasis on materials relating to foundations grew from 300 books in 1957 to 1,113 by 1972. By the latter year pamphlets, articles, and reports numbered 5,839. Uncounted newspaper clippings and other brief items are arranged by year, in subject folders.

Until recent years the heart of the collection was in the vertical file section. Long ranges of filing cabinets, completely open to the public, bulged with folders devoted to every known foundation, including recent 990-A's (official information returns to the government, recently supplanted by Form 990 and 990-AR), articles of incorporation if available, news releases and clippings, related documents of all sorts. We have sometimes surprised foundation officials with documents concerning their foundations which had long since vanished from their own files. By 1972 the entries covered some 36,600 organizations of the foundation type, of which about 26,000 would meet the Center's stricter definitions.

Some years after the Center opened we began compiling records of all known foundation grants of $10,000 or more. These were published in *Foundation News*, later noted, but also made available for recent years in a special cabinet on cards classified by subject area. The most recent (1970 and 1971) grants were published in book form.[4]

The 1970 and later foundation returns (Form 990 and 990-AR) are now supplied by Internal Revenue Service on microfilm, with a shift to aperture cards in prospect. The library is equipped with suitable reading machines, and is setting up sophisticated systems for information retrieval on grants.

[4] *The Foundation Grants Index, 1970-1971.* Edited by Lee Noe. Compiled by The Foundation Center. New York, Columbia University Press, 1972. 292 p.

The historical collections have been enriched from time to time by thoughtful gifts of foundations and individuals, disposing of collections no longer needed. The late Robert M. Lester, long secretary of Carnegie Corporation of New York, and a collector of foundation memorabilia, gave us a large part of his personal library, rich in biographies of philanthropists.

But the largest accretion, aside from the original Russell Sage Foundation contribution, came from The Hanover Bank. I had long been familiar with Hanover's Philanthropic Library. It was established in 1930, collecting books, articles, clippings, and reports on philanthropic organizations, on methods of giving, on other aspects of philanthropy, and publishing a few related pamphlets of its own. This was done "as a service to our trust customers and their attorneys," with a counseling service under Craig R. Smith, Charles N. Wonacott, and R. L. Dickinson, the last a fellow deacon in The Riverside Church. The library was open to the public, doubtless with the hope that outside users would often be wealthy persons who would be influenced to use the bank's trust department.

In October, 1958, while I was still a member of the Tenafly Planning Board, I attended a luncheon meeting of the Regional Plan Association. A table companion introduced himself as Robert M. Lovell, senior vice president of The Hanover Bank. I mentioned our pleasant relations with their Philanthropic Library, and of course our own related operations. It turned out that the bank was about to move to new and more costly quarters uptown, and was reconsidering many operations, including the library. Discreet inquiries confirmed what I had long suspected: most users of their library turned out to be needy fund-raisers instead of wealthy persons about to set up a trust. The operation was "rather disappointing" in terms of their original purposes and the bank's interests.

We had further conversations, in which trustee Julian P. Boyd, who had been Princeton librarian before he became editor of the Jefferson papers, most usefully shared. In June, 1959, after removing a small amount of confidential and reference material, The Hanover Bank turned over the whole remaining collection to the Center as a donation, asking us to select from this wealth of material whatever we desired for our own files, and to act as distributing agent for the remainder.

Our librarian, Miss MaryVie Cramblitt, and I spent a hot summer in a steamy file room downtown, going over every document. We acquired from this source 806 books, pamphlets, reports, and legal documents; 188 copies of wills, usually of foundation donors; 1,500 clippings, chiefly related to the origin and early history of foundations. We initiated arrangements whereby the remainder of the collection, which either duplicated our holdings or was outside our subject area, was donated to the Midwest Inter-Library Center in Chicago, except for the clippings, which were deposited with the Memorial Library at the University of Wisconsin at the request of Merle Curti.

Depository Libraries

Persons in other parts of the country complained about the nuisance and heavy cost of coming to New York to find out about foundations, even those in their own area. To improve this situation the trustees approved an experimental program of setting up foundation collections in certain other large cities, if an appropriate library could be induced to invite the collection and agree to maintain it. The Center would assist the library in assembling the original collection, continue to advise, and supply copies of foundation information returns (Form 990-A) for that state and perhaps its surrounding territory, but would assume no corporate relationship or financial obligation to these libraries.

The first such arrangement was made in 1959 with the Midwest Inter-Library Center in Chicago. Due to the happy coincidence of The Hanover Bank collection coming to the Center just at that time, we were able to obtain for this library not only the current reports of nearly all foundations, but in many cases historical series and other related materials.

While this library had affiliation as a depository with twenty college and university libraries in eleven midwestern states, its location near the University of Chicago campus was far from convenient for most Chicago users. A few years later it changed its name to Center for Research Libraries and to some extent its program. In the altered situation it agreed to transfer the foundation collection to The Newberry Library, in central Chicago, where it is now handsomely housed.

In 1960 and 1961 six additional depositories were set up, two in California at Berkeley and Los Angeles under auspices of the University of California, two in the public libraries of Atlanta and Kansas City,[5] and two in libraries associated with founda-

[5] In 1969 the Missouri collection was transferred to The Danforth Foundation in St. Louis.

tions: in Cleveland by The Cleveland Foundation and in Austin by The Hogg Foundation for Mental Health, in the Tower of the University of Texas. In these two cases the initiators were trustees of the Center, J. Kimball Johnson, director of The Cleveland Foundation, and Robert L. Sutherland, director of The Hogg Foundation. Under the watchful eyes of these foundation executives, these libraries established high standards of excellence.

Making initial arrangements and attendance at the sometimes impressive opening ceremonies involved heavy travel. Even in later years I tried to visit each library at least every other year, and in the alternate years we have been inviting the librarians to New York where they and the Center staff could sit down together to discuss the nature and present use of their collection, how the public could be better informed of its existence, and ways to improve its content.

At one such seminar we had a hair-raising account of the Texas Tower massacre. About noon, 1 August 1966, Charles Whitman, Eagle Scout, honor student, ex-Marine marksman, transported his arsenal of rifles, pistols, and sawed-off shotgun to the observation deck, where he beat the receptionist unconscious and began shooting. Members of The Hogg Foundation staff, on the 24th floor, rushed into the stairwell to find a man screaming, bodies piled on the stairs, blood running everywhere. They phoned in alarms, leaned from windows shouting vainly to people to take cover, finally barricaded their own door for fear the attack would come to them. In just under two hours, when he was himself killed, Whitman shot 49 people, killing 15. It was scarcely an ordinary library day.

Washington Office

For calendar year 1962 Internal Revenue Service drastically revised the reporting Form 990-A, with substantially all data on the new form open to public inspection and including, for the first time, a requirement for individual listing of all grants paid, as well as much more detailed balance sheets and other financial data. Moreover, one set of all these forms was to be filed in their Washington office.

For the Center, this was tremendous news. Now it would be possible to get our information and much more of it, in a single office instead of traveling to sixty-two locations all over the United States. At our board meeting on 1 April 1963 we discussed eagerly how far we could mine this new resource within our budget. Previously, we had been able to copy 990-A's only every three years, to coincide with *Directory* needs. Now we could probably afford to place a transcriber in Washington for months at a time, and keep annual records at least on the larger foundations.

A few weeks later, on 26 April, I had a phone call from Arnold J. Zurcher, vice president of Alfred P. Sloan Foundation and a Center trustee. The aging but still vigorous Mr. Sloan, he reported, had expressed a deep personal concern that foundations act promptly to improve their public image and counter the attack of Representative Patman.[6] Mr. Zurcher himself, one of our trustees, added that he was well aware that the Center could not speak out like a trade association, which is what Mr. Sloan with his business experience probably would like, but perhaps we could in some way contribute to a wider presentation of pertinent facts. Could I come to lunch with Mr. Case, president of Sloan Foundation, and himself—perhaps today?

I could, and on the short walk across Fifth Avenue to the Sloan offices in the International Building I developed what I called at luncheon "a wild idea." Provided they and the Center's board were both interested, we might set up a separate Washington branch office, which could serve both as an information center in that strategic place and be our research facility for mining the vast new information available, on the new 990-A forms, beginning to be filed this very month.

Our fine relations with Internal Revenue made it almost certain that they would permit us to copy these returns under a special arrangement. We could make three sets, one to remain in the new Washington office, one to come at once to New York, the third to go to the appropriate depository library. This would save the Internal Revenue offices a great deal of trouble through serving in our libraries the information-seekers who would otherwise be in their hair. Moreover, this whole new dimension in foundation disclosure should notably contribute to the public understanding and confidence which Mr. Sloan had at heart.

When I had finished, Mr. Case said, "That seems like a very sound suggestion. Now tell me about your wild idea." We tossed some tentative budget figures in the air, and he urged that I get in touch with our executive committee at once.

The committee met in emergency session on 7 May. It speedily approved "the establishment of a branch office in Washington

[6] Later discussed. See pp. 244-246, 250-253.

and authorizes the Director to seek support from the Alfred P. Sloan Foundation or others for the expenses of such an office for a five-year period." Such an office, it agreed, "should be an information and research center operating under the charter restriction of the organization itself, and specifically not functioning as a lobby for any point of view."

On 22 July Sloan Foundation notified the Center that its trustees had approved a grant of $200,000 to be spread over three years, for "expansion of its services," not specifically for a Washington office, though clearly it could be used at least in part for initiation and early support of this project. It was less than our request, based on a budget for at least five years and preferably for the full 1960 decade. Nevertheless it permitted us to start, and in mid-August J. Richard Taft was added to staff, as manager of the projected Washington Office and also to take over editorship of *Foundation News*, discussed later.

Then came a serendipity that needs a bit of history. Margaret Olivia Sage received many requests for funds upon the death of her husband in 1906. One, to which she acceded, was a plea for a bird refuge in Louisiana. Early records are obscure, but it appears that the land developer pointed out to her that The Rockefeller Foundation had already established one refuge, not large enough, however, for the great flocks of migratory birds, which were being killed off far too rapidly. He could let her have title to some 75,000 acres on Marsh Island, near the delta of the Mississippi. He neglected to tell her that he was reserving for himself a strip between the two refuges, on which he sold shooting rights.

Mrs. Sage bought the land, established it as a bird refuge, and subsequently gave title to the Foundation trustees. In 1920 the Foundation transferred title to the state of Louisiana under strict covenants concerning its use as a wild-life sanctuary, and with residual rights of recovery in case of abuse.

Under the extraordinary[7] administration of Huey Long shoot-

[7] Perhaps the most bizarre in American political history. According to David M. Potter in the *Dictionary of American Biography*, Huey Long "improperly influenced legislators by awarding state jobs to them . . . used state funds for personal and unauthorized expenditures. [During 1934-1935] the legislature enacted, without debate, a series of laws that abolished local government and gave Long control of the appointment of every policeman, fireman, and school teacher in the state. His complete control of the militia, the judiciary, the election officials, and the tax assessing bodies left all citizens at his mercy and denied them any redress—either electoral or legal." Supplement I, Scribner's, 1945, pp. 507-508.

ing and trapping contracts on Marsh Island were granted for the benefit of politicians. The Foundation tried to enforce its right of recovery. During the Long administration the Louisiana courts were deaf, but Mr. Long was assassinated at the State Capitol on 8 September 1935, by Dr. Carl A. Weiss, an outraged physician. The Foundation recovered title.

Meanwhile, oil was being discovered on nearby lands. Since this was a wild-life sanctuary, the Foundation refused to permit explorations. Then World War II broke out, and the need for domestic oil became urgent. With both the Department of the Interior and the state of Louisiana bringing strong pressure for the right to explore, in the spring of 1944 the trustees agreed, on certain conditions. There must be a minimum disturbance of wild life and any resulting revenues should be divided equally between the Foundation and the state of Louisiana, with the state devoting its revenues to "maintaining, policing, and improving Marsh Island as a wild life refuge." Any surplus was to be applied to state-wide programs of propagation and protection of wild life, and then to health and educational work in Louisiana.

Some monies were received for exploration rights, but for many years no substantial discoveries were made. Suddenly, toward the close of the Foundation's 1962-1963 fiscal year, its Marsh Island receipts mounted to $1,797,780. As a consultant to the Foundation, I was aware of this bonanza, and aware too of Internal Revenue's strictness concerning prompt appropriation of foundation income. Since at that time the Russell Sage Foundation program was averaging about $1 million a year, met from ordinary investment income, it was clear that this addition was too large for mere expansion of regular program.

We prepared a careful budget of expenses for the Washington office for the remainder of the 1960 decade, estimating the balance needed at $320,000. This would not solve their whole problem of temporarily excess funds, I said to the Foundation trustees, but it was all the Center could presently justify. . . . They voted the requested appropriation.

Dr. Young was retiring at the end of that year. In my letter of appreciation for the handsome grant, I added my regrets at his impending retirement and a very special tribute to that sagacious mixture of support, independence for me, and wise direction which had made possible, and delightful, my own work in the philanthropy vineyards. I also announced my desire to resign my formal consultantship at the time his resignation took effect; I would be finishing thirty-five years' connection with the Foundation, and his successor should start with a clean slate.[8]

Mr. Taft proceeded rapidly with organization of the Washington office. On 1 October modest quarters were leased at 1327 18th Street, N. W. By the year end these quarters were completely furnished and a staff of four busily at work.

On 3 January 1964, which was also publication date of *Directory 2* permitting national publicity for both events, we opened the Washington office. There was a small party, with guests from government, foundations, and research and educational agencies. From government came Commissioner of Internal Revenue, Mortimer M. Caplin, and Assistant Secretary of the Treasury, Stanley S. Surrey; Representative Patman was invited, but declined.

Though the Washington office functions as an important center of information for the inquiring public, its main service was in connection with the copying of the 990-A returns, which were the Center's chief source of recent information on foundations. Internal Revenue was most cooperative, permitting us to photocopy promptly these returns in a special office. One or two operators were constantly busy at this task; well over 100,000 pages were produced a year to take care of the ever-increasing number of foundations and the multiple pages required for the increased reportage.

Washington City renovation soon threatened the "old brownstone front" in which we originally located. The office was moved to larger quarters at 1001 Connecticut Avenue, N. W. in October, 1966. With the retirement of Mr. Taft to enter business on his own account early in 1967, there was a brief interregnum, during which the Center's secretary, Irene R. Kay, commuted from New York to supervise. Mrs. Lois A. Murkland was appointed director of the Washington office in July, 1967, retiring in January, 1971. Mrs. Margot Moore Brinkley replaced her.

Foundation News

As a further measure toward supplying information to a wider public, with some emphasis on significance and recency, the Center initiated in September, 1960, a bimonthly publication entitled *Foundation News*, Bulletin of The Foundation Library Center.

[8] At the insistence of the young new president, Dr. Brim, I remained a consultant, but on a per diem basis.

Said my "Beginning Note":

> *Foundation News* will ordinarily include three kinds of material. There will be "think" pieces—excerpts from an annual report, a speech, or material prepared especially for the Bulletin—related to philanthropy, and usually specifically to foundations. A substantial section will be devoted to general reporting, including developments within foundations or affecting them.
>
> Finally, about half our space will be devoted to reporting foundation grants. . . .
>
> It is hoped that this Bulletin may serve both those who disburse and those who seek foundation funds, and promote a better understanding of this unique instrument for the contribution of private wealth to public purpose.[9]

We were at this time conducting an experiment in training foundation personnel, in accordance with our ambitious original announcement that the Center would offer annually an "internship in philanthropy" to a person nominated by a foundation which presently employs him, or expects to do so. The first, and as it turned out the only, such intern was Mr. Burton Raffel, who resigned a law firm position with the expectation of making philanthropy a career. He was sponsored by Russell Sage Foundation, which made the Center a grant for half his salary. The arrangement was that our intern would spend half his time in directed reading, sitting in on significant conferences, and other learning processes; the other half would be as an employe of the Center in whatever capacity needed, with the hope that this also would be of practical training value.

Mr. Raffel worked on the Bulletin as one of his staff assignments. He proved an exceptionally able writer and editor (he is translator of a widely used edition of *Beowulf* and an authority on Indonesian poetry), and was formally appointed editor of *Foundation News*, an assignment he ably filled until his retirement to literature and teaching in the fall of 1963. He was succeeded by J. Richard Taft, as already related, in the fall of 1963. Mr. Taft remained editor until the spring of 1967, when Mr. Harvey B. Matthews, Jr., assumed the editorship, along with other duties, upon my own retirement. Staff member Mrs. Lee Noe has been grants editor during substantially the whole period of publication. *Foundation News* was transferred to the Council on Foundations in January, 1972.

[9] *Foundation News*, Vol. 1, No. 1, September, 1960, p. 1.

Twenty Viewpoints

Russell Sage Foundation under Dr. Young had financially assisted with *Foundation News* in two ways, through paying part of the fellowship for Editor Raffel as already noted, but also with a two-year grant totaling $25,000 toward initial costs.

On 11 December 1964 its energetic new president, Dr. Orville G. Brim, Jr., broached over the telephone a fresh idea related to our Bulletin. In the present situation, it seemed important to get the foundation story to a wider audience; would the Center consider for speedy Foundation publication a paperbound volume reprinting a selection of the major stories appearing in *Foundation News?* In this economical form it could be sold widely, with copies also distributed free by Russell Sage and perhaps other foundations.

My executive committee quickly agreed, and after consultations with my editors and others we selected twenty pieces from Volumes I through IV, and I wrote an Introduction.

The volume was in three parts. Four papers dealt generally and broadly with that extraordinary expression of American free enterprise, private philanthropy, and its ingenious invention, the freely operating philanthropic foundation. The nine papers in Part II identified fields in which foundations make their grants, and discussed practical experience in a few quite specific areas. Part III presented "Views on Administration" in seven papers, ranging from training foundation executives, through the intricacies of legal and tax problems, to sage advice on how to frame a persuasive grant proposal.

To get copy out I worked through Christmas Eve, one eye on manuscript, the other on the proper placing of those red and gold balls on our Christmas tree. We had a small delay in getting permission on the piece by Dean Rusk, by this time Secretary of State, dashing from country to country. In addition to the Secretary, the distinguished list of contributors included, among others, Everett N. Case, then president of Alfred P. Sloan Foundation; Mortimer M. Caplin, formerly Commissioner of Internal Revenue; Donald Young, formerly president of Russell Sage Foundation; James A. Perkins, president of Cornell University but vice president of Carnegie Corporation of New York when his paper was prepared; and Manning M. Pattillo then with The Danforth Foundation, later to become my successor as president of The Foundation Center.

The number of papers gave us our title—*Foundations—20 Viewpoints.*[10] I received first copies the 6th of March. Few books have had a faster production history, from original idea to bound copies in less than three calendar months. The collection was well received, and a reprint became necessary.

We Move

The addition of the Hanover material and the growth in use of the Center began to cramp our otherwise pleasant quarters in the Christian Science Building. We managed to rent additional space on an adjoining floor in August, 1959. This was not convenient and soon it, too, proved inadequate. In September, 1961, the Center moved into the Newsweek Building at 444 Madison Avenue, New York City, with usable floor space nearly double that in its previous location.

But even before my retirement in 1967 it was becoming obvious that a further expansion would be necessary. On some days every chair in the library was occupied and readers had to be accommodated in the reception area. In 1971 the Center moved to larger quarters in a new building at 888 Seventh Avenue.

Equipment, too, was much changed. Under the energetic and able direction of the new president, Thomas R. Buckman who assumed office on 1 July 1971, the Center has fully entered the age of electronics and computerized data banks. Changes were due with the improvement of information retrieval techniques, but in the foundation field they were speeded by the sudden shift to microfilm and then aperture card reports on foundations by the Internal Revenue Service. The new techniques should enable the Center to keep abreast of increasing demand for information about foundations and expansion of the field itself.

[10] *Foundations: 20 Viewpoints,* edited by F. Emerson Andrews. Russell Sage Foundation, 1965, 108 p.

CHAPTER 15

Foundation Watcher—People

O<small>N SEVERAL</small> occasions I have begun speeches or articles with the assertion, "I have the most fascinating job in the world. I am a foundation watcher."[1]

Of course a few other people may feel equally enthusiastic about their tasks; indeed, the more the better. But I do find it difficult to imagine another job which would offer equal insights into every field of learning, all the arts, the frontiers of scientific research, poverty and suffering, extreme wealth and privilege, nearly every type of business, the stock market, economic theory, investments, taxation, Congressional hearings and politics at all levels, education, the law, religion and philosophy—the list extends to the ultimate concerns of man and the infinities of space.

Moreover, for the foundation watcher this acquaintance comes not from lectures or libraries, but out of personal involvement, often with top leaders in the field. Some of these relationships have been touched upon in earlier chapters, but the flood began when the Center opened its doors.

The Human Tide

In the Center's first full year, 1957, library registrants numbered 1,407. Ten years later, during 1967, they totaled 5,625, and this did not include visitors to the Washington office, the seven

---

[1] Two of these, from which much of the materials in this and the following chapter are drawn, are "New Developments in Foundations," a talk at the annual meeting of the American Association of Fund-Raising Counsel in New York on 10 November 1961, printed in the Association's *Bulletin*, Vol. 7, December 1961; and "What Foundations Support," *Kiwanis Magazine*, February 1965.

regional depositories, or the countless inquiries handled by mail and telephone.

Who are these people?

Briefcase in hand, they arrive eagerly at the Center, some of them before the 9:00 o'clock opening. Most of them are seekers of funds, amateur or professional. Among such, the largest single group are presidents or development officers from colleges, seeking grants for better salaries for professors, or a new science building, or special equipment for a pioneering course in astrophysics.

Sometimes they are foundation executives and trustees, getting information on what other foundations are doing, or trying to find a field no foundation has yet entered. They are poets and playwrights, looking for Maecenas in foundation garb.

A considerable number are lawyers, researching technical data on setting up foundations, comparing charters and bylaws, or concocting new tax gimmicks so that their principals can use an institution meant for the welfare of mankind to contribute to the wealth of one client.

They are students seeking scholarships (few foundations give them directly). They are researchers, needing a final few thousands—or hundred thousands—to push on to the discovery of a new miracle drug, or to travel to central Australia for a study of the Aborigines.

More than a few of them are donors, burdened with accumulated wealth that they would gladly devote to relieving suffering or lighting a candle of new knowledge, if they could find out how.

A few are newspaper or magazine writers, who from the same set of facts may discover either that foundations are the very crown of America's creative genius, or are a threat to national survival and pawns of the Communist conspiracy.

Some visitors are from foreign countries, and each recent year groups of economists and financial officers from developing countries, chiefly Africa, sponsored by the Department of State and the United Nations, have visited us for a lecture and question period on foundations. It is first necessary to try to convince them that private organizations really do exist with the purpose of giving away money for the benefit of others, without a primary concern for American foreign policy, prestige, or economic advantage.

On the way to one such meeting, this one at the UN for the advantage of simultaneous bilingual translation, I picked up an advance announcement of a Carnegie Corporation grant to the University of Ibadan. When the inevitable questions came about grant ties to American interests I took pleasure in reading the detailed terms of this grant: "The new curriculum will introduce a new emphasis on African, and particularly West African, history . . . and will bring together 72 teachers from Nigeria, Ghana, Sierra Leone, and Gambia and about 25 African and other experts on African history." It became evident that this group were impressed and delighted to see an American foundation supplying money for a study of their own backgrounds rather than an attempt to indoctrinate them with Western culture and history.

Some Vignettes

Individuals are more exciting than categories. One was a bearded man with a long scroll, who has invented a new system of economics that will replace all religions. Another, this time a letter-writer, addressed to me this personal request:

> Could you please help me in getting a grant for the development of the Holy Ghost? I have it at the present time, in the embryo stage in front of my right eye. I can show it to you. The Holy Ghost is the maker of all so-called miracles and the supernatural. . . .

One firm-jawed lady disrupted the library with loud claims that we were supporting lies. The staff protects me as far as possible, but she was finally brought in. Her complaint was that although she had devised a brand new and absolutely perfect plan for solving labor relations, the eighteen foundations that our files indicated had some interest in that field all refused support. Having scorned her splendid project, their alleged interest in that area was obviously a lie on our part.

Another lady showed our librarian two jars of jelly, asking which was home-made and which was synthetic? Foundations, she is certain, have no more pressing cause than to help supply real, not synthetic, jellies for children.

A scientist came in, presenting persuasive arguments that if we slept in aqua-beds (a saline solution just the specific gravity of the body) we should recover the ideal rest that our remote ancestors presumably had, and that fish still enjoy, and need no more than two or three hours of sleep a night for perfect refreshment.

Another scientist believes, and has advanced his belief through articles in scientific magazines as well as appeals for foundation grants, that the south polar ice cap is growing steadily. It may soon displace enough weight to tilt the earth, radically changing the climate and spilling the oceans over what are now the land masses. This, he maintains, has happened periodically in the past, and may account for the flood legends so common to all ancient cultures. He wants preliminary funds for scientific measurement of this presumed growth; if it is actual and dangerous, the new preeminent concern for all men and nations is not hunger or war or space exploration, but application of atomic heat to melt a portion of this ice cap while still there is time.

Slightly less cosmic are these two requests, by mail:

> I need an upper and lower denture after the extractions of eight teeth—at present, I have a partial lower and upper denture which are quite worn. A dentist recommended by your Foundation would be satisfactory.

And from a Kentucky rural correspondent:

> Can you all please, please help me out to get a piano? A second hand piano will cost $50. . . . Nearly everyone around here are farmers. They consider a piano of no importance in the home, but it really is to a person with talent. I like to be respected and looked up to. *Please* help.

One day a clown came in, powdered face, big red nose, jacket spangled in rainbow colors. He has incorporated himself to give free performances to children in hospitals, and seeks foundation support.

Several times newspapers have carried feature stories on the Center,[2] and these usually stir up an immediate flood of telephone calls, letters, and visits. After such a feature story in an evening paper one researcher could not wait for dawn, but reached one of our editors working overtime. He needed immediate funds for two of his current inventions, which were absolute cures for blindness and cancer.

The same feature story produced two business-related requests. A telephone call asked for the address of The Ford Foundation, since the caller was sure it would be glad to supply funds

---

[2] Including "Information Is His Business," Stafford Derby, *Christian Science Monitor*, 11 August 1958; "Foundations Found Here," Sidney Fields in his Only Human column, New York *Daily News*, 23 June 1965; "17,000 Ways to Get Money," Ed Wallace, New York *World-Telegram and The Sun*, 7 April 1966.

for her to start a laundromat. A Long Island gentleman hoped foundations would solve his special financial problem:

> I am a small business man in the tavern business. This business is not able to borrow from the Small Business Federal Fund. I am however in need of financial assistance & can't raise it through normal lending agencies unless I wish to go to Loan Sharks.

An astrologer, "reading what a wonderful man you are and the good humanitarian work you are doing," offered his services free for a weekly mind-reading act toward support of the Center. We expressed gratitude, but declined.

One memorable day two foreign-looking visitors asked our librarian to name three foundations that "would be sure to reject our proposal in medical research." Upon her baffled further inquiry she learned that they had a desirable but reluctant donor who would support their project if it failed of support elsewhere, the proof to be three authentic rejection letters!

Extraordinary Foundations

Chuckles for a foundation watcher come also from some of the queerer names or purposes donors attach to their creations. I kept in my desk a private folder labeled "Extraordinary Foundations," and occasionally used examples to leaven articles or speeches, but always with the reservation that these oddities are a small part of the foundation picture, not characteristic, and should not be cited out of qualifying context. I present a few of them here with diffidence, and the hope that they may be used only with those cautions.

Sometimes the donor was playing with words when he named his foundation. *The Foundation Directory, Edition 3*, for example, includes at least four "backward" foundations: Lexerd Foundation (address, c/o *Drexel* and Company); The Stiver Foundation (donor, Samuel *Revits*); The Surdna Foundation (donor John E. *Andrus*), and The Munitalp Foundation, which includes meteorology in its program. The Rockefellers' Sealantic Fund is an amalgam from their estates at *Seal* Harbor, Maine, and Po*cantico* Hills. The New York section also includes S A D Foundation, which puzzled us until we noticed that the donor was Stewart A. Dunn.

Donors of small and highly specialized foundations sometimes choose modest names. Guedel's Dinky Foundation reported its

1966 income at $144, assets at $14,025. Hinky-Dinky Foundation in Omaha reported 1963 income of $953, but operating from current gifts, gave out more than $20,000 in "toys to various charitable homes and institutions."

Almost all lists citing curious purposes include Emma A. Robinson Horses' Christmas Dinner Trust Fund. Mrs. Robinson, of Olathe, Kansas, left a trust fund of $10,000 on her death in 1932 to continue the Christmas dinners for horses she had been conducting for twenty-four years. The provender was to be one bushel of oats or half a bushel of corn crops for each of 200 horses. The Kansas City *Star* on occasion carried advertisements: "Horses fed free Christmas dinner." In 1949 the courts turned the money over to Wayside Waifs, an organization that provides a home and food for all sorts of abandoned animals, because not enough worthy horses could any longer be found.

There is a Share Your Birthday Foundation in Philadelphia, designed to "encourage children the world over to give up one of their birthday presents to children of the same age in other lands." Some years ago a youngster from India arrived in Allentown, Pennsylvania, with a birthday gift he proposed to share—a baby elephant.

Columnist George W. Crane a decade ago was promoting his Scientific Marriage Foundation "to introduce congenial folk who are unmarried." All applicants (it was necessary to send 20 cents and an application blank) "are interviewed by competent local clergymen who have volunteered as counselors, and who check on the three character references each applicant must cite. . . . We try to introduce people of the same religion, race, educational and economic background, same hobbies and ideals . . ."

Sports are a central interest for a number of foundations. South African golfer Gary Player recently used $20,000 of his $25,000 United States Open winnings to set up the Junior Golf Foundation "to promote junior golf in this country." The American Casting Education Foundation helps conduct indoor casting tournaments for fishermen, but American Casting Educational Foundation helps educate casting (shot-putting) instructors and to select castors to represent the United States in world competition. A decade ago United States Brewers Foundation offered a $1,000 prize for the best antique set of full-size skittles uncovered in continental United States. It recognized that "beer and skittles" still go together in popular parlance, though few people know that skittles was the forerunner of modern bowling, extremely popular until about a century ago.

A few purposes are pleasant enough, but seem less than world-shaking in importance. James Dean in his Will set aside $10,000 to be administered by Boston's Permanent Charity Fund, a community trust, to provide for delivery to the Boston Light Vessel of "one copy of each of the principal Sunday newspapers published in Boston" every Sunday from mid-April to mid-October. The Dr. Coles Trust Fund for Ice Cream for the Pupils of Scotch Plains and Fanwood provides from the income of $1,000 free ice cream for those New Jersey school children one day a year (if the funds are adequate) until "the end of the world."

An anonymous Boston business executive organized the Lollipop Foundation to supply lollipops to console children in hospitals. It estimates an average hospital would need 25,000 in a year at a cost of $318. The Texahoma Redbud Foundation encourages the planting of redbud trees from the Gulf Coast to Canada. Two prairie chicken foundations (one in Illinois, the other in Wisconsin) are devoted to the preservation of "that magnificent bird . . . an inseparable part of American tradition."

Central Intelligence Agency

Not infrequently foundation executives came to my office for confidential conferences. They must never be identified, but the questions they raised were sometimes of great importance.

The chief executive of a small, highly respected midwestern foundation asked for closed-door treatment. During World War II, he said, he had served with the Office of Strategic Services (OSS). So when the Central Intelligence Agency asked permission to use his foundation as a "pass through" agency—giving them money for grants to specified persons who would do "research" or be delegates to meetings in sensitive areas abroad—he had complied without hesitation.

"It was a request from government," he said, "and I saw it as simply our patriotic duty. But now one of my trustees is objecting, and I was asked to get your views."

I warned him that my views would be purely personal, and not an official position. We were not unacquainted with the practice, however. A certain substantial foundation operating many excellent programs in the foreign field did not appear in our *Direc-*

tory; we refused listing because it declined to furnish financial information and did not file a 990-A. He could guess, as we did, the probable principal source of its funds. On several past occasions men arrested as spies had claimed to be researchers for named foundations on which we had no records whatever; perhaps this was why the CIA was now seeking the better cover of legitimate foundations.

As to personal advice, I opposed the whole practice, and any cooperation with it by foundations or individuals. This was not on moralistic grounds—though for individuals this might be decisive—but on appraisal of total effects. Any strategic information which could be obtained by these means had to be weighed against the poison spread in foreign minds about all of our genuinely independent research, or our efforts to aid. Glib speeches supporting American views at foreign conferences would be heavily discounted when it was discovered that any of these delegates was government-paid. At the Center we had disturbing evidence of rapid spread of these practices, which made the day of discovery inevitable.

I think he took my advice, for in the later revelations his foundation was not named. The first substantial leak was, amazingly, in the halls of Congress. At one of the Patman hearings, on 31 August 1964, Congressman Wright Patman, obviously irritated at Internal Revenue Service's delay in acting on The J. M. Kaplan Fund, startled his audience with these comments while the Acting Commissioner of Internal Revenue Harding was on the stand:

> Mr. Rogovin informed us that the J. M. Kaplan Fund has been operating as a conduit for channeling CIA funds and hence you would rather not discuss the matter for the public record. He also indicated that the Fund's operations with the CIA was the reason for the lack of action on the part of the IRS. . . .

He then added a request for audits "and addresses" for eight mysterious "foundations"—The Gotham Foundation, Michigan Fund, Andrew Hamilton Fund, Borden Trust, The Price Fund, The Edsel Fund, The Beacon Fund, and The Kentfield Fund—which collectively had contributed $923,950 to The Kaplan Fund in a given year.[3]

[3] *Hearings before Subcommittee No. 1 on Foundations.* Select Committee on Small Business, House of Representatives, 88th Congress, 2d Session. Government Printing Office, Washington, 1964. Pp. 182, 191.

After certain private conferences Mr. Patman did not proceed further on this subject in his hearings, and few persons apparently recognized its broader implications. Then in March, 1967, *Ramparts Magazine* published a devastating article revealing wide CIA operations, particularly in connection with the United States National Student Association and the heavily financed Foundation for Youth and Student Affairs.

For weeks our libraries in New York and Washington were jammed with reporters and others seeking every scrap of information on any real or fabricated foundation that had been mentioned, including those which had quite innocently contributed to activities now revealed to have had some support from CIA-related funds. After an ugly incident in which a significant page had been cut from our files, for a short period we required each user to apply at the desk for the documents, and personally return them.

The issues are not simple, particularly when one includes support from a wide spectrum of government agencies. My views are presented in a special section of Chapter 19, Afterthoughts.

What Can We Do?

Most of the conferences with foundation people and prospective donors were not cloak-and-dagger. Much more typical is the case of Mr. T. J. Jones (name fictitious).

Mr. Jones is a dark-complexioned, energetic man probably in his late fifties, who retired early after making a great financial success in his business of floor coverings. At first he enjoyed his new leisure, living winters in California and summers on Long Island. He spent his mornings reading *Barron's* and *The Wall Street Journal*, had luncheon, and played tennis in the afternoon, followed by dinner and a social evening.

Lately this program has completely palled. He realizes that merely to survive he must have some worth-while personal interest, something to get up for in the morning. So he has established a foundation, gives it about $30,000 a year in new money, and hopes that through the foundation and other volunteer services he can get himself into the stream of living.

I made a variety of suggestions, including the possibility of organizing a community foundation with his own fund as the initial stake, and himself becoming the unpaid director, thus developing wide community interests. I also turned him loose on typi-

cal foundation reports which showed highly individualized
programs in the hope that he would come upon something that
struck fire with him. Among these I carefully included The Dorr
Foundation's white marginal lines project, which at small expenditure had contributed notably to highway safety.[4]

Incidentally, one of my visitors was the daughter of the late
John V.N. Dorr, Mrs. Malcolm Oakes, seeking suggestions for
a new program for The Dorr Foundation. While Mr. Dorr was
living "he always insisted that he wanted our ideas on how the
foundation should be run, but we knew that his own enthusiasms
would take up all of our funds." Among these enthusiasms, she
related, was his idea of automatic coin collection on turnpikes.
On occasion, small boys stood in his driveway holding a little
aluminum pan for guests to toss coins into, so as to get used to
the coin idea.

Another gentleman, about to retire from a publishing house,
wished advice as to whether a present operation should be organized as a foundation. He has been obtaining, by gift or purchase, libraries of older books. One recent lot of 10,000 books
cost him $1,000—ten cents a book. He goes over them, discard-
ing the valueless, rebinding the better ones that require this attention, and listing the collection on 5x3 cards. He then sends
these cards to libraries, principally those in large universities,
offering as a gift any that they desire. He takes an income-tax
deduction on the libraries' valuation of these gifts, with which to
cover the costs of lots for which he has to pay.

Upon retirement, he may set up a formal "book salvage operation" agency to do this on a larger scale, and more systematically.
He could no longer take advantage of personal tax deductions,
but if the agency were an exempt foundation, presumably it
could give appraisals for the donated books so that the donors
would have a tax inducement. He would set aside a substantial
initial endowment for running expenses, and hoped that
contributions might come from individuals, companies, and
foundations.

A former publisher myself, I was intrigued by this project, and
considered it workable and useful for the present, if propelled
by his personal enthusiasm. But I suggested a broad charter, so
that his precise operation may not be rigidly fixed, and pointed
out that the need for storing the physical book in particular li-

[4] See p. 254.

braries is decreasing as we improve our methods of information retrieval, facsimile reproduction, and the like.

Another earnest inquirer had the distressing problem of too much money. He is the most active trustee of a new foundation set up in a midwestern town of about 800 population. The donor made the foundation principal beneficiary in his Will, and it has suddenly come into an income of about $400,000 annually from agricultural lands and oil and gas royalties. In view of wishes expressed by the donor before his death, the trustees feel that all or most of the income should be spent locally. But how does one spend $400,000 a year in a community of 800, without taking over functions the citizens ought to be doing for themselves, and perhaps working more harm than good?

We discussed, among other things, salary supplementation for high-school teachers for summer training, particularly for those in the humanities since the science and mathematics teachers are already receiving such aid through National Science Foundation; youth programs of various sorts; and in view of an interest of his own, special psychiatric services, in this case statewide and in connection with the penal system.

A visitor from Hawaii, formerly a banker and now associated with several Hawaiian foundations, recalled the interesting origin of five large Hawaiian trusts. The Reverend Amos Starr Cooke, one of the early American missionaries to Hawaii, was given the task of establishing a school for the children of the royal families of Hawaii. Among his royal pupils five died childless, leaving by their wills five charitable trusts. Four of these are special-purpose trusts and as such are not included in the *Directory* as foundations.

The largest trust, recently ruled to be an educational institution rather than a foundation, was established by the last descendant of the great Kamehameha kings, Princess Bernice Pauahi Bishop. She originated the trust in 1884 with assets of present market value of approximately $400 million. Initially set up to build and maintain a boarding school for young Hawaiian boys and girls, it has now been able to broaden its program to general educational programs in Hawaii.

The last ruler of the Islands, Queen Liliuokalani, set up a trust which has as its sole stated purpose the support of indigent Hawaiian orphans. The widow of King Kamehameha IV, Queen Emma, left by her Will a charitable trust with an income of

about $1 million a year, solely for The Queen's Hospital, Hono-
lulu's largest general hospital. The beloved King Lunalilo established the Lunalilo Trust Estate to endow a home for aged and
indigent Hawaiians. And Queen Kapiolani, widow of "the Merry
Monarch," King Kalakaua, established the Kapiolani Maternity
and Gynecological Hospital and devoted her holdings to a special endowment fund.

Incidentally, two of the Reverend Cooke's children set aside
a quarter of their earned estates in living trusts for general charitable giving. Both the Juliette M. Atherton Trust and the Charles
M. and Anna C. Cooke Trust give substantial sums annually to
tax-qualified eleemosynary institutions, primarily in Hawaii.

That grants cannot always be judged on their face was pointed
out to me at lunch one day. The executive of a large foundation
discovered substantial grants of theirs going to prison inmates
for whiskey and as spending money. Further inquiry revealed
that these payments were for a research project in which a group
of prisoners were serving as volunteers to try out the effects of
alcohol on diabetes.

About Large Gifts

In my rather extraordinary job I received a number of phone
calls and letters, usually from Madison Avenue publicity agents,
asking me to declare authoritatively that the lordly gift they
were about to publicize was the largest ever given for this or that
particular purpose. But what really broke this patient camel's
back was the request from one such person that I list the
fifty largest gifts in history. I replied:

Sir:

I should like to nominate for a place among your fifty largest gifts
in history the two mites which a lady in Palestine dropped into the
collection box nearly two thousand years ago.

Perhaps you remember what an observer said at the time: "This
poor widow has put in more than all those who are contributing to
the treasury. For they all contributed out of their abundance; but
she out of her poverty has put in everything she had, her whole
living."

Indeed, you might wish to place this gift at the head of the list.
Certainly it is one of the largest in terms of capacity to pay. Besides,
it has by the power of its example brought to philanthropy many,

many millions of dollars, particularly from people of small incomes who nowadays, even statistically, give "more than they all."

Sincerely yours,

F. Emerson Andrews

Other Activities

Speeches in a typical year might run to a dozen or more for major occasions. The range included such a variety as National Science Foundation, the Junior League, College and University Business Officers, National Industrial Conference Board, Conference of Southwest Foundations, National Religious Publicity Council. . . . Though preparation was sometimes a chore, most of these events I enjoyed, with the chance they gave of renewing contacts, making new friendships, and hopefully increasing understanding of foundations. I attended nearly all conferences in the field of philanthropy, and was usually on the steering committees, helping arrange speakers and program.

In 1961 the National Bureau of Economic Research and the Merrill Center for Economics arranged a general conference on philanthropy at Merrill Center's luxurious estate in Southampton, Long Island. Most of the guests were leaders in their areas of philanthropic knowledge or practice, and the sessions were lively and productive. Aside from sharing a room with a gentleman with a resounding reputation for snoring, I found living conditions most enjoyable. We operated under the sensible conference schedule of sessions mornings and evenings, with the afternoons free for tennis, ocean swimming, or being lazy. Willard L. Thorp was the able and genial conference director, and composed for us a special "Merrill Center No Mater Song" to the tune of the Whiffenpoof Song, a portion of which ran:

In Southampton by the sea
We've discussed philanthropy
In a squash court where one
knocks the ball around,
In the manner of pedantics,
We soon bogged down in semantics
And it took some time to
get up off the ground.

Chorus
We're philanthropists who've lost our way—
Bah, Bah, Bah.

For Federal grants are here to stay—
    Bah, Bah, Bah.
To the Merrill Center we have come
In search of the millennium
Why aren't we all born deaf and dumb?
    Bah, Bah, Bah.

    We're all for more exposure
    What we want is full disclosure
        Like foundation garments of the
        latest styles.
    I might dream the form I see
    Is my 501 (c) (3)
        As it wanders all about among
        the files.

        Repeat Chorus

    We've talked for many hours
    In the room among the flowers
        We've gathered many thoughts
        quite hard to come by.
    The Faculty will pass
    Every member of the class—
        Soon the Merrill Center'll have
        some new alumni

        Repeat Chorus

Manuscripts

Another chore, and often it was heavy, was advance reading of most manuscripts dealing with foundations, and sometimes the whole broad area of philanthropy. I took this task seriously, for everything dealing with foundations should be as accurate as possible, and in the Center we did have unrivaled source material. I did not attempt to change value judgments, but names, dates, statistics came in for careful checking. Though usually I received thanks, the sometimes devastating criticisms ruined some beautiful friendships. But others were made.

One of the most rewarding events of that sort happened almost by accident. Marion R. Fremont-Smith, the lovely lawyer lady who was assistant attorney general and director of public charities for the Commonwealth of Massachusetts, was in my office discussing charities in general and her new directory of Massachusetts charitable agencies in particular. We got to deploring

the inadequacies of either registration or any degree of supervision of charities in most states. Suddenly I had an idea. The
only substantial treatment of the field had been Eleanor K.
Taylor's book which we published at Russell Sage Foundation
back in 1953, now hopelessly out of date. Across the desk from
me was the one person in the United States best equipped to do
the job that now needed doing. I began to talk.

In 1965 Russell Sage Foundation published Mrs. Fremont-
Smith's *Foundations and Government: State and Federal Law
and Supervision*, a major contribution to the field.

CHAPTER 16

Foundation Watcher
—Foundations

Tнis chapter deals more particularly with the program of the Center and the decade's major developments affecting the foundation world.

Legal Instruments of Foundations

Almost before we were in official existence, Carnegie Corporation of New York suggested a study that in their view urgently needed updating. Back in 1939 a collection of trust instruments, charters, by-laws, and other legal documents of twenty-nine foundations, prepared by Edward C. Elliott and M. M. Chambers under auspices of The Carnegie Foundation for the Advancement of Teaching, was issued in processed form for limited distribution under the title, *Charters of Philanthropies*. In 1948 this material was substantially revised by Professor Chambers, and was reissued with an analytical introduction as a 247-page pamphlet, under the same title. This second edition was out of print, and newer forms such as the company-sponsored foundation and the "mixed" family-corporation foundation had sprung up.

The Center now had extensive material of this character. The Carnegie officers suggested that we prepare a replacement of this material, and our trustees approved. Russell Sage Foundation voted a grant of $2,500 to underwrite the costs of preparation and agreed to act as publisher under a combined imprint. Early in 1957, about a month after we opened our doors to the public, I was immersed in charters and by-laws, making a final selection.

The pathfinding service of the earlier volumes was gratefully acknowledged, but my plan of arrangement was quite different. Separate chapters with introductory notes grouped documents of the various types: acts of Congress, acts of state legislatures setting up foundations, wills, trust instruments, corporate resolutions, certificates of incorporation, constitutions, by-laws, letters of gift. A final chapter introduced selected operational documents, such as a grant notification form, agreement with consultants, publication arrangement.

Variety was a criterion. We included significant instruments from at least one perpetuity, dissolving fund, discretionary perpetuity: at least one company-sponsored foundation engaged in unrelated business activities, association of foundations, "captive" foundation; at least one research foundation, special-purpose foundation, community trust, scholarship fund. Several documents were included for historical interest, such as the Act of Congress setting up Smithsonian Institution and Benjamin Franklin's Will. Documents of Nuffield Foundation and Calouste Gulbenkian Foundation (in England and Portugal, respectively) seemed important for comparison values. The effort was to present a broad sampling of each type of document. Evaluations were not made, though seriously faulty draftsmanship was cause for exclusion.

The preface discussed recent developments among foundations, available processes and choices in setting up a foundation, and the origins and nature of this study. It reported my resistance, "not always with entire success," to individualistic appeal of some of the examined documents. The *Agreement* of The Luling Foundation described the motives of a donor in terms so divergent from some popular assumptions that, although I could not justify it for the main text, my Preface quoted this paragraph:

WITNESSETH:

That I, Edgar B. Davis, a bachelor, believing that the kind and gracious Providence Who guides the destinies of all humanity, directed me in the search for and the discovery of oil near Luling, Texas; and in our successful management and favorable outcome of the business; and believing that the wealth which has resulted has not come through any virtue or ability of mine but has been given in trust; and desiring to discharge in some measure the trust which has been reposed in me. . . .[1]

[1] *Legal Instruments of Foundations.* Compiled by F. Emerson Andrews. A Foundation Library Center Study. Russell Sage Foundation, New York, 1958, p. 20.

Albert M. Sacks, Professor of Law at Harvard University, whom I had grown to know and admire in connection with one of our Ford Foundation projects, served as legal consultant to the study. Though designed for persons desiring to set up foundations, their lawyer and banker advisers, it was not to be a substitute for skilled legal advice; "no single document is presented as a model of its kind, but a variety are offered in the hope of stimulating comparison and improvement."

I delivered manuscript to Russell Sage Foundation at the close of 1957, less than a year after beginning work. On 2 May 1958 the printer put on my desk a first bound copy. *Legal Instruments of Foundations* was published on 19 May 1958.

Two Million for a Word

On 13 March, while *Legal Instruments* was in press but not yet published, representatives of The Rosamond Gifford Charitable Corporation, a new foundation in Syracuse, New York, came to me with a legal document problem in which $2 million hinged upon a single word. Rosamond Gifford, they reported, was a maiden lady of firm opinions, considerable wealth, and no close relatives. She intensely disliked federal taxation, and made out her income-tax check to "District Director of Infernal Revenue." When she died in 1953 her Will, after some minor bequests, granted the whole remainder of her estate to "a corporation which shall be created, managed and operated exclusively for religious, educational, scientific, charitable or benevolent uses, which corporation shall be called THE ROSAMOND GIFFORD CHARITABLE CORPORATION."

The foundation was duly set up in June, 1954, began completely proper operations, and was ruled exempt by Internal Revenue Service on 1 August 1956. But in March, 1957, the Service disallowed the whole of the charitable deduction on what was soon acknowledged to be the inclusion of the single word "benevolent" in the Will. The Service declared that "benevolent" was a broad word which could be stretched to include noncharitable expenditures, and that therefore the whole sum of more than $5 million willed to the foundation was fully taxable. It levied a tax assessment of $2,146,085.87, of which the foundation as chief beneficiary was forced to pay the major part. It had promptly made a claim for refund, and after delays of about a year the case was now about to come up for trial. Did the Center have information that would be useful, and what were our views?

I reported that we had just finished a study of legal documents during which I had personally read many hundreds of them. I knew, as they doubtless did, that "benevolent" was not regarded as the full equivalent of "charitable" in England, but was widely used in that sense in the United States. I had sympathy with Internal Revenue's attempts to keep certain foundations from skirting the letter of the law for the financial advantage of their donors, but in this case there seemed no possible doubt of the full charitable intent of the Will, and the attempt to collect $2 million on a technicality should be resisted to the utmost. Much more was involved than their own urgent situation. The word "benevolent" appeared in the New York State charters of The Rockefeller Foundation, Russell Sage Foundation, and doubtless in many others. We would be happy to be of any possible assistance in helping them get a favorable judgment.

It was agreed that I should enter the trial as an expert witness; indeed, since the whole case turned on use of a single word, their only witness. Meanwhile, both the Center and their lawyers would search the charters of New York foundations—since local usage had an important bearing—for "benevolent." By the morning of the trial we had from New York State alone 56 corporate charters and eleven trusts in which the word "benevolent" occurred.

The hearing was before Judge Stephen W. Brennan in Federal District Court in Syracuse, on the morning of 19 May 1958—by one of those impossible coincidences that are always occurring, the precise date Russell Sage Foundation had set for publishing *Legal Instruments of Foundations*.

The stipulations concerning the facts were placed on the record with agreement on both sides, though the government lawyer (definitely the adversary type!) objected to about half the paragraphs as being "irrelevant and immaterial," and even to Judge Brennan's jurisdiction.

Then I was called, and lawyer Lewis C. Ryan for the Gifford Corporation asked usual qualifying questions concerning name, address, occupation, college degrees, experience in the foundation field, any publications in this area, and what was my latest such book.

"The most recent, sir, is *Legal Instruments of Foundations.*"

He held up a copy, which I had brought along on the plane, and asked when this book was published.

"This morning."

The fact was established that its preparation had involved extensive research among the charters and similar instruments of foundations. But when questioning began about the appearance of the word "benevolent" in charters of New York State foundations the government lawyer objected that since the witness was not a professional lawyer, his testimony would be "incompetent, irrelevant, and immaterial." Judge Brennan leaned over his desk and mildly observed that he believed the witness was quite able to read, and this was all that was required for the present testimony: objection overruled. Amid showers of objections, always overruled, I got into the record the fifty-six "benevolent" New York State charters, with attested copies as an exhibit; the eleven trusts; and the eight such charitable foundations incorporated by special acts of the New York State legislature, with photostatic copies of the laws as a marked exhibit.

In cross examination, in a further effort to discredit the witness, the government lawyer suddenly asked for a separate count of conjunctive and disjunctive use of the word "benevolent." Fortunately, I had foreseen this point, and had in my hands an annotated list with the precise context of the word. I said I could not give him a count, because in some instances it was neither "and" nor "or" but "and/or" or other constructions. I could read the actual entries.

He asked me to do so. So I started on the list of fifty-six corporations, and when I came to the word "benevolent," spoke it emphatically. He soon saw that this was bringing the wide use of that word to the court's attention much too prominently, and asked me to stop. Judge Brennan ruled that since he had requested it, I should continue—and with rising titters in the courtroom, I did go through all fifty-six *benevolents.*

The government had also only one witness, the local Internal Revenue agent. At the close of the hearing (it was not a jury trial) both sides were asked to prepare reply briefs within a reasonable period, but the government indicated that it might wish to await decision in the somewhat parallel *Hight* case in Connecticut, now on appeal to a higher court.

I was scarcely back in the office when in came a graduate law student, introducing himself as special assistant to Harold R. Medina, judge of the Court of Appeals for the 2nd circuit. He had heard of the Center, and wondered whether we might have in our collections any charters that related to the *Hight* case now before the judge, which involved the word "benevolent."

He was, I think, surprised at my informed comments on the subject, and aghast when our librarian produced—only a few minutes later, for we had not yet filed the material—a foot-high pile of pertinent photostated charters. He retired to a special office we loaned him, and took copious notes. On 18 June 1958 the Court of Appeals ruled against the government in the *Hight* case, with this pertinent comment from Judge Moore:

> 'Benevolent' is not a word of art connoting 'non-charitable' or 'non-tax-exempt.' To the contrary as used in ordinary speech and writing it is associated and is synonymous with 'charitable.' In granting tax deductions for bequests . . . Congress could not have intended to encourage bequests for eleemosynary purposes only to have them defeated by narrow construction.[2]

In early December Judge Brennan rendered a similar decision in the Gifford case, emphasizing "primary purpose" and "tangible evidence of that intent." We received generous credit in the news story reporting the decision:

> The Foundation trustees are extremely grateful to F. Emerson Andrews, director of the Foundation Library Center of New York City, who appeared at the trial as a witness for the Foundation. He testified, in substance, that the language of the Gifford will was similar to that used in the creation of many of the largest foundations in the country.[3]

The refund did not come through until 28 July 1959. By this time, with accumulated interest the check for one word amounted to $2,415,071.49.

More About Benevolent

But the battle was not yet fully won. After the two decisions, but before payment was made, the *Federal Register* of 26 February 1959 included among its "proposed regulations" for foundations this "example":

[2] U.S. Court of Appeals, 2nd Circuit, *H. Wadsworth Hight* v. *United States of America.* No. 136, Oct. Term, 1957, before Medina and Moore, circuit judges, and Galston, district judge.

[3] *Herald-Journal*, Syracuse, N. Y., 10 December 1958.

For example, if an organization is created for 'benevolent' purposes, the term 'benevolent' being, in its generally accepted sense, a broader term than 'charitable,' will not be regarded as synonymous with 'charitable' as used in section 501 (c) (3) in the absence of proof as to State law.

When this proposal reached my desk I wrote to the Commissioner of Internal Revenue, commending most of the proposed regulations but with respect to this item citing the recent contrary *Hight* decision and adding out of our own experience:

> As director of The Foundation Library Center it has been one of my duties to prepare a study entitled *Legal Instruments of Foundations* which cites many of these documents from many parts of the United States and in preparation of this material I examined some thousands of others. The word "benevolent" appears in many of the charters and other fundamental documents of foundations in many parts of the country, and it would be damaging indeed if all of these were now to be subjected to review.
>
> More seriously, [in case this general statement is also applied to Sec. 170, deductibility of contributions] I call to your attention the fact that the word "benevolences" is almost universally used among churches to identify the portions of their total contributions which are used for the charities they support rather than strictly congregational expenses.
>
> In support of this position I enclose a recent (1957) edition of *Statistics of Giving* prepared by the National Council of the Churches of Christ in the U.S.A. Our series runs back to the year 1922 and all include the word "benevolences." As you will see, 52 Protestant denominations in the United States report giving for "benevolences" in amounts approaching $400 million for this particular year.
>
> This seems convincing evidence that in all states in the United States the general public commonly understands "benevolences" and "charitable contributions" to be synonymous. I hope you will remove the section beginning "For example" from the *Regulations* in their final form.[4]

Of course I spoke of this matter, with its vast implications for religious giving, to my friends at the National Council of Churches, and supplied a copy of the letter. What additional protest they may have made I do not know, but the *Regulations* as published in final form omitted the offending paragraph.

[4] Excerpt from letter of F. Emerson Andrews to the Commissioner of Internal Revenue, 20 March 1959.

A Foundation Directory

The greatest single service the Center performs in making its information about foundations broadly available consists in publication of its periodical *Directories*. Work on the first such *Directory* was begun in mid-1957, after the closing date for the filing of 1956 990-A returns. Ann D. Walton and I were the editors of this first edition, with Marianna O. Lewis assistant editor and responsible for most of the field work. But it was a vast task extending over several years, to which everybody in the Center contributed as their schedules permitted.

An earlier chapter has mentioned our initial difficulty with *Directory 1*: the Presidential ruling that stopped us from photographing returns, requiring expansion of field staff and heavy extra expense. Another difficulty arose in California.

Mrs. Lewis phoned from Los Angeles to report that in that district director's office public portions of many of the returns showed nothing but the name and address of the foundation with none of the required attachments or financial information. The office, moreover, was not inclined to supply the missing data. Mrs. Lewis had ferreted out the principal reason—football!

The University of Southern California had lost its Conference membership on evidence of widespread payment of athletes. It appears that a "foundation" had been established to which enthusiastic alumni could make contributions to be passed on to promising football material. This "foundation" had apparently included on its 990-A Form names and payouts which had been seen by the press, though this detail was not then required on the public copy. What irate alumni did to the District Director for permitting this unrequired listing to be seen we do not know, but obviously he was taking no further chances, and even required data and attachments were usually lacking.

I got in touch with Internal Revenue Service in Washington, which has always been extremely cooperative, recognizing that the Center is performing services not only useful to the public, but which spare their own offices a great deal of expensive searches for reports, correspondence, and "have actually saved the Government money." They agreed that even a private citizen, let alone our organization, had a right under the law to the information we were requesting. Presently, however, they were stressing decentralization; would I begin at the local office, then regional, and finally if necessary their national level?

We pried from the Los Angeles office acknowledgment of the inadequacy of their records and a promise to do better in the future, but because of low staffing, they could not correct in the near future the present filings. For all of our Directories it is established policy to report for every included foundation, if available, corporate name and address; donor; general purpose and activities, with any special limitations; assets, grants, and total expenditures for the most recent available year; officers and trustees. *Directory 1* went to press with a weak California section, entries for southern California foundations being usually extremely slender. College football can have strange side effects.

Other obstacles sprang up. Particularly bothersome were the not infrequent letters, usually from a law firm, threatening suit if we dared include even the name of their foundation-client in our proposed *Directory*, and demanding prompt assurance that this would not be done. Having already cleared policy with the trustees, I was prepared with a prompt reply. In what it regarded as the public interest, the Center would include in its *Directory* every foundation which met its size and other qualifications. We would use in their case only information from government records, which we believed to be in the public domain. They were certainly at liberty to enter suit, but this would seem an odd way to keep the name of their foundation unknown. Such threats have been received in connection with all the *Directories*, over a period of more than a decade, but no suit has ever been entered.

Even Cupid aimed arrows at the *Directory*. Marianna Olmstead, assistant editor and chief field worker, became Mrs. George Lewis in August, 1959. In return for helping induce Robert J. McCracken, minister of The Riverside Church and then a trustee of the Center, to perform the lovely service, I suggested that she might at least keep on reading galley proof in the back of the church until those unmistakable first notes of the wedding march, but doubt that she did this.

Then on 24 June 1960, less than three weeks before publication day, Mrs. Walton, who shared with me prime editorship, became Mrs. John A. Willis. So our book came out with even the name of one of its principal editors wrong. However, she did continue to use Walton as her business name during the remainder of her Center service.

With these and other problems, preparation of the *Directory* took longer than had been planned. It finally included 5,202 foundations—all those we could discover with assets of at least $50,000, or making grants totaling at least $10,000 in the year of record. First copies would be off press early in July, 1960.

My public-relations friends pointed out how poor a time summer was for publishing any book except hammock fiction, and to release it on 11 July, the very day when the Democratic National Convention was opening, would ruin any chance of news coverage. I insisted on making it available as a public service, on this earliest possible date.

In spite of the Convention, it did not go unnoticed. In *The New York Times* Fred M. Hechinger did a fine page-one story with a page runover and charts; there was also an editorial, and I turned out to be the day's "Man in the News." Other newspapers, radio, *Newsweek*, the Kiplinger *Letter*, all contributed to a fine start for *The Foundation Directory, Edition 1*. Among comments from foundation people was this from Ralph Hayes, director of The New York Community Trust: "The result is triumphant and it must be a source of enormous satisfaction to have forged an instrument so distinguished and serviceable."

Directories 2, 3, and 4

Immediate wide use of the *Directory* and increasing growth and change in the field made desirable a prompt start on *Directory 2*. Russell Sage Foundation, publisher of the *Directory* and impressed by the flood of orders it was receiving, offered an assistance grant of $30,000 to cover extra costs of starting *Directory* work earlier, and the trustees instructed the staff to begin work in the summer of 1961.

For *Edition 2* Mrs. Walton and Mrs. Lewis were the listed editors, and for *Edition 3* Marianna O. Lewis alone. I continued to write the analytical introductions, but surrendered as much of the detail as possible to our able editors. *Edition 4* was prepared after my retirement, but I was drafted to do once again the analytical introduction. It was edited by Marianna O. Lewis, with Patricia Bowers assistant editor; published in 1971, Columbia University Press is the distributor.

Each edition has been wholly reset, but has followed the general pattern of *Edition 1*, which proved very serviceable. Some tightening in definition has been made, and size level of included foundations has been raised from the $50,000 in assets of *Edition 1* to $100,000 for *Edition 2*, $200,000 for *Edition 3*, and $500,000 for *Edition 4*, with also coverage of any foundation that made total grants of $10,000 or more in the year of record for *Editions 1* through *3*, raised to $25,000 in *Edition 4*.

Information swelled, partly from better cooperation and fuller reporting to us from the foundations themselves. But also records required by the government, and the portions open to public inspection, were amplified by changes in reporting forms and regulations. The greatest such advance has already been noted in connection with our Washington office.

The table below suggests this growth. But because of minor changes in *Directory* specifications and major changes in government requirements (particularly for statement of assets at market value), its totals cannot be taken as more than a rough measure of growth.

COMPARISON OF FOUR FOUNDATION DIRECTORIES

Directories	Number of foundations	Assets (millions)	Grants (millions)
Edition 1 (1960)	5,202	$11,518	$ 626
Edition 2 (1964)	6,007	14,511	779
Edition 3 (1967)	6,803	19,927	1,212
Edition 4 (1971)	5,454	25,181	1,513

A Mythical Foundation

The Center has never retreated from its position of including in the *Directories* all foundations meeting type and size qualifications. But we did recognize that such listings sometimes result in mass mailings of quite inappropriate appeals, and other abuses. Each volume included strong advice against such uses, and every listed foundation was invited to supply detailed information on its fields of interest and any limitations it might have, geographical or other, in the hope of reducing nuisance mail to tolerable proportions.

It seemed desirable to determine precisely how the *Directory* was being used. Publication of *Edition 2* in January, 1964, gave us an opportunity to conduct a controlled experiment. I invented a foundation, gave it a deceased donor and modest endowment, named no trustees, and (not to mislead legitimate fund-raisers into wasted effort) made it clear in the *Purpose and Activities* paragraph that this foundation was not in a position to entertain present appeals of any sort. Its name was not divulged even to most members of our own staff. Any mail received by this mythical foundation must originate from the *Directory* listing. After three years (when we called it dissolved and cancelled the postal address) this was the record:

MAIL RECEIVED IN THREE YEARS
FROM A DIRECTORY LISTING

Category	1964	1965	1966	Total	Percent
Appeals for funds	10	9	14	33	17
Magazines and reports	3	5	3	11	6
Book advertisements	1	8	3	12	6
Supplies and services	5	13	18	36	19
Investment opportunities	14	40	46	100	52
Total	33	75	84	192	100

Under the safeguards indicated, no flood of mail materialized. In exactly three years only thirty-three appeal letters were received, an average of less than one a month. Several of these were "repeat" appeals, sometimes within the same year. One such correspondent opened his second letter with "To confirm our telephone conversation . . ." although the mythical foundation had no telephone. One careless fund-raiser addressed a highly emotional appeal to the donor, whom we had carefully indicated as deceased.

Three of the eleven magazines and reports were the Center's own annual Reports, sent by unwarned staff; only one appeared to be a first step in a fund appeal. The twelve book advertisements dealt chiefly with foundation-related titles, notice of which was useful to foundation executives. The thirty-six offers of supplies and services were an extraordinary group, ranging from information on fund-raising organizations and an invitation to a foundation conference to two kinds of floor finishes, office equipment, and an orchestra for special entertainments. Another advertised imprinted Christmas cards, still another was auctioning off a college, complete with campus and buildings; and on 23 December came the final offer of chemical pellets to melt snow off foundation sidewalks.

One addressing firm urged our mythical foundation to use a

list of foundation addresses at $20 per thousand names. With that address imprint on their envelope in hand, we checked all mailings received in 1965 and 1966 and found that at least fourteen organizations had rented this list, for they used the identified address plate.

But the big category, accounting for over half of all mail received, was investment opportunities. There was heavy concentration in California savings and loan associations, one such organization sending almost identical mailings every month throughout most of the three years.

The total for three years was 192 pieces, fewer than six letters a month, or a bit more than one letter a week. Much of this mail was in such categories as services or investments, some of which might interest the average foundation executive, and none of which requires answer or acknowledgment.

It is probable that the negligible appeal mail would have been heavier if the mythical foundation had been given assets upwards of a million, and had either declared wide general purposes or refused to express any. But the experiment strongly suggests that inclusion in *The Foundation Directory* will not subject a small foundation, if it provides a careful statement of purposes and limitations, to a burdensome volume of mail that requires answering.

The Investment Policies of Foundations

In September, 1962, Ralph L. Nelson was commissioned by the Center to do a study of foundation investments, with a supporting grant from Russell Sage Foundation. He based his study on examination of investment holdings of many foundations derived from their reports in the Center, from tabulations newly available from the Patman inquiries, and from a questionnaire, amplified by personal interviews. Focusing on large foundations endowed by individuals or families, his basic group included some 133 foundations which together account for the major part of endowment, income, and spending of all foundations.

Cooperation from most of the foundations was excellent, but there were some refusals to respond, and a few violent objections to the whole project. All through the welfare field one encounters well-intentioned "do-gooders" who maintain that the less the public knows the better; some facts may be unsavory, and even neutral knowledge may be used against you. I think this is a mistaken view. In the present case some of Dr. Nelson's findings were available just in time to counter some of the extreme charges made by Congressman Patman. For instance, instead of foundations having reached "massive, undreamed of proportions," they accounted for less than 1 percent of financial asset holdings in the country, and though many of the large foundations concentrate on common stock—and usually the single stock of their donor—even corporation stock holdings of all foundations are less than half those of noninsured pension funds, and only 2 percent of the stock holdings of individuals.

The report indicated only a slight recent trend toward diversification by most of the large single-stock foundations. However, their income record was found good, for usually a man has become wealthy enough to endow a large foundation only through association with a company making excellent profits, and for many years his foundation may enjoy an income rate above the market average. The question arises, however, whether trustees, some of whom may also be associated with the company, could act objectively in the sole interest of the charity if the situation changed; for such reasons diversification seems desirable.

It has been objected that attempts to dispose of large blocks of stock would drive down the price, harm the company, and reduce assets for the foundation. In private conversations I have suggested that this is not necessarily so, and indeed several large foundations are finding a way. For example, six large foundations, each possessing a sound stock, could meet on an appointed day and agree to exchange with each other $50 million of their stock at the average market price for the day. At day's end each would have disposed of $250 million of its own stock and acquired $50 million in each of five other desirable issues, with no effect on prices since the "sales" would not go through the stock exchange (incidentally saving brokerage fees!) and need not even be known until the foundations issue their annual reports.

Such exchanges are taking place, but usually between pairs of foundations. In the spring of 1972 The Kresge Foundation traded 175,000 shares of its common stock with The Ford Foundation for 257,325 shares of Ford Motor Company common stock. A problem has developed, however. Many of these large stock holdings are in shares on which dividends are very low at current prices. With the high pay-out requirements of the Tax Reform Act of 1969, foundations are not eager to obtain or hold such stocks. So recently a more frequent practice has been to place upon the market large blocks of foundation stocks in secondary public offerings. The new giant, The Robert Wood Johnson Foundation, participated in at least two million-share offerings of this sort in 1972.

The Investment Policies of Foundations was published for the Center by Russell Sage Foundation in May, 1967.

Some Foundation Problems

One provision of the Revenue Act of 1950 denied tax exemption on income of a foundation for a taxable year in which accumulation out of income was "unreasonable in amount or duration." Foundations were greatly concerned over how "unreasonable" might be interpreted by Internal Revenue Service and the courts. Tension eased as many years passed without knowledge of any severe application of the Code provision.

Then in 1962 it became known that The Danforth Foundation, a fine midwestern foundation then tenth largest in the United States, had had to pay some $558,000 in assessments, including penalty charges and interest, as a "nonexempt" corporation for the years 1951 and 1952. This Foundation had acquired greatly increased assets, and therefore income, just when the new Act was going into effect, and also appointed a new executive director, Dr. Kenneth I. Brown, in January, 1951. Dr. Brown was not able to work out a new program speedily enough in those initial years to spend all of the increased income. But since those two years the Foundation had spent both income and enough of principal to more than exhaust the surplus created in 1951 and 1952.

The Foundation appealed to the U. S. District Court in St. Louis for recovery of the assessment. I agreed to serve as an expert witness in the hope that this case might help produce a reasonable definition of "unreasonable." I put into the testimony my statements made prior to the passage of the 1950 Act on the desirability of foundations being required to spend their approximate income, but with a reasonable period allowed. In the case of sudden substantial new income, it was not in the public interest to require fast disbursements, often resulting in wasteful or at least unimaginative programs; good or bad faith should be judged by the record over a period of years.

In this hearing there were numerous witnesses. Don K. Price was particularly effective in detailing the time problems of The Ford Foundation in some of its major programs. But the decision was finally against The Danforth Foundation. No clear definition of "unreasonable" resulted, but the adverse decision put all foundations on further warning.

This and other storm clouds spurred more foundations into attending, and even helping organize, meetings and conferences at which their mutual problems could be discussed. The Center was called upon for ever larger participation in these activities. In 1964 I helped organize the "First Biennial Mid-Continent Conference on Philanthropy" under auspices of Metropolitan College, St. Louis University. But my steadiest such participation was as "permanent" steering committee member of the New York Foundations Luncheon Group, beginning in 1956 (I had made a speech before the group in 1954, the second in their records) and extending to my retirement in 1967.[5]

---

[5] In 1965 I prepared a brief history, *The New York Foundations Luncheon Group: An Historical Note*, which also included a listing of some 86 meetings, the speakers at these sessions constituting a small Who's Who of foundations and philanthropy.

CHAPTER 17

Philanthropy Abroad

Many persons from all over the world came to see us at the Center, usually seeking funds. We became well acquainted with needs abroad, from these visitors, from our own information on American foundations (chiefly the large ones) which met some of these needs, and we kept abreast of other private agencies and the vast overseas programs of the government.

None of these sources, however, satisfied my own interest in how the people themselves in various countries looked at philanthropy, their private attitudes, personal giving, institutions similar to the foundation, related laws and government programs. Questioning visitors was not enough; real insights required visits abroad and face-to-face contacts with thoughtful persons. My earliest intensive view of foreign attitudes came in connection with the Royaumont Conference.

The Royaumont Conference

At the joint invitation of The Ford Foundation and the European Cultural Foundation a meeting was held at Royaumont, some twenty-five miles from Paris, from 1 to 3 December, 1961, to investigate the present status in various European countries of laws affecting philanthropy, and to consider what actions, if any, were appropriate in this area.

Royaumont is the partially restored ruin of a Cistercian abbey built by Louis IX in 1228. We reached it in a special bus from Paris at night in a driving rain. The ancient stone gates were too narrow for a modern bus, so we sloshed on foot, baggage in hand, up the dark entrance drive along an unseen stream gurgling dangerously close, toward a distant light. A warm welcome awaited us, and our quarters, while austere, were not uncomfortable. I had a long and narrow monastic cell with steam (hear it CLANK) heat. The W.C. was down a long corridor, and halfway between this and the next floor, which it also served. The food was superb.

The conference was chaired by the late George Nebolsine, who wrote the report.[1] Chairman Nebolsine, Shepard Stone, and I were from the United States. The other fifteen delegates represented seven European countries and four international agencies.

It soon became apparent that few common denominators existed. In France there were only minor legal concessions to charity, and special laws made even the completed gifts of living donors subject to reexamination in the settlement of their estates. The French representative, upon hearing some examples of American giving, declared angrily, "That is a clear prerogative of government. Individuals have no right to interfere!"

Tax and other inducements which so greatly encourage giving in the United States were extremely limited, or did not exist, in most of Europe. Gifts from individuals were not tax-deductible at all in Austria, Luxembourg, Norway, Portugal, Sweden, Switzerland; nor in England except under a complicated seven-year covenant agreement. In most countries charitable gifts from companies were not recognized at all; in France certain such gifts were deductible up to 0.5 percent of income, as contrasted with the 5 percent in the United States.

The representative from the Council of Europe suggested that foundations might be organized under international law, an idea abandoned when the danger was pointed out that the least liberal arrangement might then become the common denominator. An American representative suggested a possible Atlantic Foundation to function internationally so far as the Atlantic Community of Nations (NATO) was concerned, with its funds from various nations and the implication that America might be a heavy contributor. This suggestion was received without enthusiasm, and I sensed a suspicion that such a foundation would be chiefly an instrument of NATO policy, politically oriented. On the bus back to Paris one of the participants said loud enough for me to hear, "We mustn't let those Americans buy us with their money."

Count Denis de Rougemont, speaking in French, proposed a

[1] Nebolsine, George, *Fiscal Aspects of Foundations and of Charitable Donations in European Countries.* European Cultural Foundation, Amsterdam, 1963, 130 p.

directory of European foundations and creation of a European journal similar to our *Foundation News*, with a continental counterpart of The Foundation Center, with which he and the others were apparently quite familiar.

The conference was going off in forty different directions when the British contingent got their heads together and on the final day came up with four suggestions, unanimously adopted: (1) that a spring conference should be set up, chiefly of foundation personnel, not concentrating on legislation but upon program and international extension of activities; (2) that possibility of an information service on European foundations should be explored; (3) that closer association should be promoted between foundations and international cultural associations; and (4) that a small task force should be created to deal with tax incentives in various countries.

A somewhat similar conference was held in Berlin in 1964, which I did not attend. But two Ditchley Conferences in England, convened in 1966 and 1972, were much in the Royaumont pattern, and are reported below.

Royaumont itself has been further renovated, and is now the headquarters of Fondation Royaumont, organized in its present form in 1964 by Isabel and Henri Goüin, specializing in the social sciences, particularly anthropological research. M. Goüin, with whom I have visited both here and in his Paris home, believes that France will soon see a substantial growth in foundations.

Some British Foundations

After the Royaumont Conference I spent some time in London, visiting nearly all the larger British foundations. Mr. Leslie Farrer-Brown, who had been at the Royaumont Conference and was Secretary (which means staff head) of The Nuffield Foundation, received me cordially and was helpful with further appointments. Nuffield was at that time the largest foundation in England, and though it may now have surrendered financial priority to the newer Wolfson Foundation, it is still the one that in breadth of program and general organization most nearly resembles the leading American foundations.

William Richard Morris, bicycle-repair shop owner and genius, built Morris Motors into a fortune and became Lord Nuffield. In an act of faith that must have few equals, he summoned his advisers one morning in 1943, in the midst of the blitz of London in World War II, and asked them "to put before him by next Monday morning the legal papers necessary and the names of persons who ought to head such an organization" to which he would give £10,000,000.[2] Its handsome headquarters are Lord Nuffield's own lodge, set among gardens in Regent's Park. Its objects include "the advancement of health . . . advancement of social wellbeing . . . care and comfort of the aged poor . . . advancement of education . . . other charitable purposes." Under its early able directors, first Farrer-Brown and then the lean, energetic schoolmaster Brian Young, it has supported constructive, imaginative programs in Great Britain and the Commonwealth countries.

Sir George Haynes, director of the National Council of Social Service, also a Royaumont delegate, explained how his organization is involved in Britain's queer substitute for a charity deduction for individuals, the seven-year covenant. This is a written agreement under which a donor contracts to give a stated amount for a minimum period of seven consecutive years. This transforms a taxable transfer into one on which the tax is rebated to the recipient exempt agency. If the donor makes his contract with an organization such as the National Council of Social Service he is not committed to the same charity, but may specify each year how he wishes his gift distributed.

At the Wolfson Foundation I found in charge Sir Harold Redman, a lieutenant general who had had major responsibilities in defending Gibraltar during the war. At this point the Wolfson Foundation was relatively new—it had been established by Isaac Wolfson, industrialist, in 1955—and was following a pattern of support for education and special charities based upon receipt of appeals. We discussed the view of many American foundations that the limited funds available to them should preferably be devoted to low visibility causes, that cannot hope for either individual or governmental support, and the general proved a very interested listener.

As he drove me to my luncheon appointment he found out that in my otherwise crowded schedule I should have one morning free. He turned to his liveried chauffeur,

"Mr. Cook," he said, "tomorrow you have a different job. Call for Mr. Andrews, and take him wherever he'd like to go. You be thinking, too, what he ought to see."

[2] Conversation with Sir Geoffrey Gibbs, chairman, The Nuffield Foundation, 18 November 1966.

The next morning was that rare thing for London, a sunny day in December. I had a wholly delightful "Cook's tour" of London. We saw the standard sights speedily and efficiently, and at St. Paul's my Mr. Cook rather insisted on our going deep into the crypt to examine the iron carriage made of captured Waterloo cannon to convey Wellington's bier to the church.

In what looked like a private house on Queen Anne Street I found the Wellcome Trust, which with an income then about £800,000 (in England, foundations are rated by income; assets are often not even reported) was among the top three. There is also The Wellcome Foundation Limited which is not a foundation at all in our sense, but the collection of pharmaceutical industries "founded" by Sir Henry Wellcome, from which the Trust derives its income.

Dr. Frank Green, scientific secretary, gave me a brief history of the Trust. Its donor, Henry Solomon Wellcome, was born in Wisconsin in 1853, grew up in Garden City, Minnesota, learned "pill making" from an uncle, knew elder Dr. William Mayo, traveled for McKesson and Robbins. On a trip to Britain he set up with Silas Mainville Burroughs an importing and then a manufacturing drug firm. Burroughs died in 1895. Wellcome went on, the complete autocrat, to great wealth. His Trust was set up in 1936, limited to health and medical research, broadly defined.

With no time to travel out of London, I had arranged dinner and an evening with Lewis E. Waddilove, director of the Joseph Rowntree Memorial Trust, who came down from York. Perhaps because this is a venerable trust, I had expected a grey-bearded ancient; Mr. Waddilove proved to be a relatively young man, earnest, energetic, and a Quaker with an obvious "concern" for the welfare of others. He reported that of the original three trusts, two still survive. One, the Social Service Trust, is intentionally not tax exempt, so that it may pursue objectives not charitable under British law, including active programs for temperance and against gambling. The Joseph Rowntree Memorial Trust was in the early 1960s supporting adult education, international relations, religious work, and social research.

The donor, Joseph Rowntree, sent a memorandum to his trustees in 1904 which would do credit to the most modern thinking:

> I feel that much of current philanthropic effort is directed to remedying the more superficial manifestations of weakness or evil, while little thought or effort is directed to search out their underlying

causes. . . . The Soup Kitchen in York never has difficulty in obtaining adequate financial aid, but an enquiry into the extent and causes of poverty would enlist little support. . . .

I hope that the Institutions to which contributions are made from these Trusts may be living bodies, free to adapt themselves to the ever changing necessities of the nation and of the religious Society of which I am a member. . . . At the same time, realizing not only that 'new occasions teach new duties,' but that 'time makes ancient good uncouth,' I have given to the Trustees and Directors of these foundations, very wide powers and very few directions of a mandatory nature as to their exercise.

Sir Donald Allen, executive head of the City Parochial Foundation, an elderly gentleman not unwilling to be regarded as the dean of British charitable trusts, received me most cordially and seated me before a grate fire in his cozy office in Temple Gardens. The City Parochial Foundation was established in 1891 as an amalgamation of numerous London charitable trusts. Since many of these funds were devoted to technical schools which at the time of my visit were beginning to be supported by tax funds, substantial changes were in process.

Among projects were lodging hostels (Sir Donald described his visit to one London lodging house where the men were sleeping in a common room on mattresses crawling with bugs) in which they would supply sanitary and individual quarters, but also endeavor to find out why the occupants were reduced to public aid. Support includes the usual welfare range—the handicapped, old people, the deaf, youth programs, coordination of social services. Among the stranger special funds is The Pony Riding for the Disabled Trust, which believes that those who cannot walk receive splendid physical and psychological lift out of their scheduled pony rides.

An informing afternoon was spent with Mr. C. P. Hill, Commissioner of Charities for Great Britain. His vast assignment was to administer the new Charities Act of 1960, supplanting all previous British legislation in this area, including the Statute of Queen Elizabeth I in 1601. It provides for registration of all charities in Britain except certain in the educational field covered by a different act, and will be the first such complete registration since the Domesday Book. Mr. Hill thought that the trusts alone might run over 250,000, which he proposed to index in three ways: alphabetical, geographical, and by subject area. He had on his desk a copy of our *Foundation Directory*, and expressed gratitude for the information it supplied so pertinent to their own project.

I examined some of the day-sheets for registrations then beginning to pour in. They were divided into twelve size classifications based upon averaged annual income; the lowest category, with less than £5 income annually, had the largest number of registrants. I suggested that though complete listing might be necessary, a *de minimis* rule ought to be applied to cut the paper work on a group where more than half a million would be required to equal the spending power of The Nuffield Foundation alone.

One evening I had dinner with Miss J. H. Lidderdale, the extremely able and informed assistant to Lord Nathan, who had herself much to do with preparation of that most significant of recent (1952) British publications in this field, *Report of the Committee on the Law and Practice relating to Charitable Trusts*, popularly known as the Nathan Report. As a result of her account of British charities in general and the hearings in preparation for the Nathan Report, I was the more delighted when in 1964 the late David Owen, at the conclusion of his book on British philanthropy, presented to The Foundation Center the full oral and documentary evidence offered before the Parliamentary Charitable Trusts Committee in London, upon which the Nathan Report is based.

Down Under

On personal journeys I usually managed some informal investigation of foreign philanthropies. In December, 1958, I had the fine excuse for a long journey of visiting my eldest son, finishing a graduate year in Australia at the University of Sydney.

I went by way of New Zealand. Here cradle-to-grave social security (at least on paper) supplies most fundamental needs and social services out of the tax monies of the welfare state. But this protection was far from complete, and the Labor Government widely criticized. A breakfast companion reported a recent operation for which he paid £94 (about $265) for specialist, anesthetists, and other items not on the covered list.

No deductibility from income tax was available for charitable gifts, either individual or corporate. Also, there were gift duties; here gift duties to "charity" were exempted, but that term strictly defined, so that, for instance, it did not include education, and if the donor died within three years of date of the gift, it was ruled a gift in contemplation of death and became a part of the taxable estate.

High-pressure fund raising, chiefly for health agencies, was just beginning. The Labor Government was offering to match gifts triply to establish homes for the aged; a lawyer reported to me a wealthy client who rewrote his Will to include £100,000 for such a home, thereby escaping estate duties on this amount and costing the hated government three times his gift.

A few trusts existed, some akin to foundations but usually for quite specific purposes. One of the largest was the J. R. McKenzie Trust, to which the McKenzie business (retail chain stores) was contributing about one third of its profits. Tax laws have recently been liberalized, with deductions for minor gifts starting in 1962. Under the McKenzie Trust sponsorship an excellent directory of New Zealand trusts has been issued, including fifty-nine such organizations.[3]

In Australia, individual philanthropy was more highly developed. According to the controlling statute, "gifts of £1 and upwards to public benevolent institutions and to approved research institutions for scientific research, etc." are deductible, without a top percentage limit. But "benevolent institutions" must be individually declared so by the government, and church contributions are not deductible at all, unless for a specific purpose such as a building which has been ruled as deductible.

I had an instructive hour with Sir Edward Hollstrom in his office in Taronga Park, Sydney's superb zoo and one of Sir Edward's largest benefactions—without tax deduction, for animals are not charitable. As perhaps Australia's chief philanthropist, he was receiving requests for as much as £200,000 in a single day. These came personally, since he had not thought of setting up a foundation.

A Darwin plane failure brought son Frank and me back into Sydney. On the way to our free hotel we passed Hyde Park, crowded with people, all holding candles. We got off, to see perhaps the most colorful fund-raising enterprise I have ever witnessed.

"Carols by Candlelight," sponsored by a radio station and a newspaper, was in its thirteenth year. It was the 14th of Decem-

[3] *A Directory of Philanthropic Trusts.* New Zealand Council for Educational Research and J. R. McKenzie Trust Board, Wellington, New Zealand, 1964. 68 p.

ber, a lovely spring evening in Sydney's Christmas season. At least 3,000 people were gathered on benches and on the grass, holding lighted candles and singing the traditional English Christmas carols, including those stressing snow and ice. On a central stand were a robed chorus and a living creche, replete with animals, acting out the lines of the carols when appropriate. Each person paid two shillings for his candle and music sheet. Proceeds went to a hospital for women and children.

Australia published its first directory of foundations in 1968[4] It describes 226 trusts and foundations; 14 of these are located in other countries but make some of their grants in Australia. Annual disbursements of the 187 located in Australia and furnishing data on disbursements totaled about $A24 million. Admittedly incomplete, this directory is an excellent beginning and indicates a considerable recent expansion of the foundation idea "down under."

Japan

On the way back to the States we spent some time in Japan, where philanthropy in American terms is rudimentary or unknown. The family is still the resource for elementary needs, as in most Eastern countries, but since World War II the nation is in rapid transition.

Until the end of that war Shintoism was the official religion, the Emperor its god, state revenues its chief support. After the defeat the Emperor ceased to be divine and the new constitution specifically forbade governmental contributions to any religion. At the time of our visit the vast Shinto shrines were trying to survive on wedding fees and the meager yens of worshippers who have no tradition of religious giving.

There was also no general tradition for corporate giving, but some eight great corporations which controlled most of business in Japan were contributing to hundreds of charities, usually making certain that their names were prominently displayed. They could deduct these contributions if made as a capital expenditure for a project approved by the Minister of Finance. Frequently they acted through an association which decided which causes should be supported and made a lump sum donation.

Individual giving is not common, though the tourist, seeing on

4 Hart, E. K., *Directory of Philanthropic Trusts in Australia.* Australian Council for Educational Research, Victoria, Australia, 1968. 274 p.

the Ginza kimono-clad girls with canisters for community chests and like causes, might think otherwise. Newspaper drives for calamity funds are sometimes run, but get most of their take from foreigners, in Japan or abroad. There is a Japanese Red Cross which collects "memberships" rather easily; for a member has the special privilege of attending the annual meeting at which the Emperor will appear. At the time of our visit this was an unusual privilege, for he otherwise appeared only in the New Year's crush at the Imperial Palace.

The Vaqf

As a foundation watcher, I became aware of a near-equivalent to foundations in Islamic countries under the name *vaqf* (alternative spellings, *waqf*, *wakf*, plural *vakif*), and gathered information from foreign visitors and by correspondence.[5]

The *vaqf* closely resembles the charitable trust of Anglo-Saxon law, but is under religious rather than secular sanction. It has had a long history, and according to tradition was recommended by Mohammed himself in the seventh century. The root word means "to cause to stand still, to render firm," and perpetuity is characteristic, though in recent land reforms of the United Arab Republic many *vakif* were destroyed.

A *vaqf* may be set up for any purpose recognized as laudable both in Islam and by the religion of the founder. The *both* is important. Apparently a Christian could not set up a *vaqf* for either a mosque or a church—the former being contrary to his own religion, the latter to Islam.

Three categories of usage are recognized: first and foremost, a man's duty to his own family; second, maintenance of God's worship according to the tenets of Islam; finally, charities in the everyday sense, including works of public utility. The first usage is directly contrary to our conception of a charitable trust, the beneficiaries of which should be a general class, not related to the donor. Responsibility for family being primary in Mohammedan countries, the opposite view is taken.

Accumulation of income is forbidden. If a *vaqf* is set up for children yet unborn, income is not accumulated but goes to the poor until the birth of the first child. The founder may appoint himself the first *mutawali*, or trustee, and assign to himself re-

[5] Summarized in my article, "On the Nature of the Vaqf" in *Foundation News*, Vol. 5, September, 1964, pp. 6-7.

muneration not more than that which he appoints for subsequent trustees, and not exceeding the customary fee, usually 10 percent of income.

No estimates are available of the number or accumulated wealth of the *vakif* in the world today, but they exist in considerable numbers, and some with great wealth, in Turkey, Saudi Arabia, India, Iran, and other countries with substantial Mohammedan populations.

Binational Foundations

In many countries educational commissions have been set up to aid in the selection of Fulbright fellows, frequently bearing names that make them look like foundations: e.g., Australian-American Educational Foundation, United States Educational Foundation in Finland, United States Educational Foundation in Pakistan.

In 1965 Senator J. William Fulbright proposed in a Senate bill that up to $1 billion of the approximately $3 billion in non-convertible foreign currencies currently owned by the United States be used for creation of binational foundations. With half their trustees American citizens and half nationals of the given country, these organizations would operate like American private foundations, using income for "scholarships and travel within their respective countries, for internal educational and cultural projects, for the construction of educational and scientific facilities, for the translation and publication of books and magazines, and for similar type activities not involving expenditures abroad."

Such a binational foundation in India seemed near creation under a Presidential order, but the mere fact of some American representation on a board spending exclusively American funds roused in India violent opposition in both academic and governmental circles. With its abandonment the Fulbright bill also was shelved. I had been in correspondence with Senator Fulbright and had on invitation consulted with the House Committee on Foreign Affairs, but this hopeful idea seems presently dormant.

Canada

With common backgrounds, philanthropy in Canada does not greatly differ from that in the States, but develops more slowly with less wealth and a small population. Private and corporate giving are both increasing; I have already referred to service with the Committee on Corporate Giving in Canada.[6]

Foundations are increasing in numbers, and are of all types, as in the States. Among the largest are the J. W. McConnell Foundation (assets $42 million), Donner Canadian Foundation ($33 million), J. P. Bickell Foundation (limited to Ontario, $29 million), the Eldee Foundation ($23 million), The Atkinson Charitable Foundation (also limited to Ontario, assets $14 million); and two substantial community trusts, Vancouver Foundation ($12 million) and The Winnipeg Foundation ($8.7 million). No complete directory exists, but over 100 "foundations and similar grant-giving organizations" are listed in the nearest approach to such a volume.[7]

The largest "foundation" is The Canada Council, organized in 1957 not as a private foundation but set up by the government with initial capital of $100 million, half of which went as capital gifts to universities; the remainder is held as endowment, with income (together with annual government appropriations in recent years, and some current contributions to capital or income from individuals) devoted to "the arts, humanities, and social sciences."

Brooke Claxton, then its chairman, invited me to be the speaker at the Council's annual meeting in 1959. I described foundations in the States and then raised a question as to why we in the States at that time had set up as our single tax-supported foundation National Science Foundation without even a sideglance at the arts while their single such foundation stressed the arts. (Of course in a changed political climate we did establish in 1965 our own National Foundation on the Arts and the Humanities.) Their reply was that in Canada public support for the theater, orchestras, the dance, books, came from a smaller population, and the arts to survive had greater need of subsidy.

As private foundations in the States have increasingly attempted the difficult role of Maecenas, I have continued to follow the longer Canadian experience with lively interest. Recently I asked Mr. Jean Boucher, director of The Canada Council, about possible problems in this field.

[6] See p. 129.
[7] *Canadian Universities' Guide to Foundations and Granting Agencies*, compiled by Jeffrey Holmes and Lorraine Matte. Association of Universities and Colleges of Canada, Ottawa, Canada, 1969. 110 p.

In the arts, he reported, the individual rather than the institution is the necessary key. About 80 percent of their arts grants go to individuals, 20 percent to organizations. Difficult situations arise among these persons—drinking up the grant, failure to answer correspondence, complete inability to organize their lives. Nevertheless, because it is precisely this sort of individual who is often able to make a major artistic contribution, a foundation operating in the arts field must somehow manage to accept the heavy risks involved in individual support.

Latin America

I have managed only three visits to Latin America, and can therefore speak little of its philanthropy from personal knowledge. But as a consultant to Russell Sage Foundation, I was in close touch with the first directory of Latin American foundations, and with its efficient editor, Miss Ann Stromberg.[8]

Mainly from this source it is possible to report that philanthropy in Latin America is beginning to grow, and in most of these countries, unlike Europe, tax laws have recently become favorable.

Foundations are rapidly increasing in numbers, though many are still small and often they represent a mixed picture, being sometimes little more than pension or aid funds of companies, and are often beneficiaries of fund-raising campaigns or government subsidies. Some 800 legally incorporated foundations were identified, with relatively complete information obtained on 360. Of the 353 for which the founding date is known, a startling 52 percent have been organized since 1960—more than 81 percent since 1950.

The assets and income of foundations are tax exempt in every country. "In twelve countries full tax deductions for contributions to foundations are permitted; in another five countries partial tax deductions are allowed."[9] In only one country, Bolivia, no deductions are permitted; in Venezuela companies may deduct contributions of up to 5 percent of net income, but not individuals.

A brief visit to the Sears-Roebuck Foundation in Mexico City

[8] Stromberg, Ann, Editor, *Philanthropic Foundations in Latin America*. Prepared by the Pan American Development Foundation. Russell Sage Foundation, New York, 1968. 215 p.
[9] Idem, p. 6.

in the spring of 1969 proved illuminating, at least as to the functioning of a company-related foundation in Latin America.

I was cordially received by Mr. Jorge Lemus Espana, general secretary of the foundation which was established in 1956. Mr. Lemus Espana is an affable, well-built executive-type man, also director of personnel and public relations for the company, and in command of perfect English.

Present program, he explained, emphasizes scholarships, and by now they have had 170 graduates. They select poor boys usually from large families who could not otherwise go to college, and support usually extends through six years. Good scholastic records are required, but family need rather than very superior marks is the criterion. Some preference is given to students intending to take business courses, and a few of the graduates have been employed, but medicine and other unrelated disciplines are also supported. "We don't want our program to be too selfish."

They also support boys' clubs somewhat like the 4-H clubs in America. Mr. Lemus Espana, when he took over the foundation assignment about two years earlier, spent some time in Chicago acquainting himself with programs of the United States Sears-Roebuck Foundation. He indicated that there is almost no intercommunication among foundations in Latin America.

Office conferences with persons concerned with Latin American philanthropy have been numerous, including those with L. Ronald Scheman, of the Pan American Development Foundation. In addition to preparation of the directory already noticed, this Foundation is endeavoring to stimulate and coordinate private philanthropy in Latin America by a varied program including matching of grants for some endeavors, offering management services, and the like.

A stranger proposal, antedating formation of the Pan American Development Foundation, came from a gentleman convinced that the Latin American countries ought to meet many of their needs through their own philanthropy, and the way to accomplish this was for me to write a pamphlet encouraging such giving, with an introduction by President Kennedy which he was sure he could obtain, and a blessing from our State Department. Without venturing an opinion on whether the time was now ripe for promoting this idea, I said that any such document would have to be written by a Latin American thoroughly familiar with the thinking and culture of the countries concerned.

The Ditchley Conference

In November, 1966, I attended an international foundation conference held at Ditchley Park, near Oxford, England. It brought together representatives of some twenty-five charitable foundations from Britain, continental Europe, and North America, some of whom were old friends from the Royaumont Conference.

In addition to full plenary sessions, the conference endeavored to study in some depth three specific areas: the juridical and fiscal position of foundations, their domestic role particularly with relation to operations of government in similar fields, and their international role. I had the initial talk, and was reporter for Group A, chaired by the now experienced administrator, Sir Harold Redman of the Wolfson Foundation.

Ditchley is a fine manor house set in wide fields where we could see flocks of sheep under the early morning mists. It is maintained by The Ditchley Foundation, which endeavors to provide "opportunities for men and women from both sides of the Atlantic and elsewhere to meet quietly for the discussion and study of problems of common concern." One day when Sir Harold and I were hurrying back from a brisk walk around the adjoining lake we cut through the servants' quarters and noted one call bell still labeled, "Prime Minister's Room." During World War II Ditchley was a secret headquarters for Winston Churchill.

Chief findings of the conference are reported in its official document.[10] But in our section we smoked out what I have come to regard as the most significant handicap to foundation development in certain European countries. The official proceedings could refer to this problem only obliquely.

In certain countries, perhaps especially France, Italy, and Spain, income-tax reports appear to be often a matter of maneuver and negotiation, with few individuals reporting full income. Therefore, when a wealthy man proposes making a large gift to set up a foundation, his lawyer or banker immediately points out that if this is done, the taxing authorities will inquire where such an accumulation originated, since over the past twenty years reported income was only minor. One European delegate seriously proposed that the conference recommend leg-

[10] *Foundations and Government.* Ditchley Paper No. 9. The Ditchley Foundation, Ditchley Park, Enstone, Oxford, England, 1966. 18 p.

islation preventing tax authorities from examining any past years after the record had been sanctified (and closed) by a large charitable gift!

A second Ditchley Conference on British and American philanthropy was held at Ditchley in the spring of 1972, with attendance of a distinguished group of philanthropic and foundation leaders from both countries. I did not attend this conference, but was assigned the background paper for the American group. My task was to compress into "25 or 30 pages" a résumé of philanthropy in the United States, its history and structure.

For this paper I included a very brief glance at history and then described the present situation in the economic terms of "the suppliers"—individuals, corporations, foundations—"the demanders"—principally religion, education, welfare, health, the arts, foreign aid—and "the marketing mechanism"—voluntary agencies, federated giving, professional fund raising. A final section looked at taxation, supervision, and the probable future.[11]

Other European Developments

I took advantage of the 1966 European journey to visit foundations in Britain and other rainy places. These included extended London visits with Brian Young, second director of The Nuffield Foundation, Sir Harold Redman at the Wolfson Foundation, and Tom Green, head of the Charity Commission. Mr. Green reported that his office had registered (November, 1966) 62,000 exempt charities, but these include some fund-raising organizations; new registrations were still coming in at a rate of about 100 a week. Because of personnel shortages, reports are requested only once every five years. The commission's files are open to public inspection, but no central directory is planned.

I had planned a visit to Holland where a directory of European foundations was being prepared with assistance from the European Cultural Foundation. However, its editor undertook another assignment, and that project has been delayed. Until late 1969 the nearest substitute was *European Independent Non-Profit Organizations with Biomedical Interests* issued in 1965 by the European office of the U.S. National Institutes of Health, and actually including nearly all the larger European foundations.

[11] "Philanthropy in the United States: History and Structure," in *Philanthropy in the 70s: An Anglo-American Conference.* The Council on Foundations, New York, 1973, p. 89-114.

A trip to Paris included a luncheon with M. Henri Goüin and officials of his Royaumont Foundation. There I also talked at greater length with M. Michel Pomey, who had been at Ditchley, and who has produced *Les Fondations en France & aux Etas-Unis*,[12] a comparative study of foundation development in the two countries, presenting also information on the few known such organizations in France.

In Sweden in 1970 a directory of foundations was issued which includes about 700 organizations of the foundation type, many of them scholarship funds.[13] They are also indexed by categories.

In 1971 the National Council of Social Service issued a directory of approximately 2000 British trusts.[14]

In 1971 Fondazione Giovanni Agnelli issued a revised edition of its directory of European foundations,[15] first issued in 1969. The English edition is available through Columbia University Press. It describes 296 foundations in 16 European countries.

Fondazione Giovanni Agnelli has begun an intensive program looking toward assembling information about foundations in Italy and in Europe generally in its own offices, becoming a European center for such data. Staff members of this Foundation recently described the Italian situation in *Foundation News*.[16]

The recent spread of the foundation movement in many countries of the world makes especially appropriate action of the trustees of The Foundation Center to remove from their charter the original limitation to foundations in the United States. In 1969 new staff was added to collect information on foundations in all countries.

[12] Issued by Fondation Royaumont, Paris, 1966, 91 pp. A new directory, *Fondations*, was published in 1971 under auspices of the Ministry of the Interior.

[13] *Svenska Kulturfonder*. P. A. Norstedt & Söners förlag, Stockholm, Sweden, 1970. 288 p.

[14] *Directory of Grant-Making Trusts*. The National Council of Social Service, London, 1971. 854 p.

[15] *Guide to European Foundations*. Prepared by the Giovanni Agnelli Foundation, Franco Angeli, Editore, Milan, Italy, 1973. 401 p.

[16] Laureti, Pasquale, and Ann Parneti, "Foundations in Italy," *Foundation News*, Vol. X, No. 1, January 1969, pp. 12-15.

CHAPTER 18

The Gathering Storm

I‌N the earlier years at the Center I was able to read every 990-A return, and at all times staff was instructed to send over my desk all the returns of large foundations and any others that had special interest or questionable items. We were not policemen or informants, but all the records were freely open to public inspection, and we ourselves were well aware, simply from the statistical record, that some foundations were grossly violating the ethics of philanthropy and even existing laws.

For example, the son of the donor of one foundation "sold" to his father's foundation, for cash and listed Wall Street securities, more than 2 million dollars' worth, at his valuation, of stock in a closely held family corporation. In the year of record the foundation realized in dividends, from its $2 million assets, only about $500 for its charitable purposes. Charity should have had at least $100,000.

Another foundation gave some $4,000 in "grants to worthy college students," all of whom were actually identified on the form as sons or daughters of the named trustees. In other cases the listed salaries of trustees (though in most foundations they serve without pay) seemed princely in terms of time applied to their tasks.

Not all the sins were on the foundation side. One company-sponsored foundation which matches employe contributions to colleges and schools suddenly received a tremendous list of contributions to a local church-related school, all duly certified and with full matching required. On investigation it discovered that members of that church had been instructed to make their contributions to the school, which would then rebate them to the church as their usual religious contribution, but meanwhile collect an equal sum from the company-sponsored foundation. Said the foundation official to the church dignitary: "Not illegal; just immoral."

There had been no investigation of foundations since the close of the Reece hearings in 1954. As we entered 1961 seven years had passed, during which a flood of family foundations had been given birth, often with the midwifery of skilled lawyers who were more concerned with financial advantages for the donor than the public welfare. At the Center we were painfully aware that storm clouds were gathering, and must soon break.

Mr. Patman Attacks

The first sign of the direction from which the storm might come was a brief and relatively mild speech by Congressman Wright Patman of Texas, delivered in the House on 2 May 1961.[1] It was titled "A Fresh Look at Tax-Exempt Foundations" and had as its main theme the "disproportionately rapid growth" of foundations. Other speeches followed in rapid succession, and soon he was attacking foundations on a broad front, and furnishing some extraordinary statistics, such as an alleged 45,124 foundations in existence at the close of 1960. I knew this was the precise number of total Information Returns for all exempt organizations reported by Internal Revenue Service for the given year.

Still hopeful that this investigation would listen to facts, as had the Cox Committee, I wrote to Mr. Patman, giving the source of his figure, noting that the first dozen names in the present alphabetical list included only one foundation (there were six A.A.U.W. organizations, an orphanage, a seaman's club, a service center, the "A.A. Society," the A.A. Suburban Group for the other eleven), and citing our own estimates of total foundations. He went on putting into his printed reports the same figure with amplification to a probable 250,000 for foundations Internal Revenue had overlooked. He supplied detailed financial data on 522 named foundations, allegedly selected across the board, and calmly concluded that his totals were "1 percent" of the foundations. We checked his named list with the *Directory*, finding all but six, but noting that it was far from an across the board se-

[1] *Congressional Record—House*, 87th Congress, 1st Session. Vol. 107, No. 73, 2 May 1961, pp. 6560-6562.

lection; his little "sample" possessed 92 percent of the assets of all the foundations in the *Directory*, and an estimated 90 percent of the assets of all foundations. His reports, concentrating on income and expenditures, alleged tremendous Treasury loss which "the widow with a cottage instead of a palace" must make good, with no hint of any public benefit from these expenditures.

Most of the press scare-headlined malefactions, but a few papers checked on facts, criticized inaccuracies, and noted that these were not even reports *of* the Small Business Committee, but simply the personal reports of its chairman to the members, most of whom never saw the documents before release to the press. In some of these refutations The Foundation Library Center and its *Directory* were mentioned as fact sources; the list of investigated "foundations" was enlarged to 534 in December, 1962, and now included The Foundation Library Center. Of course our record as a "foundation" looked deplorable; we were spending much less than receipts (it was the period of building our ten-year Sustaining Fund) and all the money we did spend was for operation.

We were specially favored with endless inquiries. They covered staff salaries, costs of the *Directory*, who subscribed to *Foundation News*, names of all the foundations we were transcribing in Washington, names of the foundations which supplied confidential information for the Nelson study (this one we declined), and much else.

There were pluses. Aided by his subpoena powers, Mr. Patman obtained and published some financial data we had been denied. His castigations of the Treasury and Internal Revenue Service had undoubted influence in promoting better supervision and liberalization of public access to information.

The Patman Hearings began in Washington on 21 July 1964, but it was not a hearing for foundations. Typically, the chairman would question, usually for a whole day, a government official: Douglas Dillon, Secretary of the Treasury, on the first day; Mortimer M. Caplin, former Commissioner of Internal Revenue, the second day; a representative of the Securities and Exchange Commission on the third. He would ask these gentlemen whether they were enforcing the law in their fields, and demand examples of foundations possibly violating a wide variety of statutes. Sometimes the government official would be asked whether he was familiar with the operations of a named organization. When he was not, Mr. Patman or his research assistant immediately read into the record their own statement concerning it, and the foundation was given no opportunity to reply.

The Center's experience may illuminate how such a procedure can be manipulated. I received an urgent phone call from our Washington office, informing me that a further hearing was suddenly called for Monday morning the 10th of August; only Bertrand M. Harding, Acting Commissioner of Internal Revenue, was to be called, but it was rumored the Center would be involved. I took a dawn plane, and was almost the only person present related to foundations; apparently none of the many discussed that day had been notified; only the press, and Internal Revenue Service.

In the afternoon Mr. Patman read and handed to the press, while I had to sit silent, a long memorandum on the Center.[2] It included a number of false implications based on absolutely truthful statements. Examples: "Contributions to charity have been nil." They would be illegal under our charter. ". . . the Foundation (sic) did not make full disclosure with respect to capital gains or losses in its tax returns for 1958 through 1961 . . . despite the fact that Treasury regulations *require* a detailed statement." [Italics mine. Such statements were *not* required until 1962, but the switch to the present tense makes the second statement "true" though completely misleading.]

At a subsequent trustee meeting it was decided to make no formal reply to these allegations. One of our business members said that this was about par for many Congressional hearings, and would not mislead informed readers. Besides, a refutation must repeat the charge, which is all most readers will remember.

The Treasury Report

Under the Patman lash the Treasury Department, acknowledging some past neglect of the exempt field from which little revenue could be expected, began tightening its procedures, conducting more field investigations, and working on a comprehensive report on foundations with legislative recommendations in mind.

---

[2] *Tax-Exempt Foundations: Their Impact on Small Business.* Hearings before Subcommittee No. 1 Foundations. Select Committee on Small Business, House of Representatives, 88th Congress, 2d Session. Government Printing Office, Washington, 1964, pp. 157-165.

For policy discussions it appointed in 1963 "an informal advisory committee . . . to assist in its study of problems relating to tax-exempt foundations. The study is intended to consider both the legal and administrative aspects of such problems." The committee, efficiently chaired by lawyer and Assistant Secretary of the Treasury Stanley S. Surrey, consisted of fifteen persons, principally lawyers and foundation executives or trustees, with three of its members nominated by Mr. Patman. I was a member.

Discussions, which were off the record, were extremely lively, as the composition of the committee guaranteed. The Treasury put on our agenda specific cases of abuse, problem areas not covered by present laws, and certain broad policy questions. The committee members collectively possessed legal acumen, wide experience in actual conduct of foundation affairs, and extremely divergent political and economic views. The Treasury listened, in the persons of Chairman Surrey and members of its legal and tax staff. No report was ever issued, or planned, but I suspect the discussions contributed to better understanding on both sides—the operation of foundations, and problems of the Treasury in its unwelcome task of supervision.

Meanwhile the Treasury was working on its own extensive survey. Its statistical sample was carefully drawn, consisting of all foundations with assets of $10 million or more, and a stratified random sample of smaller foundations, weighted to represent the whole field. Since its own files of Form 990-A were not separated by type of exempt organization, facilities of our Washington office were widely used, and acknowledged. Its *Report*,[3] prepared for both the Committee on Finance of the Senate and the House Committee on Ways and Means, was issued on 2 February 1965. Among its major findings were these:

> The Department's investigation has revealed that the preponderant number of private foundations perform their functions without tax abuse. However, its study has also produced evidence of serious faults among a minority of such organizations . . .

> Private philanthropy plays a special and vital role in our society. Beyond providing for areas into which government cannot or should not advance (such as religion), private philanthropic organizations can be uniquely qualified to initiate thought and action, experiment with new and untried ventures, dissent from prevailing attitudes,

[3] *Treasury Department Report on Private Foundations.* Government Printing Office, Washington, D.C., 1965. 110 p.

and act quickly and flexibly. Private foundations have an important part in this work. . . .

The contention that foundation holdings have become an excessively large part of the national economy in recent years finds little support in the relevant data. . . . Hence, there would appear to be little present factual basis for the assertion that foundation lives should be limited because foundation wealth has become disproportionate.[4]

Six major problem areas were identified, and solutions proposed. For my own trustees I prepared this brief analysis:

(1) *Self-dealing.* Almost complete prohibition of self-dealing is proposed, and long overdue.

(2) *Delay in benefit to charity.* Foundations would be required to spend their whole income in the year received or the following year, would be required to spend the equivalent of income if their assets include non-income-producing stocks or other property, and could not call contributions to another foundation an . expenditure for purposes of avoiding accumulation penalties.

(3) *Involvement in business.* Foundations would be sharply restricted in such involvements, including the holding of 20 percent or more of the stock of a business unrelated to the charitable activities of the foundation.

(4) *Family use of foundations to control corporate and other property.* To prevent abuses in this area income-tax deductions would not be permitted for gifts of stock or other property closely controlled by the donor until the foundation disposes of that asset, devotes it to active charitable operations, or donor control over the property terminates.

(5) *Financial transactions unrelated to charitable functions.* Loans in either direction would be severely restricted, and trading activities either speculative in nature or so numerous as to constitute a business would not be permitted.

(6) *Broadening of foundation management.* After the first 25 years, the Treasury Department "recommends" that the donor and related parties would not be permitted to constitute more than 25 percent of the foundation's governing body.

The Treasury adopted the very sensible policy of asking any affected foundation to submit in writing its own views, with detail on special problems the proposals might create for it. These

[4] *Treasury Department Report*, pp. 2, 5, 13, 14.

replies were published in two massive volumes totaling 771 pages.

The Center was extremely busy in the weeks and months following issuance of the *Report*. We took no official position on any of the proposals, but made available all of our pertinent information.

At the request of Russell Sage Foundation, where I was still officially a consultant, I prepared a then-anonymous commentary. In general I thought the *Report* able, judicious, and in all respects worthy of serious consideration. Most troublesome of the recommendations would be the requirement speedily to reduce stock holdings to less than 20 percent in any business, and to reconstitute boards of trustees to not more than one fourth representing donor or donor business. The latter would probably be completely unworkable for company-sponsored foundations, and an unnecessary hardship on some others.

Side effects might be serious. And should not most of these regulations be at the state level? The federal government then had available only the inappropriate sanction of removing tax exemption. This simply robbed charity of many dollars, and did not punish individuals guilty of infractions. The Tax Reform Act of 1969 now spells out further penalties, including heavy liabilities on errant trustees and managers, but the chief enforcing agency is still Internal Revenue Service, for which such duties are not appropriate. To date the states, with a few exceptions, have inadequate legislation and supervisory machinery.

Again, withholding deductibility on gifts of stock to controlled corporations might seem a justifiable policy, but to what extent would it dry up future large contributions to charity? Finally, the regulatory proposals were limited to foundations, with no mention of application to other exempt institutions, such as colleges, hospitals, churches. When the 1950 Revenue Act taxed unrelated business income to foundations, the churches moved massively in. Unless corrective measures apply generally to the whole charity field, they may do no more than transfer the evils they were intended to cure.

This memorandum, with some Russell Sage Foundation changes, had limited circulation. After my retirement it went on the public record.[5]

[5] "Views on the Treasury Report," *Foundation News*, March, 1968, Vol. IX, No. 2, pp. 29-33.

More from Mr. Patman

After its hearings in 1964 Mr. Patman's committee continued to require annual reports and sometimes detailed information from its group of studied foundations, but for two years held no hearings and issued no reports.

However, on 21 December 1966 Mr. Patman issued *Installment 4* of his peculiar personal reports to his committee on foundations, Installment 5 on 28 April 1967, Installment 6 on 26 March 1968, and Installment 7 on 30 June 1969.

Also, the committee held a second series of Hearings in nine morning sessions in late October and early November, 1967. Almost the sole subject of these hearings was a sort of super foundation which called itself Americans Building Constitutionally (ABC), "the purpose of which is to help citizens of the United States make full use of the rights guaranteed them under the Constitution." The "rights" contemplated were principally rights to avoid paying taxes.

A tremendous documentation had now built up, consisting of more than 4,200 pages of printed Hearings and Reports together with a flood of speeches in *Congressional Record*, special magazine articles, acres of press clippings. The new president of the Center, Manning M. Pattillo, felt that it was time that this material be digested and given preliminary appraisal. He asked me to undertake this task. I pointed out that it was too soon for any final evaluation: the committee had not disbanded and its energetic chairman might well initiate further activities,[6] and only a longer historical perspective would reveal what might be the ultimate effects of work already done on legislation and foundation development. Nevertheless, since I was one of the few persons who had read all the vast documentation and had kept currently familiar with the complex operation, and moreover could now speak as an individual and not as an officer of the Center, I agreed to undertake the task.

The first full summer of "retirement" found me holed up in Vermont, surrounded by government documents and devoting most mornings to this task. I finished the manuscript in late August, 1968, and it was published by the Center as its Occasional

---

[6] An eighth Installment, this time for the Subcommittee on Domestic Finance of the Committee on Banking and Currency, appeared in August, 1972.

Paper No. 3 at the year end.[7] Its concluding sentences made this assessment of the Patman operation as of the close of 1968:

> Objective studies of foundations by public authority are desirable, and should be conducted from time to time. A high standard in this respect was set by the "Nathan Report" in Great Britain, and in the United States the Cox Report produced much direct testimony and related conclusions that are of permanent value.
>
> The Patman investigation has had some positive benefits, particularly in terms of calling attention to abuses in the field, stimulating fuller reporting and public disclosure, and providing some added financial data. It has also indulged in rabble rousing, misleading the public with gross exaggerations and misrepresentations. Possibly later activities of the Committee may present more balanced findings. At this stage the investigation has utterly failed to present a rounded picture of the place of the private foundation in American society or even in the domestic economy. It has set up a most unfortunate example of how a Congressional investigation should never again be conducted.

Since my pamphlet had severely criticized some of the statistics in the Patman reports and many of the conclusions based upon them, rejoinder was expected. Indeed, one of my foundation friends, a former editor with experience with Mr. Patman, shook his head and said I had done a fine and needed job, but a very rash one. Another friend, happening into the office of Mr. Olsher the director of the Patman foundation study, reported back that his desk was littered with separated pages of my pamphlet, every one of which was apparently being closely scanned.

After some months I had a brusque letter from Mr. Olsher, raising five points. One of them will require some revision because of use of figures not revealed in published reports; but the revision may be even more damaging to the conclusion drawn. The others I answered item by item, and took particular delight in one of them.

He asked what my authority was for a statement on page 19 that "The Rockefeller Foundation pointed out that an alleged accumulation on their part of $91 million was, in fact, the sum of grants made *in excess* of total income," and enclosed the Rocke-

[7] Andrews, F. Emerson, *Patman and Foundations: Review and Assessment*. Occasional Paper No. 3. The Foundation Center, New York, 1968, 62 pp.

feller 990-A for 1951. I replied that my authority was a news release sent out by The Rockefeller Foundation, and quoted the
pertinent paragraph. As to his submitted form, it confirmed the
error. It is true that Line 21, accumulation of income, did include
the $91 million item, but Line 24, disbursements out of principal,
had the same figure to the penny. Apparently he was using a
Xerox copy, which he had also supplied to me, and forgotten that
Xerox prints red figures black. Surrounding data clearly indicated that the Line 21 figure was negative. And, I took delight in
adding, if his staff had not been carefully warned, as has the
Center's staff, of this danger in handling Xerox copies, then he
would do well to go over all his statistical data and find out in
how many other cases a similar error had been made.

Though my letter requested certain additional data from him
"at your early convenience," no reply has ever come. Mr. Olsher
left Mr. Patman's employ on 1 April 1969, reportedly quite
promptly upon discovery that he had accepted a grant from a
large Texas foundation.

When Mr. Patman subsequently issued his Seventh Installment
it still included the egregious Rockefeller error.[8]

Ways and Means Committee Hearings

With the Patman paper finished and the winter snows upon us,
Mrs. Andrews and I loaded our station wagon with both winter
and summer clothes and in mid-January set out for Mexico. We
were having a most lovely holiday in that country when the
phone rang in our Mexico City motel—New York calling. It was
Dr. Pattillo reporting that the Ways and Means Committee had
just announced hearings on general tax reform, with the first
week to be devoted to foundations. The hearings would start on
18 February. I might be needed; could I come up?

We surrendered the rest of our holiday in the tropics and
started north. Of course we arrived at the tail end of the biggest
snowstorm in the New York area in a decade, and I had to hire
a snowplow even to get my car into the driveway. But I was
home in time, had the weekend to prepare my testimony, and on
Monday flew down to Washington.

[8] *Tax-Exempt Foundations and Charitable Trusts: Their Impact on Our Economy.* Seventh Installment. Subcommittee Chairman's Report to Subcommittee No.
1. June 30, 1969. Washington, Government Printing Office, p. 81.

When the hearings opened on Tuesday 18 February 1969 the first witness was Congressman Wright Patman, who spoke vigorously on his familiar theme that "philanthropy—one of mankind's more noble instincts—has been perverted into a vehicle for institutionalized, deliberate evasion of fiscal and moral responsibility to the Nation." He also disclosed that he was introducing into Congress a bill which, if passed, would (1) tax all foundations in the amount of 20 percent of gross income, including capital gains; (2) limit to 3 percent foundation ownership of outstanding shares of any class of stock of a corporation, or to the same percentage its share in interest in the capital or profits of a partnership; and (3) require annual disbursement of net income.

Dr. Pattillo next presented a general statement concerning foundations, their history, their growth, their place in organized philanthropy and in the American economy. He estimated present foundations at about 22,000, with assets of $20.5 billion and annual grants amounting to $1.5 billion. He pointed out their great diversity, the difficulties of defining foundations, and described in broad terms their fields of activity, with appraisals of strengths and weaknesses and a glance at future development.

My testimony followed, and I made the point that I was testifying as "a private citizen and a lifelong student of foundations, able and willing to express his own views." It had been agreed that I should discuss primarily the six specific proposals concerning foundations which were made in the *Treasury Report*. My testimony closely followed the memorandum and special article cited above,[9] and need not be repeated.

Several members of the committee stressed the view that government was now doing nearly all the things for which foundations used to assume responsibility, and with larger funds and under public controls. Were foundations of any use any more, with their smaller sums? I asked permission to give "just one interesting example."

MR. ANDREWS: I just drove up from Mexico City to attend this hearing and I am still a little driver conscious. All over the United States now as I drove along the highways I found very helpful white lines on the margins of the highways as well as a white line in the center.

[9] See p. 248.

Do you gentlemen realize that as little as twelve or fourteen years ago there was not in the United States—I believe this is correct—one marginal white line on any highway? We had center lines.

A small foundation in Connecticut, the Dorr Foundation, was then headed by its donor (who has recently died) who had engineering training. He had an idea. He went to the Connecticut Highway Department and said, "Gentlemen, why don't you put white lines on the edges of your highways?"

They said, "No, that would be three times as much white painting and we are trying to avoid head-on collisions and that is what the center line is for."

He said, "Gentlemen, I think you are wrong. I think we motorists driving at night are blinded if we have to look at that white line in the center, and this results in accidents. Will you let me do an experiment, taking a road on which you have accident statistics, and with my money if you need it, paint white lines on the side?"

Well, this happened on a prominent highway in Connecticut close to New York and it was to Mr. Dorr's amazement as well as the highway department that accidents dropped something like 65 percent on that newly marked highway.

MR. COLLIER: Are you prepared to believe that if it hadn't been for that it would not have come about?

MR. ANDREWS: It would have been five or ten years before you and I would have been more safe. . . . This is one of the most important things foundations do. They buy time.

Before this tax-writing committee I stressed the danger of directing regulatory efforts at only one segment of the exempt field, concluding my formal testimony with this statement:

> Gentlemen, I recognize that broadening the regulatory effort to the whole charity field will take political courage. But without such broadening, even the best of these measures may do no more than transfer the abuses they were intended to cure.[10]

I remained for most of the rest of the hearings in the week devoted to foundations. Much of it presented excellently the case for private philanthropy and for foundations, but it became increasingly evident that many members of the Ways and Means Committee were impressed by the instances of abuse which Mr. Patman and others had cited, were openly critical of the Ford

[10] *Tax Reform, 1969.* Hearings before the Committee on Ways and Means, House of Representatives, Ninety-First Congress, Part 1 (February 18, 19, and 20, 1969). U.S. Government Printing Office, Washington, 1969. Pp. 95, 98, 99.

Foundation grant to former aides of Robert Kennedy, and with the necessity of extending the 10 percent surtax their immediate business, were minded to seek additional revenue wherever it could possibly be found.

Nearly all the foundation witnesses agreed to many of the Treasury recommendations, usually including absolute prohibition of self-dealing, expenditure of investment income (though with two- or three-year carrybacks and carryforwards instead of the unworkable single year proposal), the desirability of stock diversification. All resisted a direct tax on foundation income; it was pointed out that any revenue so derived would be directly taken from foundation beneficiaries, and in many cases these deficiencies would have to be made up by government.

At a later session John D. Rockefeller, III, gave testimony chiefly in defense of the unlimited charitable deduction. His testimony as to the desirability of private philanthropy and its ability sometimes to enter a field (example, population control) long before government is ready, was excellent. On the unlimited charitable deduction he testified that although he had qualified for it every year since 1961, "I have deliberately paid a tax of between 5 and 10 percent of my adjusted gross income in each of those years."

However generous this action was on his part, some of us thought he had given his case away. If he felt conscience-bound to pay a tax in spite of no legal liability, why should those without his scruples be legally exempted? Mr. Patman was more severe: "My disgust with Mr. Rockefeller's statement is matched in magnitude only by his audacity in offering it as a defense of an inequity which this nation should no longer tolerate."[11]

A Commission on Foundations

In April, 1969, chiefly at the urging of John D. Rockefeller, III, a private Commission on Foundations and Private Philanthropy was set up, consisting of thirteen persons prominent in business, education, law, and art, chaired by Peter G. Peterson, head of the Bell and Howell Corporation. It was charged with studying legislative and tax problems as they relate to foundations and to the larger question of the direction philanthropy is taking in this country. It was hoped that its report could be presented in time

[11] Letter to Wilbur Mills dated 5 May 1969, printed in *Tax-Exempt Foundations and Charitable Trusts*. Seventh Installment, p. 39.

for the scheduled autumn hearings before the Senate Committee on Finance.

In September the commission requested that I prepare a position paper on "The Role of Foundations in 1975." I demurred, pointing out that the commission had been intentionally set up without representation from the foundation field. It was alleged that for this difficult job of prophecy my own long experience was essential. I completed the paper in two weeks.

After reservations as to the dangers of prophecy and with assumptions—which proved substantially correct—as to what would be the main provisions of the Tax Reform Act of 1969 as finally passed, I predicted somewhat slower growth in numbers, particularly for company-sponsored foundations, than the recent 8.5 percent annual increase: assets rising, but not spectacularly; grants rising more sharply, and perhaps reaching $4 billion a year by 1975. As to where grants would go I believed that "foundations with conservative boards will yield to pressures and bury their grants in projects safely unquestionable, which should have received support elsewhere. But substantial funds will be committed still to the more venturesome projects, where failure is possible and criticism probable, but the potential rewards of success are very great in terms of advancing human welfare and pushing forward the frontiers of knowledge."

The paper was not acknowledged—an experience shared by many other persons cooperating with this hurried and harried commission—so that I have no way of knowing if it proved helpful. But Mr. Peterson did make a personal report before the Senate Finance Committee, his testimony and the prodding questions of the Senators occupying a full day. In the main Mr. Peterson found the pending tax bill punitive and ill-considered. But he scored the ultraconservative investment policies of many foundations, and proposed a required pay-out, with invasion of capital if necessary, of from 6 to 8 percent. He deplored the apparent lack of concern in both Houses for the pluralistic concept in decision-making and the hasty passage in the committees of a bill without consideration of its side-effects on total philanthropy. He thought the really pertinent question to be how people could be encouraged to give more of their money or of themselves to the improvement of society. The full report was published in 1970.[12]

<hr/>

[12] *Foundations, Private Giving, and Public Policy.* Report and Recommendations

The Tax Reform Act of 1969

In addition to Mr. Peterson's day, the Senate Finance Committee heard extensive testimony on foundations, from both friends and bitter foes. I neither testified nor attended these sessions, but was well aware that in the Senate, as in the House, a severely critical attitude prevailed. Indeed, it was in the Senate bill that a proposal was made to limit the tax-exempt life of all foundations to forty years; but this radical proposal was defeated before the bill's final passage.

What deeply concerned me, as I read these discussions and reflected on the types of questions which had been asked me in the House, was the realization that for the first time in America we were facing what I had previously encountered only in Europe— big government, feeling that it alone should undertake nearly all projects for human welfare, and that the private sector should be heavily taxed and closely supervised, if it was to be allowed to survive at all. This was not an attitude shared by all members of both Houses, or perhaps even a majority; but it was vigorously expressed in both tax-writing committees.

President Nixon signed into law the Tax Reform Act of 1969 on 30 December 1969. It is a massive document, so complicated that full interpretation will take years and many lawyers—indeed, it has been called "the lawyers relief act of 1969."

With respect to foundations, it can only be described as severely punitive. Among included provisions is an "audit-fee tax" of 4 percent of net investment income, including realized capital gains. Grants may not be made to individuals without prior governmental approval of the procedures involved. Disbursements must equal at least investment income within a year, with invasion of capital if such income did not reach a set percentage, increased over several years, of asset holdings. A needed tightening of restrictions on self-dealing between donor and foundation was spelled out. Reporting requirements were broadened.

Some years must pass before it can be ascertained whether these restrictions will unduly discourage foundation initiative and enterprise; it is certain that the funds they have available for welfare purposes have been reduced by the amount government now deducts.

---

of the Commission on Foundations and Private Philanthropy. Chicago, University of Chicago Press, 1970. 287 p.

Reporting to Internal Revenue Service

The storm that had been gathering for more than a decade had broken in the 1969 hearings and the passage of the Tax Reform Act of 1969. But this might not be the end. A substantial part of the public had apparently been convinced that nearly all foundations were established for the financial advantage of donors and engage widely in dubious practices, with little regard for the public interest, and that they represent "public money" since their income is tax exempt. Foundation defenders were not always heard—for scandal is more newsworthy—when they pointed to the tremendous good foundations have accomplished, to the fact that their grants for education and many other needed services save tax funds, and expressed the belief that the abuses, though certainly needing correction, are not numerous, and are usually acts of the smaller foundations involving relatively small dollar amounts.

But though individual abuses had been unearthed and highly publicized, no general survey had been conducted. No one really knew how numerous, in fact, these abuses are, what are their chief kinds, and what proportion of the field they represent. Trustees of The Foundation Center believed this information was urgently needed, and authorized a special study in May, 1969. Unfortunately the Congressional storm and other urgencies prevented early assignment of regular staff to this project. In October I was asked whether I would be willing to undertake it as a special project. Recognizing its importance, I agreed, and began work at once.

I proposed to examine in detail the Information Returns (Form 990-A) for the latest year available, usually 1968 or 1968-1969, of 1,000 randomly selected foundations, which would constitute approximately a 5 percent sample of the foundations then in operation. The sample was geographically stratified: each state was assigned substantially the same proportion in the sample as its total foundations bore to the national total. Within the state every foundation was taken following a given letter, up to the state's quota. New York, for example, having about 27 percent of all United States foundations, was assigned 270 foundations, beginning with the letter E.

Then each Form 990-A was examined with care, including arithmetical checking. Work sheets arranged by states included coded data on size as determined by assets, expenditures with relation to investment income, degree of reporting accuracy, payment to trustees, reported possession of 5 percent or more of the stock of any corporation, and had a final column labeled "Dubious Practices." If such were found, a special card gave a detailed picture of that foundation and the one or several practices which cast doubt upon its record. In all such cases the full files of The Foundation Center were examined, to see whether previous records might shed further light upon the questioned acts.

Research was completed in December, and the full report is available at the Center and the depository libraries. Its chief findings were published in *Foundation News*.[13]

The study confirms the view held by all recent students of foundations, but not by the general public, that most present foundations are small—90 percent of the sample possessing less than $1 million in total assets. The expenditure picture is in general good, with 88 percent spending at least 80 percent of investment income, and many of them more than income. Fees to trustees are rare, and usually small; 98 percent of the sample paid none, and only seventeen foundations, nearly the additional 2 percent, less than $5,000 per annum. Three foundations (less than half of 1 percent) made more substantial payments, and data were lacking for two more.

Reporting left much to be desired. Only 59 percent of the returns examined were fully acceptable, even with some allowance for honest misunderstandings. An additional 37 percent showed minor omissions of required data, or statistical error. More than 4 percent were severely and inexcusably remiss, unless there were filing or copying failures in the documents used by the study.

Holdings of 5 percent or more of the stock of one or more corporations involved 7.5 percent of the foundations, with this item unknown for three others. But among these 75 to 78 foundations are a great many of the derelictions which are charged as "Dubious Practices."

Dubious practices appeared in 4.7 percent of the examined returns. This ratio might be reduced under more complete reporting, but in some cases such reporting might disclose further faults. Most of the dubious practices involved manipulation of stock to the donor's advantage, and usually to the disadvantage of charity.

[13] "Foundation Reports to the I.R.S." *Foundation News*, Vol. XI, No. 4, July-August, 1970, pp. 125-129.

A large percentage of the abuses disclosed could have been corrected under then-existing law if complete reporting had been enforced and the returns thoroughly inspected. One may hope that the stiffer provisions of the Tax Reform Act of 1969, with its broadened reporting requirements and its liberal funds for inspection and enforcement, may halt nearly all these abuses, and do much toward restoring public confidence.

CHAPTER 19

Afterthoughts

For several years I have been enjoying two major retirement blessings, time to think and a new freedom to speak out. Of course the record suggests I have not been wholly reticent in the past. But for the official head of an organization to express controversial views on any topic may cost the organization needed friends. And those views, no matter how carefully described as purely personal, are inevitably taken to be an official position.

In this closing chapter I shall set down with complete frankness my views on certain subjects. I do not ask agreement. These are not dogma, but one man's opinions, and an invitation to further thought.

On Creativity

Creativity is the finest flower of the human intellect, through which the great advances of mankind have come. It may blossom in art forms—poetry, painting, the drama, music, dance; in scientific discovery—the wheel, the pendulum, electrical energy, relativity; in medical research—circulation of the blood, insulin, DNA; in social invention—courts, the corporation, zoning, democratic government. Creativity of any sort adds to the joy of living, and may make possible a worth-while personal contribution. How can it be stimulated in ourselves and others?

The mind seems to work on two levels, the conscious and the subconscious. We can set it to work, as in adding a grocery bill. Consciously adding, it is often correct; sometimes it is wrong. But when addition becomes automatic, proceeding without thought of individual numbers, the answer is always right. The subconscious mind appears to be a flawless mechanism that works even when we sleep. Out of its wide universe of knowledge and experience this machine brings up toward consciousness answers that correctly combine all the data it has assembled.

I have elsewhere suggested[1] that poets and statisticians have in common one factor that often makes their work singularly creative—a major obstacle. In the case of at least the traditional poet, this obstacle is the requirement of meter and rhyme. The trite, common word that first flashes into his conscious mind and would be used in prose fails to fit the meter, or perhaps the end rhyme. To find a metrical fit the poet turns the whole idea around and around, looks at all sides of it, considers alternatives, perhaps even the negative of the original idea. Meanwhile, his subconscious mind is at work. Suddenly a whole new idea flashes from the subconscious into consciousness. We call this "inspiration."

Similarly, the research scientist who takes the trouble to do his own statistical work (and except in vast projects where team work is necessary this task should not be delegated) often faces a similar obstacle. For when a tabulated trend seems uniform and then suddenly the next item breaks the pattern, the tabulator, like the poet, must pause. His rhythm is broken. Data must be checked; if right, a reason for the break must be sought elsewhere. All components of the erratic figure and all the surrounding data must be examined freshly. The tabulator's fingers stop and his mind works. Out of such forced study and seeming idleness, major discoveries may rise. The subconscious has time to work its prescient miracles, and science shifts from storage bin to creativity.

Science has sometimes been defined as organized knowledge. But creative science springs not so much from a body of organized knowledge (which also is a definition for an encyclopedia) as from the *process* of organizing knowledge. The process may be more important than the inert factual data with which it deals.

When we train students who show promise of research capacity it is not important that we store their brains with the maximum number of previously discovered scientific facts. It is important that these students conduct major experiments for themselves, even though the "discoveries" they make may have

---

[1] "The Poetry of Science," in *Saturday Review*, 5 October 1957, which elaborates this thesis with an example from philanthropy.

been made a thousand times before; they should pass through the process of organizing knowledge in the field of their interest, and be encouraged to explore aspects new to themselves.

In our day it may be more important for race survival to discover the fundamental laws of attraction and repulsion among men and nations than how to make a still more destructive H-bomb. But the social sciences are scarcely yet science; the simplest relationships involve such multiple interactions that even the computer cannot reduce them to precise mathematical formulas. Major discoveries in such areas may well spring from a trained mind, delayed and hindered by inadequacy of data to the point of bringing subconscious appraisals to the threshold of consciousness. The problem of proof remains, but the creative leap has been made.

Foundation Doctrine

As the storm clouds gathered in the early 1960s it began to be suggested that thoughtful people in the foundation field ought to propose a code of ethics for foundations.

Viewpoints differed. I had the lively duty of presiding at a 1965 session of the New York University Conference on Charitable Foundations where former Commissioner of Internal Revenue Mortimer M. Caplin came out strongly for such a code, with suggestions on content. He was immediately followed by Dr. Donald Young of Russell Sage Foundation, expressing the view that anything in the nature of a uniform code was inappropriate for a group so radically divergent in organizational patterns and programs.

My own position was against a "code of ethics" where a group of self-righteous foundations might try to legislate for the whole field. On the other hand, a "code of practice" through which experienced foundations shared their views about the field and their own operating principles might indeed be useful.

In fact I had closed 1963 by pecking out on my typewriter a possible such code as a trial balloon. This went promptly to the Center trustees, asking whether they thought such a document would be useful, whether the Center should have any part in it even as a personal expression, and hoping that they would "examine it, puncture it either completely or wherever necessary, add patches, and give us the benefit of your thinking."

Then on 29 January 1964 Congressman Patman sent to his

group of investigated foundations, which now included the Center, his Foundation Questionnaire 1. My "code" happened to cover many of the same points, except that his questions were full of trick wordings such as whether tax exemption should be revoked for "questionable" accumulation of funds or "inefficient" operation. The trustees ruled that the Center should make no official reply since we were not a foundation and our charter specifically forbade the Center from acting for or representing any foundation or group of foundations, but I might offer to make a purely personal reply if Mr. Patman so requested. This was done.

Meanwhile my suggested code of practice was set in type for possible use in *Foundation News*, if the board approved at our April meeting. A few weeks earlier I had luncheon with the head of one of our large donor foundations. He rather stunned me by insisting that I was regarded as "the conscience of the Foundation field," and no matter how carefully such a document was declared to be personal, it would be treated as an official statement of The Foundation Center. He objected strongly, not at all to its content, but to publication or distribution in any form because of this "official" status. I carried his objection to our board, and it was decided not to publish.

Now that I am no longer president of the Center and can speak for myself alone, I have dug the proof from the files. My views have not changed on the points it presents, and it is here offered as a merely personal view:

A CODE OF PRACTICE FOR
PHILANTHROPIC FOUNDATIONS

1. A foundation is a nonprofit organization having a principal fund of its own, managed by its own trustees or directors, and established to maintain or aid educational, charitable, religious, or other activities serving the common welfare.

2. Tax deductibility of contributions to foundations, as to other charities, was designed by the Congress to stimulate such giving and is wholly proper and in the public interest.

3. However, these provisions were adopted before the incidence of the very high rates of taxation presently making possible such anomalies as costless giving. Manipulations of gifts so as to achieve extreme results call into serious question a charitable intent, and should be avoided.

4. Exemption from taxation of the investment income of foundations, as of other charitable agencies, is a proper means of expand-

ing the sums available for expenditure in the public interest. It should be noted that in the case of most foundations, the possible tax on net income would not be large, and might be none.

5. Acceptance of tax and other legal benefits does not diminish the sole responsibility of the properly constituted trustees to administer the foundation in accordance with their own best judgment, nor does it make any of their funds "public money" to be controlled by public authorities.

6. Foundations should account for their stewardship. Such accountability should include prompt reporting of the availability of the new social asset and, when operation has begun, full and regular reporting of programs supported, grants paid, other expenditures incurred, and an audited balance sheet. At least for larger foundations, such reports should be published annually, and made widely available.

7. Funds donated to a foundation should be administered exclusively for charitable purposes. They should not be loaned to, or otherwise used for, the personal advantage of donor, trustees, officers, relatives, or associates of these persons.

8. In most foundations trustees serve without pay beyond their expenses; but trustees who render services in any other capacity may be paid for those services. A practice of some foundations in paying all their trustees an annual fee is not objectionable if the fee is clearly modest in terms of time required by the office.

9. Investment policies of a foundation should be governed solely by the needs of its charitable program. Safety, current income, and capital gain in terms of keeping abreast of monetary inflation are considerations that need to be weighed in terms of total program purposes.

10. Investment diversification, particularly for long-term and perpetual foundations, seems a desirable policy. This might take the form of putting no more than 5 percent of its total common stock investment into any one corporation stock, and holding in portfolio no more than 1 percent of outstanding stock of any single business corporation.[2]

11. To avoid possible conflict of interest or suspicion thereof, foundations with substantial holding of stock in a business related to the donor or trustees should vest that stock in an independent fiduciary or a separate finance committee of the Board, with full

---

[2] These very low limits, which would present severe difficulties for a few foundations, were not suggested for legislative enactment, but as guidelines which most foundations could voluntarily adopt.

power in either delegate to vote that stock or to dispose of it, with a sole concern for the charitable purposes of the foundation.

12. In accordance with the proven values of individual initiative and dispersal of decision-making, programs of foundations should be governed by the trustees, subject only to any legally controlling instrument and the broad definitions of charity and the general welfare. It is proper for a living donor to serve on this board and actively participate in these decisions.

13. Where a trustee is officially connected with a prospective beneficiary, he should withdraw from the meeting considering that proposal until the vote has been taken.

14. Before voting a grant, a foundation should make certain of the integrity and competence of the persons involved, the responsibility of the organization, and the potential worth of the project.

15. After voting a grant, a foundation should make no attempt to influence appointments or internal policy of the organization, should avoid trustee membership on its board, and give counsel only if asked.

16. When requesting progress and financial reports, a foundation should avoid any suspicion of control over the nature of findings or their dissemination. If there should ever be complete misapplication of funds or other malfeasance, discontinuance of further payments or action for recovery is warranted.

17. Foundations with resources and programs broader than the personal charities of the donor should include in their board membership trustees of broad and diverse interests, and make provision, through rotation or otherwise, for board renewal in terms of both age and fresh viewpoints.

18. Small foundations often function effectively under guidance of the donor and his associates, especially in their local communities. But unless eventual corpus will yield income large enough to warrant professional staff and to attract men of stature as trustees, the fund should either be liquidated within a reasonable period after the donor's death, or—if perpetuity is desired—administration should be transferred to a larger continuing organization, such as a community foundation, or another foundation or agency operating in the chosen field.

Taxation and Philanthropy

Early in the 1960s I began suggesting in speeches and writings that this was the decade in which, because of mounting governmental costs, all tax exemption would be examined, including those extended to philanthropy. This has been happening, though vested interests through effective lobbies have thus far prevented any substantial changes. In my view it makes little sense that most of the wealthiest individuals in the country manage to pay a low income rate through tax devices such as the depletion allowance, tax-free securities, favorable treatment of capital gains. In 1965, for example, thirty-five persons, all with incomes exceeding $500,000 and five of them with incomes above $5 million, paid no income tax at all.

The depletion allowance, which can be claimed long after the total original investment has been written off, needs more drastic revision than has been made in the Tax Reform Act of 1969. Philanthropy, too, has been involved in some of the extreme cases, chiefly through contribution deductions claimed on greatly appreciated assets. This needs to be included in an overdue total examination of the field.

State and local taxation present problems quite as severe as federal. A recent tabulation indicated $16.2 billion of tax-exempt property in New York City. But proportionally, the situation in some small communities is worse, particularly where large estates representing much of their taxable area have been willed or sold to exempt agencies such as schools, churches, old folks' homes. Municipal services are still required, and only in a few cases have the agencies voluntarily offered to offset these costs.

Adjustments of some sort are inevitable. Full information on the nature and dimensions of the problem is required, including detailed data from all educational and religious agencies, which in the past have been exempt from such disclosures. First local steps might include voluntary payment of costs of services and abandonment of such special privileges as exemption from tax of property commercially used. This might afford time for a review of the whole problem and a reasonable solution, in place of radical changes now proposed such as elimination or drastic across-the-board reduction of all exemptions.

Particularly with respect to philanthropy, tax "exemption" is in some respects a misnomer. Government at its various levels has the right to impose taxes. In the light of varying and usually increasing needs for revenue, government from time to time levies taxes upon selected segments of the economy. Examples are profit-making corporations, individuals, estates, donors of large gifts, residential and business property, travelers, theatergoers, purchasers of alcohol, tobacco, gasoline, and now in many states, consumers generally.

Charitable agencies have traditionally never been taxed. Federal codes have carried in some form the proviso of the first corporation tax in the Revenue Act of 1894:

> . . . nothing herein contained shall apply to . . . corporations, companies, or associations organized and conducted solely for charitable, religious, or educational purposes.

This exemption has had minor modifications, particularly with respect to foundations, where profits from unrelated business activities are fully taxed and exempt status may be lost by indulgence in prohibited activities, unreasonable accumulation, or similar infractions, and a 4 percent excise tax has newly been levied by the Tax Reform Act of 1969.

But why in America (and almost only in America) have taxing authorities not only exempted these organizations with respect to their own incomes but encouraged gifts to them from individuals, corporations, and estates by making such gifts deductible from taxed income?[3]

The public policy involved appears to include a recognition that some of the funds so generated will reduce expenditures of government for the same purposes; a desire to encourage a wider range of welfare activities than would be possible or appropriate for government; a wish to decentralize power and to distribute decision-making; a hope that experimentation may be stimulated; and a need to protect sensitive areas against punitive taxation.

The *quid pro quo* consideration needs expansion. It may be moot whether a private agency usually spends dollars more effectively than a public agency in the same field, though I think the probability strong. But under our present tax inducements the private agency has not only the dollars not taxed against its own and contributors' incomes, but large additional sums which flow to these purposes from donors who, without these inducements, would have kept their money for personal expenditures.

All these sums, the monies not taxed away and the augmented contributions, are indeed monies affected with the public interest: they must be spent for welfare purposes and not for private advantage, and their use should be open to full public scrutiny.

---

[3] I have discussed these subjects with particular reference to foundations in more detail in "Foundation Funds—Whose Money?" in *Foundation News*, Vol. IV, No. 1, January 1963, pp. 5-6.

But they are not "public funds" subject to public controls, to be spent, as the Reece Committee tried to insist, only for what "the public currently wishes, approves, and likes." Granted our tax history, it seems a reasonable assumption that tax concessions have been made in favor of private philanthropy, not only to increase the funds available, but so that decisions on use might benefit from the responsible but diverse judgment of the trustees or governors of these respective institutions.

These considerations were not kept adequately in mind in the so-called Tax Reform Act of 1969.

Philanthropy and the Law

In forty years of foundation watching I have had frequent occasion to deal with lawyers and the legal problems of foundations, and have written several articles for law journals. One of these said that if the mother of philanthropy is religion, the law has long been its special guardian. I did not say "guardian angel," for though this title was often appropriate, I have also a few criticisms.

The first is a matter of ethics, applying to a few lawyers and not to law as a whole. These gentlemen utterly, and sometimes honestly, forget whom they are serving. When they are paid with a foundation check, is it not clear that they have a sole duty to that organization as a public trust, devoted wholly to exempt purposes? Advice to donors may be appropriate on the form and timing of donations, but once the asset is within the foundation, its management and expenditure should be with a sole concern for maximizing charity. If a conflict arises between the foundation's best interest and the financial advantage of the donor, should not the lawyer decide that conflict in favor of the foundation from which he receives his pay?

As a realist who has examined many recent examples, I know that in many cases this is too much to expect. But from this problem of individual ethics we turn now to more general considerations.

Originally, the law defined for the western world what philanthropy (or charity) was. More recently the guardian law has specially concerned itself with its ward's income, particularly in the matter of tax privileges. But it has not yet developed in the field of philanthropy an expertise comparable with its resources in criminal law, corporate law, tax law—or even such a specialty as bottomry. Many law offices have occasional need to organize and obtain tax exemption for a new charitable organization, or to advise upon the acceptability to Internal Revenue auditors of particular actions or grants, if the organization is a foundation. These occasional services for a client, sometimes in his selfish interest, give the practitioner little opportunity for a continuing and broad view of the place of philanthropy in American life.

Perhaps as a consequence, the law has too often become a restrictive influence, particularly on foundations. Lawyers, serving as trustees or legal advisers, succeed in limiting the programs of these organizations, not merely to what reasonable opinion would regard as within the law, but to innocuous acts which no one could question. To a distressing degree the programs of some foundations are determined, not upon the greatest public good, but upon sure avoidance of any possible tax question. The device of tax exemption, designed to encourage and expand private enterprise in philanthropy, has constricted and narrowed it.

For a foundation, as for Caesar's wife, merely to remain above suspicion is scarcely the whole of a useful life. The law has indeed the right and duty to warn of dangers in particular enterprises, but in all of life advantage must be balanced against hazard, or no man would venture from his door.

Custom, tradition, and precedent are basic in legal training, and this conservatism has been an important stabilizing force. However, one wonders whether conservatism is the precise quality most valuable for astronauts, or poets, or atomic scientists, or framers of a new society. If philanthropy's precocious child, the foundation, has set for itself the special task of crashing new frontiers and finding some of the essential and ultimate answers of man's relationship to his fellowman, it may have to get on with these tasks and depend upon the guardian law to defend its right to break precedents to do so.

Government in Philanthropy

The tremendous expansion of government into areas formerly regarded as the province of private philanthropy has utterly changed focus and relative dimensions. A few comparative figures from the President's proposed Federal Budget for 1973 suggest the new orders of magnitude, with a few caveats. Not included are state and local expenditures from tax funds for education, health, and welfare; for education, these far exceed the federal amounts. Also, at this writing it is not clear in what directions the Congress may alter this budget.

Of the total proposed budget of $246 billion, almost a third ($78.3) goes for national defense. The still substantial sums related to philanthropy include:

CHIEF PHILANTHROPY-RELATED ITEMS
IN THE PRESIDENT'S BUDGET FOR FISCAL 1973

Item	Billions
Health	$18.1
Veterans' benefits and services	11.7
Education and manpower	11.3
Public assistance	10.3
Community development and housing	4.8
Social and individual services	2.3
Food for peace	.8
Total	$59.3

As a private citizen I find a mere million dollars hard to comprehend, but as a foundation watcher I have become accustomed to occasional grants of one million or more, and the Center's recent tabulation of grants of all foundations in the United States was up to $1.6 billion a year. However, these alleged large spenders, the foundations, have been able to grant for all purposes, including education, health, welfare, international activities, scientific research, religion, and the humanities, less than 3 percent as much as the federal government budgets for similar items.

"The federal government." Let it not be overlooked that you and I pay 38 percent of those sums out of our individual income taxes. (The 1973 estimate for corporations is an additional 14 percent, which comes out of dividends we might otherwise receive.) While a large share of our tax dollars recently went to the Vietnam War and other expenditures that are scarcely welfare, nevertheless our 38 percent of the $59.3 billion related to welfare amounts to $22.5 billion. We individuals are compulsorily paying for social programs fourteen times as much as all the foundations in America annually spend. In this perspective we shall look at government involvement in some of these areas.

Private Contributions to Tax-Supported Agencies

An earlier chapter[4] described an informal survey I conducted for The Ford Foundation in 1956 which marshalled arguments for and against private contributions to tax-supported institutions. In the intervening years events have shifted the weight of some of these factors (e.g., to what extent can we restore the balance by contributing to the private sector).

I share neither of the extreme views—that the welfare state should take care of substantially all educational and welfare needs, or that government operations are necessarily unimaginative and expensive, and the private sector should always take charge.

For the short term, leverage and timing are important. If a public institution has the better man or the only adequate equipment for a certain research project, the funds should go there. If equal facilities are available through a private institution, many donors will prefer the latter.

But I view with some dismay a recent trend among public agencies, and notably the National Foundation on the Arts and the Humanities, to require matching of many of its grants from private contributions. This procedure is supposed to limit government monies to projects the public also will support, and is in fact welcomed by some agencies as a pressure tactic to force local givers to support these particular causes so that their dollars may be matched. But also it results in government agencies with their vast resources being able to determine which programs should be supported even by private funds, tending to dry up free money. If decentralization of decision-making is important, we the people might better insist that government funds—ours—be used to match programs which we, who are close to the local situation, deem important enough to initiate and partially support.

International Affairs

The President's Budget set up $4.1 billion for international affairs and finance—which compares with $106 million from all foundations for international activities, broadly defined.

A substantial portion of these funds is spent, chiefly through the Agency for International Development (AID), to help devel-

[4] See pp. 161-163.

oping countries increase their natural resources and to train their technicians and educators. Disturbing evidence of waste has been uncovered, and any funds from government are always under suspicion of being given primarily to advance some national interest of our own. Nevertheless the ends served by these funds are so essential that we should continue and even increase them, but with more careful administration.

Another substantial portion supplies arms to nations presumed to be our friends. Believing that war has no place in the modern world and that killing for settling international disputes is indefensible, I object strenuously to these expenditures on moral grounds. But on merely practical grounds they may also be attacked. Too often in the past the very weapons we have supplied to a presumed friendly nation have later been used against us. Moreover, any arms we supply to nations in our group are soon matched or overmatched by armaments supplied to nations in the other power bloc. We end with substantially the same balance of power, but a tremendous increase on both sides of the dangerous powder.

However, as a foundation watcher my chief concern with government expenditures "for international affairs" has been with the results of programs of the Central Intelligence Agency (CIA) and similar agencies. An earlier chapter[5] has detailed my own long acquaintance with some of these operations. I have expressed violent objection to the CIA practice of hiring spies under the disguise of researchers for fake or real foundations. Damage to legitimate research, and to the American image abroad, must far outweigh the value of the meager information so secured.

Indeed, it is my understanding that when the Peace Corps was being organized, Sargent Shriver would agree to head it only if President Kennedy would issue a direct order that the CIA could not under any circumstances make arrangements with or even talk to members of the Corps; for its whole usefulness abroad would be lost if it did not remain absolutely pure from even suspicion of such involvement. When Education and World Affairs was started with Carnegie Corporation and Ford Foundation funds it carefully set up a similar prohibition against such involvement.

Other levels exist in the use of government funds abroad. The State Department supports cultural projects, including ex-

[5] See pp. 201-203.

changes of scholars and artists. When it sent the eighty-eight-year-old Robert Frost to Russia in 1962, even the most suspicious European could scarcely suspect that this was a spy mission. Similarly, funds spent abroad by National Science Foundation seem usually to be expended for the advancement of science without prominent national frontiers.

We end with a mixed picture of almost countless billions of American money spent abroad by government: for outright war, for armaments to "friendly" countries, in loans, for educational, economic, and technical aid, for scientific research, for exchange of scholars, for cultural purposes. One could hope some items could be removed entirely, others drastically reduced, a few actually increased, and all more efficiently managed.

One could also hope that a larger portion of the desirable projects could be handled by private funds—foundations, churches, other institutions, in some cases individuals. Government money is always open to greater suspicion of narrow national interests, and government itself has said that private dollars go much further, both in actual accomplishment and in winning friendships.

Children and Giving

My own personal philanthropy began with trouble about a nickel. Father had great confidence in the power of money to accomplish any objective, so when he wanted my brother and me to attend Sunday evening Christian Endeavor sessions, he gave each of us two nickels, one for the collection plate and the other to pay us for going.

That extra nickel deeply troubled me. Hadn't Jesus even sneaked away from his parents to go to the Temple, and then said to them, "Wist ye not that I must be about my Father's business?" I thought of returning the extra nickel with indignant protest. Then I had another idea; I could double the Lord's income by slipping the extra nickel, now my own, beneath Father's nickel, and keeping quiet about it. So, Sunday after Sunday, I did this. But the process left a scar, and later, when I had children of my own, led me to do a great deal of thinking about children and giving.

Every family, in my view, should have a threefold plan. First, certain jobs are expected of every child without pay, as his contribution to the family as a going concern. Second, an allowance should be given weekly to take care of minor expenses and teach the handling of one's own money. It may be quite small at first, increasing with the age of the child. Finally, there is a schedule of pay jobs from which the child may earn—but only at his own election to do the work—extra funds for luxuries for himself or gifts for others.

Probably all his giving should come from this third source, or certainly from such earned funds plus a part of his allowance, in either case as a personal decision and at a personal sacrifice. I oppose the practice of many churches of passing a collection plate in Sunday school among very young children, who are expected to drop in their parents' nickel or dime. True, these schools cost money, as do public schools, but the parents should directly support both. We do not expect kindergartners and first-grade pupils to drop tax dimes into a basket to pay for their lessons in reading and arithmetic. All the giving children do, if it is to have validity as training, should involve choice and sacrifice on their part.

Schools, both church and public, should share with the home the great and necessary task of teaching children the joys, problems, and satisfactions of true giving. Of course care must be taken. The school pressure "drive" with the home room expected to make a 100 percent goal may be embarrassing to children from low-income families. But opportunities to give to special causes of a sort children themselves can understand, and to which they can sometimes contribute work as well as money, should be made available.

When our three boys were growing up we had the good fortune of enrolling them in the Riverside Church school in New York, which avoided the traditional collection basket routine and tried to offer special opportunities for making gifts meaningful. In one class a teacher happened to be presented with $100 by a friend to spend in a way that would do some good.

"You may have it," she said to her class of eight-year-olds, "if you can think of a very good way to spend it."

The excited children made many suggestions. Why not feed the starving millions in India? Well, $100 is 10,000 cents, and even this many among 10,000,000 starving persons would give each only one thousandth part of a single penny for one day. Vast as $100 might seem, it was not scaled to that need.

Perhaps each child should take his share and spend it? With seventeen in the class, that was only $5.88 apiece; they agreed it was better to pool the money and do something more worth while.

After a week to think, they agreed to go to a community center in a poorer part of the city and see if it had needs they could meet. They did, and took notes, asking questions of the children. Their final list included lockers for clothes; window boxes with flowers in them; balls—particularly a football and a big soft ball for the very young children; jumping ropes; tops; a table and chairs; and books. They bought carefully, and themselves painted the table and chairs to make the money go further.

When the work was all done and everything delivered, several of the children expressed views on whether useful giving was easy or hard. It wasn't easy, thought Louise, because "You nearly always have to do some work to be kind." Mary said, "You have to think and find out things."

The experiment would have been still better if it had been the children's own money. But it suggests situations homes and schools can create so that children may share in giving and learn to give wisely. If we are to preserve in America our Fifth Freedom—our traditions of independent giving—children from the earliest ages must learn the ways and joys of giving.

Philanthropy's Future

Does private philanthropy have a future in America, or will it sink into insignificance in the expanding welfare state? Just before retirement I addressed myself to that important question in a speech where I called private giving "The Fifth Freedom."[6] President Franklin D. Roosevelt had added the "Four Freedoms" to the phrases that have echoed their way into history: Freedom of Speech, Freedom of Religion, Freedom from Want, Freedom from Fear. Perhaps we need now, I said, to look at a Fifth Freedom which undergirds the other four—the Freedom to Give.

Through a long history the United States has developed, by practice and in law, this essential freedom to give. Endowed with this freedom, American philanthropy has in the past founded most of our educational institutions, built most of our hospitals, ministered to the needy, wholly supported our varied religions, financed medical research and social experiment, and sometimes played Maecenas to writers and artists.

This Fifth Freedom is still a strong and independent part of our culture. But the winds of change blow near gale force. Big government has invaded with massive funds many areas previously supported by private charity. Income-tax incentives

[6] Presented in Appendix A, pp. 283-291.

designed to increase public and corporate giving have in some cases been flagrantly abused, so that now this whole structure is being critically examined.

We can no longer take this Fifth Freedom for granted. Average voluntary giving has remained close to 2 percent of personal income throughout most of this century. But involuntary giving to much the same causes (except religion) has climbed in the same period from near zero to more than double voluntary giving by the federal route alone. How far will the pendulum swing in the direction of increasing government services? How far should it swing? These are not the same question.

All needs and services are supplied from one of four sources, or a combination of them. First, through individual effort—self-help and mutual aid. (In the wilderness, my guide and I must set my own broken bone.) Second, with the techniques of the market place. (I can pay a doctor to set my bone.) Third, through government. (I may get free service from a veterans' hospital, or through medicare.) Finally, through philanthropy. (If I am poor, I will be cared for by a hospital supported by the local community chest and contributed funds.)

A logical basis may exist for deciding which services we should perform for ourselves, which we should pay for, which are so general that government should supply them, and which are appropriate for private charity. But logic is not necessarily decisive. Where the need is real and it is not met adequately by the techniques of the market place or by private philanthropy, government moves in. This will occur almost always when voluntary giving does not rise to the needed level to meet reasonable requirements. We, the same people and corporations, still furnish the dollars to meet it, but through taxes, with no choice, no control, and no credit.

But not all the winds of change blow against private philanthropy. Now that government is taking care of most of the primary needs, private philanthropy is freed for activity in those vastly important areas of prevention, discovery, and the enlargement of man's capacity for joy and work.

Private initiative has been the key to American progress. Only a portion of that initiative has been directed toward making profits. It has also expressed itself in political inventions, medical discoveries, voluntary associations of a thousand kinds, educational experiments, and basic research into the ultimate facts of the physical universe and of man and his relationships.

Givers need to consider what their share should be in supporting existing free enterprises in religion, health, welfare, education, the arts, research, and possibly initiating fresh ventures. This is not a duty, for government will take over any essential services in these areas which fail of private support, and add them to our tax bill. The Fifth Freedom is an opportunity.

In my view it is an opportunity we should seize with enthusiasm. It ministers indeed to the needs of others, but is essential for ourselves. I have sometimes startled friends by expressing a degree of satisfaction with a world full of problems. It is important that we struggle desperately against the evils that exist, but we shall not conquer them all, and it might be disastrous if we did. An imperfect world is a necessary condition for the growth of the spirit of man.

Altruism has had little research at any level. A few biologists have tried to look into the evolution of tendencies in animals which are of disadvantage to survival as an individual, but definitely of advantage in the survival of its group. On this subject Caryl P. Haskins wrote me:

> The problem was first attacked, I think, by J.B.S. Haldane a number of years ago in what he called his "case of the broody hen" (the broody hen or pheasant defends its eggs and chicks up to a point, but, if its own survival is very seriously threatened it abandons them, thereby, in terms of population needs, giving preference in survival of one capable adult individual for a number of relatively helpless young—probably a good exchange).
>
> This case, of course, represents a compromise of values. There are many others—as the social insects—in which the evolution has gone nearly all the way in the direction of group benefit, and has become, in this sense, almost wholly altruistic. . . .
>
> A number of workers have taken the matter up since, but none, I think, has done a really thorough job of it, nor examined in detail its implications for the evolution of similar altruistic habits among men.[7]

When adequate research has been done on the place of philanthropy for man in modern society, the findings may prove startling. In a closely related field psychologists are issuing pronouncements in such sweeping terms as "Love or perish." The need of the individual for active participation in that broader

[7] Letter to the writer from Caryl P. Haskins, president of Carnegie Institution of Washington, dated 3 February 1966.

love of mankind that is philanthropy may be more basic and stronger than we yet dream.

I am emphasizing now the importance of philanthropy, not for the many causes requiring support, but to the donor: to us as individuals, satisfying an essential need for our own moral growth, psychological development, and perhaps even physical health.

As to the place of philanthropy in future society a distinguished economist has this to say:

> When we look ahead, we can see further changes in the respective roles of government, market, and philanthropy in meeting the problems created by the continual change about us. But that private philanthropy will continue to play an essential role in our society—feeding and exercising and strengthening with its teaching and its example, the spirit of brotherhood basic to social existence; using its independence of thought and its initiative and its "venture" capital to seek and discover and test new ideas and better ways to do things —of this we can have no doubt.[8]

I share Dr. Fabricant's conclusion, but think that if philanthropy in America is to hold and even improve its position, at least three things are necessary. The askers should interpret their causes more clearly, involving donors as understanding partners, and where possible as participants. Donors need a deeper understanding of the values of philanthropy to themselves, and of its place in our culture. Finally, children should be taken into adult counsel on family giving, and led toward selective, sacrificial giving for themselves.

The Fifth Freedom is worth saving. It can strongly undergird a free America and help build a better world.

---

[8] Fabricant, Solomon, "An Economist's View of Philanthropy," *Proceedings of the American Philosophical Society*, Vol. 105, No. 2, April, 1961, p. 166.

APPENDICES

The Fifth Freedom[1]

IN January 1941, before an excited Congress standing on the brink of war, President Franklin D. Roosevelt added the "Four Freedoms" to the phrases that have echoed their way into history. Freedom of Speech, Freedom of Religion, Freedom from Want, Freedom from Fear became a rallying cry for World War II.

Now we need to look at a Fifth Freedom, which undergirds the other Freedoms. It is the Freedom to Give—the freedom we in America possess to use our strengths of mind and body and bank account for our fellowman, reshaping more nearly to heart's desire our own communities, and perhaps the world.

It might be assumed that this is a freedom men have long had, everywhere. But this is not true, in any of those terms. I had a sharp lesson on that subject at the Royaumont Conference a few years ago. For nearly a week a score of us, the others chiefly fiscal officers of a dozen European countries, discussed laws and practices governing charitable donations in those countries. It immediately became apparent that the tax and other inducements which so greatly encourage giving in the United States are extremely limited, or do not exist, in most of Europe. Gifts from individuals are not tax-deductible at all in Austria, Belgium, Norway, Sweden, Switzerland; nor in England except under a complicated seven-year covenant agreement. In most countries charitable gifts from companies are not recognized at all; in France

---

[1] Address before the National Council on Philanthropy, San Francisco, 7 October 1965. Printed, *Proceedings* of the Conference. Reprinted: *Bulletin,* American Association of Fund-Raising Counsel, February 1966; *Forum* of the Association of Secretaries of the Y.M.C.A., May 1966; *Io Triumphe,* Albion College Alumni Magazine, fourth quarter, 1966. Excerpted, *Reader's Digest,* August 1966.

certain such gifts are deductible up to 0.5 percent of income—as contrasted with the 5 percent in the United States.

More startling are the limitations on the fields to which, usually, qualifying gifts are restricted. Upon hearing some examples of American giving the French representative declared angrily: "That is a clear prerogative of government. Individuals have no right to interfere!"

Through a long history the United States has developed, by practice and in law, this essential Freedom to Give. Endowed with such freedom, American philanthropy has in the past founded most of our educational institutions, built most of our hospitals, ministered to the needy, wholly supported our varied religions (for here we have no tax-supported established church), financed medical research and social experiment, and sometimes played Maecenas to writers and artists.

This Fifth Freedom is today a strong and independent part of our culture. But the winds of change blow near gale force. Big government has invaded with massive funds many of the areas previously supported by private charity. Income tax incentives designed to increase public and corporate giving have in some cases been flagrantly abused, so that now this whole structure is before Congressional investigation. We must no longer take this Fifth Freedom for granted, but explore its present values, and decide what should be its future.

II

Dollar dimensions of the Fifth Freedom are easily stated. Though complete accuracy in this field is not possible, the estimate of the American Association of Fund-Raising Counsel for 1964 is not far off: total giving, $10.6 billion, of which $8.5 billion (80 percent) came from living donors, $819 million from foundations, about $671 million in the form of charitable bequests, and $610 million from corporations.

These sums are unequaled elsewhere in the world. But before we sink into self-gratulation, let's reduce billions and millions to comprehensible size. We shall assume a perfectly average Jones family of four. Since we are now a nation of practically 200,000,000 people, the four Joneses would have 1/50,000,000 of all our national totals.

The Jones family gave to charity $170 for the year. This was out of a family income of $9,828, bringing their charity to a little less than 2 percent of income. Using Internal Revenue's analysis of itemized deductions, we find that most of the Jones's $170 went to their church; in fact, $104. They gave $24 to nonsectarian charities including the community chest, Red Cross, and various health agencies. Mr. Jones's alma mater, Clearwater College, got a check for $6.00. Clearwater Hospital received $3.00. The remaining $33 went to a variety of other organizations such as the library, the Fourth of July celebration committee, the police fund, and others.

Philanthropy reduced to this dead average does not look exciting. But averages conceal much, like the good steak-cooking average of the bride who served the first steak raw and burned the next. Some families in their charities are like Mrs. Green who reported in a survey I once directed:

> I never give to anything, not even the church, I just take care of my home and family, that's enough. Charity starts at home, I say.

—and ends there. Others are more like Mr. Bailey, in the same survey. Out of retirement income of $400 a month he gives over 10 percent, and declares:

> I get a big kick out of giving. . . . I just want to do so much good in the world, that's all.

Here we add an important footnote to philanthropy, that applies equally to stingy Mrs. Green, generous Mr. Bailey, and the average Joneses. All gave substantial sums for health, education, general welfare, and even sent money abroad. They did it involuntarily, by the tax route. Not including state and local taxes, much of which goes to education, this is the picture for the Jones family.

Mr. Jones paid a federal income tax of $1,395. Out of this the government spent $357 for medical research, hospital construction, school aid, scholarships, public assistance, and the many other "philanthropic" purposes that fall within the budget of the Department of Health, Education, and Welfare. Forty-six more of Mr. Jones's dollars went for international affairs, chiefly foreign aid.

Average voluntary giving has remained close to the present 2 percent throughout most of this century. But involuntary giving to much the same causes (except religion) has climbed in the same period from near zero to more than double voluntary giving by the federal tax route alone.

III

After individuals, the next largest givers in America are foundations. Because they are numerous and some of them bear names of wealthy families—Ford, Rockefeller, Carnegie, Duke, Kellogg, Sloan—a popular misconception exists that they have tremendous assets and are able to make almost unlimited expenditures. Actually, foundations are able to give only 8 cents out of the dollar of private philanthropy.

But among American institutions they are the only important ones free from the political controls of legislative appropriations and pressure groups, and free from the necessity of tempering programs to the judgments and prejudices of current contributors. They have sometimes been called the "venture capital" of philanthropy. Some of them do spend a substantial portion of their funds in pioneering ventures.

The catalogue of benefits that we owe to imaginative exercise of the Fifth Freedom by foundations (but of course also to the dedicated persons who did the work with foundation support) is almost endless. Examples would include: public libraries, growing largely out of gifts of buildings by Andrew Carnegie and his Carnegie Corporation of New York; the conquest of hookworm, the discovery of insulin, the successful war against yellow fever, chiefly with Rockefeller funds; *John Brown's Body*, perhaps our finest epic poem, written on a Guggenheim Foundation fellowship; New York City's Regional Plan, developed by Russell Sage Foundation when there was no interstate planning agency; the reform of medical education, sparked by the explosive survey made by Abraham Flexner for Carnegie Foundation for the Advancement of Teaching; better salaries for college teachers, brought to the national conscience by The Ford Foundation's massive gift of $260 million; and, just yesterday and today, support for research on DNA (deoxyribonucleic acid), a key to genetics and perhaps to life itself.

IV

The next largest component is one often forgotten—charitable bequests. The cited estimate of $671 million is probably too low. Amounts vary radically from year to year because they can be affected by single estates of $100 million or more, but government figures for 1961 were a resounding $951 million.

This near billion dollars annually sinks into the broad stream of charity, leaving scarcely a ripple. True, a substantial part of it may have gone into new foundations or toward increasing assets of existing ones, and thus serve long-lasting later purposes. But far too often charitable bequests in wills are after-thoughts, or simply repeat lifetime patterns of giving. For many people a final bequest may be the only really large gift they can ever make, their most important exercise of the Fifth Freedom. They should here harvest, not merely the matured securities, but the matured wisdom of a lifetime.

V

Corporations, giving now some $610 million a year, are a relatively new giant in giving. Corporate gifts were not federally tax-deductible until 1936. Except under war emergencies, giving had been minor before then, and beset by legal questions. Climbing from around $30 million in the late 1930s, it rose speedily under wartime excess profits taxes, recently reached a plateau of around $500 million, and now appears again to be slowly mounting.

The pattern is very different from that of the Jones family. Until quite recently, local welfare, chiefly through community chests and united funds, received the biggest slice of the corporate dollar. Now, for many corporations, education is a contender for top place. Religion, which fared so well with the Joneses, gets very little from corporations.

VI

Here, in broad outline, are the dimensions of the Fifth Freedom, the classes of donors, and something about the fields they severally favor. But this is not a static picture. Radical changes are just ahead, which need to be appraised.

The growing role of government may be the most important such factor. Government expansion in welfare fields took its first long stride with passage of the Social Security Act in 1935, but 1966 is already a striking year. A vast program of medicare for the aged goes into effect. Educational aid, including a new scholarship program, represents massive expansion in one of philanthropy's favorite areas. The 1967 federal budget for the National Institutes of Health alone is set at $1.150 billion.

Where a need is nearly universal and vast sums are required, it may be best to have as our almoner the tax collector, for he has also persuasive powers over stingy Mrs. Green. It is open to debate whether better judgment would be exercised by a vote-conscious Congress or a rather careless average Mr. Jones. But how far will the pendulum swing in the direction of increasing government services? How far should it swing? These are not the same question.

All needs and services are supplied from one of four sources, or a combination of them. First, through individual effort—self-help and mutual aid. (In the wilderness, my guide and I must set my own broken bone.) Secondly, with the techniques of the market place. (I can pay a doctor in a hospital to set my broken bone.) Thirdly, through government. (I may get free service from a veterans' hospital.) Finally, through philanthropy. (If I am poor, I will be cared for by a hospital substantially supported by the local community chest and contributed funds.)

A logical basis may exist for deciding which services we should perform for ourselves, which should be paid for, which are so general that government should supply them, and which are appropriate for private charity. But logic is not necessarily decisive. When the need is real and it is not met adequately by the techniques of the market place or by private philanthropy, government moves in. It has moved perhaps too massively into medical research, but this occurred only when voluntary giving clearly did not meet the reasonable need. We, the same people and corporations, furnish the dollars to meet it now, but with no choice, no control, and no credit.

VII

Another cloud on the horizon of the Fifth Freedom lies in the area of tax adjustment. Throughout American history philanthropic organizations have gone untaxed, at the federal and state and local levels. Even more important is the deductibility allowed to contributors, greatly increasing the flow of funds to the "exempt" organizations.

The public policy involved probably includes the *quid pro quo* of reducing government expenditures; a desire to encourage a wider range of welfare activities than would be possible or appropriate for government; a wish to decentralize power and to distribute decision-making; a hope that experimentation may be stimulated; and a desire to protect sensitive areas against possible punitive taxation.

These liberal tax provisions were written into law when tax rates were low. Now that they have climbed to the stratosphere, the temptation is great to abuse them—and this abuse may be within the letter of the law. The Internal Revenue Service is understandably irked, as are many suburban communities which in recent years have found their large estates becoming tax exempt as schools, convalescent homes, homes for the aged.

Within this decade our whole system of tax exemption is certain to come under critical scrutiny. The first attack is already being made on foundations, politically the most vulnerable. Unlike churches, colleges, hospitals, they have no vast bodies of members, alumni, and other supporters to vow voting vengeance on attackers.

Abuses have occurred, among foundations and elsewhere, which need correction. The Ways and Means Committee is presently considering Revenue Code revisions. But let this be remembered. It is not possible to correct an abuse by forbidding it with respect to only one type of exempt organization. The identical abuse will simply be transferred to another type of charity—until its tax shelter is also removed.

Some changes in the law to correct the severe abuses are certain, but if the Fifth Freedom is not to be crippled, its values must be widely understood and care taken in the nature of the changes approved.

VIII

Thus far, the current winds of change seem to be limiting exercise of the Fifth Freedom. They are also giving it exciting new possibilities.

Consider this very old story. At the top of a cliff a busy highway took a sharp curve, and people were always falling off. The villagers below took care of them. They even bought an ambulance by private subscription, and added a wing to their hospital, to try to save more lives. One day an old man sitting by the side of the road said to them, "Why don't you go up to the top of the cliff and build a fence?" But the cries of the injured were sharp in their ears, and they were too busy to take time out to build that fence.

Now, through social security and other measures, the government is to a large extent taking care of the people who fall off the cliff, and is running the ambulance at the bottom. Increasingly, private philanthropy is freed to build the fence of prevention at the top of the cliff.

Gift money can be spent in three ways. We may give to help people *in trouble* (give for relief). If a man has lost his leg, we can supply money to feed his family while he is out of work. Second, we can help people *out of trouble* (cure, rehabilitation). We can supply the man with an artificial leg, so that he can work again and support himself. Third, we may help people *avoid trouble* (prevention). We could have taken safety measures at the factory, so that the man would not have lost his leg.

If the last includes searching out the ultimate causes of personal and social catastrophe and building resistance to these disasters by making men more healthful, able, and creative, we have well covered the possibilities of the Fifth Freedom. Under present conditions, government is taking care of most of the task of helping people in trouble, much of the area of helping people out of trouble, but very little of the third area of prevention, discovery, and the enlargement of human capacity for joy and work.

Private initiative has been the key to American progress. Only a portion of that initiative has been directed toward making profits. It has also expressed itself in political inventions, medical discoveries, voluntary associations of a thousand kinds, educational experiments, and basic research into the ultimate facts of the physical universe and of man and his relationships. Givers need to consider what their share should be in supporting existing free enterprises in religion, health, welfare, education, the arts, research, and possibly initiating fresh ventures in these areas. This is not a duty, for government will take over any essential services which fail of private support, and add them to our tax bill. The Fifth Freedom is an opportunity.

The amount given matters, of course. But even small gifts, made wisely, have had great effects. Consider John V. N. Dorr and his idea about highways.

Until 1954, highways in America might have a central white stripe, but that was all. Mr. Dorr went to the Connecticut Highway Department and proposed that they also paint marginal white lines on their highways. They demurred. The center stripe was designed to prevent head-on collisions, and marginal lines would merely triple the cost, and be useless. Engineering-trained Mr. Dorr thought otherwise. At night, he pointed out, to look for the center stripe is to be blinded by the lights of approaching cars. Anyway, he had a small foundation—the Dorr Foundation established in 1940. If they would lend him a road (one on which accident statistics were available), he would pay for the painting.

This was done. After six months even Mr. Dorr was surprised —accidents had dropped 65 percent! Of course Connecticut painted marginal lines on its highways. The Dorr Foundation went with its startling evidence to other states, to national meetings on highway safety, and to Canada. Now you and I drive all over America on roads with white marginal lines, the result of one small but creative exercise of the Fifth Freedom.

The Fifth Freedom is worth saving. Powered by individuals, corporations, and foundations, and even sometimes "using resources largely of brains and imagination" (to quote the late Mr. Dorr), it can strongly undergird a free America and help build a better world.

Notes on a Few Books

Tㅑᴇ chapter on Beginnings records my expectation that a good portion of my time would be devoted to writing, but without the slightest inkling that most of these writings would be in the field of philanthropy. However, of 21 books thus far published, all but eight are directly concerned with philanthropy and foundations, and are described at the appropriate places in this text.

This appendix discusses briefly the remaining eight, which include children's books, mathematics, a religious novel. The reader interested primarily in philanthropy may skip or skim this appendix, included to show principal other interests and perhaps biases.

An Excursion in Numbers

My first published book was actually in mathematics, a subject in which I had had less than no interest until one idle hour in January, 1934. That wintry afternoon I remembered hearing long ago, perhaps from a teacher in high school, that one could count by twelves easier than by tens.

This was not a new idea, particularly in England, where Sir Isaac Pitman, Thomas Leech, and Herbert Spencer had advocated the dozen system, all before 1900. In America, a few efforts had been made looking toward duodecimal counting and some school arithmetics gave exercises in various possible number bases. But in the 1930s few people had ever heard of the idea, much less used it.

I tried out this half-remembered idea. I found I needed two

new numerals, one for the old quantity ten (I used Roman X and called it *dek*) and another for eleven (I used *E* and called it *el*). Of course, the new *10* was not ten, but a dozen. And since my age was just turning 33, that was a more comfortable *29*—two dozen and nine.

That evening I announced to Mrs. Andrews that the mess of scribbled figures on my desk represented an important discovery —not to some mathematicians, perhaps, but one they had never adequately introduced to a possibly waiting world. I, a writer, would make this discovery known.

That was a rash boast. I wrote an article which was promptly rejected by all the appropriate magazines. Finally I sent it to one of the most unlikely magazines, but one in which I had been previously published, *Atlantic Monthly*. After some hesitations, they published it in October, 1934, under the title, "An Excursion in Numbers."

It was an excursion in a sense I had not anticipated. Both the *Atlantic* and I were deluged with letters. Wrote editor Sedgwick, "We hoped, at best, for a limited group of appreciative readers, but found instead that x = Infinity." They were from all sorts of people, a sea captain, a missionary, a few mathematicians, Hendrik Willem van Loon who found the idea undoubtedly right, but was "too old and too hopelessly set in my respect for the sacred number 10 to adopt the duodecimal system," from a Wall Street securities analyst who invited me to lunch, sure that a person who was willing to examine figures unconventionally would be able to supply him with a magic formula for outguessing the Street's wild gyrations of that Depression year.

Not all the correspondence was favorable. The most violent objection came from a lady who found my proposal blasphemous, for did I not know that the Lord had ordained counting by tens with the Ten Commandments in the Old Testament? Realizing that mathematical arguments were useless in this case, I wrote back acknowledging the Ten Commandments in the Old Testament, but stoutly affirming that in the New Testament there were the Twelve Apostles.

In the preparation of the "Excursion" and the two additional mathematical articles the *Atlantic* demanded I had accumulated much material, enough for a small book. So I wrote the book, titled it *New Numbers*, and took it to my former employer, The Macmillan Company, where I still had many friends. It came back promptly, and six other publishers were unanimously un-interested. Then Harcourt, Brace and Company, after viewing a pile of letters I brought to their office, gave me a contract.

The day *New Numbers* was published, 19 September 1935, Faber and Faber of London cabled an offer for a British edition, which was issued the next year. The reviews here and abroad were excellent, and when the Harcourt edition went out of print, a revised edition was published by Essential Books in 1944. Meanwhile, it was stimulating other books here and abroad. In England came J. Halcro Johnston's *The Reverse Notation*;[1] in France, Jean Essig's *Douze, notre dix futur*.[2]

So, in spite of myself, I was launched on a mathematical career which has lasted to this day. Figures are fascinating, but they are not my central interest. The account of the more important sub-sequent developments is carried elsewhere in some detail,[3] so it can be much abbreviated here.

A small group of regular correspondents formed, which soon was calling itself The Duodecimal Society of America. One of its members, the late George S. Terry, had the Monroe Calculating Machine Company build him a machine with two extra cogs— making it a perfect duodecimalian—and produced his monumen-tal *Duodecimal Arithmetic*, published by Longmans, Green and Company in 1938 and making available adequate tables of loga-rithms to the twelve base, trigonometric functions in terms of the duodecimal circle, and other needed apparatus. Then he gen-erously offered to fund an official Society with a $5,000 gift, with me as president.

I was in no position to devote extensive time to what was a marginal interest. But in late 1941 came a letter from Ralph H. Beard, an executive of the New York Telephone Company, who had just read *New Numbers*. An enthusiastic organizer was found. On 5 April 1944 The Duodecimal Society of America held its first official meeting. It was chartered "to conduct research and education of the public in mathematical science, with par-ticular relation to the use of Base Twelve in numeration, mathe-matics, weights and measures, and other branches of pure and applied science." Over protest, I was made president; in this field

[1] Johnston, J. Halcro, *The Reverse Notation*; Introducing Negative Digits with Twelve as a Base. Blackie and Son, Ltd., London, 1937.

[2] Essig, Jean, *Douze, notre dix futur*. Dunod, Paris, 1955.

[3] In various issues of *The Duodecimal Bulletin* and most recently in "My Love Affair with Dozens," *Michigan Quarterly Review*, Vol. XI, No. 2, Spring 1972, pp. 104-110.

my only merit, I said at our first annual meeting, is "bringing a valid and important idea to the attention of abler minds."

The Society survived the Depression and the War, due chiefly to the indefatigable efforts of Ralph H. Beard, who served variously as secretary, treasurer, editor of *The Duodecimal Bulletin*, president, and board member up to the present. Membership was never large; one recent year its 166 members came from 30 states, the District of Columbia, and seven foreign countries. A Duodecimal Society of Great Britain was formed in 1959.

Two of the stranger uses of duodecimals may merit mention. During World War II I received an urgent request from Army Transport Service to help their clerks, who needed to figure cargo cubages on cases measured in feet and inches, to "straighten us out with a few demonstrations; it would add greatly to the speed and efficiency of our work."

One of our members, Mr. Velizar Godjevatz, developed a duodecimal musical notation. We may briefly note that in simple piano music, for example, the curiously-named "octave" has twelve, not eight, tones, produced by seven white and five black keys. A confusing set of signs—sharps, flats, naturals, clefs—indicate which of those twelve keys is actually to be struck. As a first step in a sensible notation Mr. Godjevatz proposed a stave in which each note has its own line or space, easily identified:

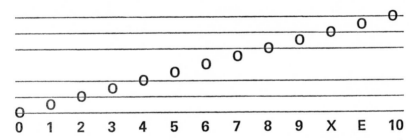

I am not musician enough to evaluate Mr. Godjevatz's proposal. But the Society received a warm commendation of this proposal from George Bernard Shaw, whose early writings were largely musical criticism:

Ayot Saint Lawrence, Melwyn Herts
21st October 1949

Dear Sirs:

I am much obliged to you for sending me Mr. Godjevatz's book entitled The New Musical Notation. I have read it through and followed its argument attentively. I know most of the new notations from that of Rousseau to the latest, as their inventors sent them to me because I was a prominent professional critic of music 60 years ago. I am greatly taken by Mr. G's plan. It is enormously more readable, writable, logical, graphic, and labor saving than any I can remember. Its adoption would save a world of trouble.

Wagner in his last days was still complaining that he could get nobody to transpose his clarinet parts for him. Reading music is said to be like riding; unless it is learnt in childhood it is never learnt at all.

Mr. G's plan would teach people to count duodecimally with two new digits: eight nine deck ell ten; and this by itself would recommend it, as duodecimal arithmetic is a coming reform.

I am no longer a reviewer, but if my valuation of the plan will help to call attention to it, you may quote this letter as much as you please.

(Signed) G. BERNARD SHAW

Mr. Shaw's prediction that "duodecimal arithmetic is a coming reform" has not proved true in Britain, which is changing to decimal coinage and weights and measures; and in the United States we have always had decimal coinage, and are under strong present pressures to change to decimal weights and measures. We shall almost certainly do so, without even considering the more fundamental change to a different number system better suited to many practical purposes, including measurements, time, the circle, packaging, divisibility. But for me this detour into numbers has been a fascinating excursion, bringing unexpected sidelights, interests, friendships. And the idea itself is absolutely valid. Counting by dozens is better.

Numbers, Please

Over the years this side interest blossomed into a number of magazine articles—two more in the *Atlantic*, two in *Mechanix Illustrated*, more than a dozen in *The Duodecimal Bulletin*, a few lectures, and one more book. Miss Helen Jones, juvenile editor for Little, Brown and Company, learned I had done some popular writing in mathematics. What was needed, she wrote, was a book that would explain arithmetic to children; not a textbook, but a supplementary book for outside reading. Would I like to try it?

That summer I borrowed all the arithmetic books used in the local schools, consulted teachers, looked at the new math. Then I wrote *Numbers, Please*. It tried to say that numbers are a second language which we use almost as much as our letter-language, and what we do with those numbers can be fun as well as useful. Instead of teaching rules it explained all the simpler operations, and included some of the queer ways people used to count and still do in some parts of the world. It was published in 1961 by Little, Brown and Company and continues to sell well.

I Find Out

The *Numbers* book was not my first venture into the juvenile field. We had three sons, Frank, born in 1935; Peter, in 1937; and Bryant, in 1938. There were illnesses and worries, and moments when we felt like turning in a recalcitrant child for a good green trading stamp. But mostly the house in Tenafly was full of laughter and high spirits. We had great fun in rediscovering the world with each of our children, and in notebooks and diaries we set down some of these experiences. Baby record books friends gave us were not much help in this respect. They had spaces for height and weight, diseases, relatives, and pictures—physical development, but not intellectual.

So I dreamed up a baby record book that would help parents accompany their children in these voyages of discovery. The title page read: *I FIND OUT: The Autobiography of* _____. There was an introductory Word to Parents explaining that this "is a record book in which, with your help, your child will write the exciting autobiography of his own first years. It is a key to help you unlock the door to your child's growing world, enter, and explore it with him."

The manuscript had an extraordinary history. Over four years it was refused by fourteen publishers. Then it was accepted, but with a contract I rejected. A year later the publisher agreed to the contract revisions I had stipulated and would print an initial edition of 100,000 copies. The book, handsomely illustrated by the late Pelagie Doane, was published in 1946.

After modest initial sale the publisher ran into financial difficulties and "remaindered" the book. This was illegal as he did it, under my special contract. The American Arbitration Association decided every point in my favor, and ruled that royalty must be paid on the amount received. Because of the publisher's financial difficulties, I accepted as part of the settlement rights to the book and ownership of the plates. A few months later it was placed with World Publishing Company, and before it went out of print had sold a total of 300,000 copies. Royalties from that book were set aside for the boys' education, since they were its inspiration. That helped mightily with later college expenses.

The Gingerbread House

We had made-up stories in our house, some of them continued over weeks and even months. Whenever possible, I put humor in my made-up stories, and disagree with the school of child psychologists who insist that stories must be exactly true, and limited to a predetermined age vocabulary.

In our house we soon had a Mimi the Kitten who could talk well enough to be understood by Waddle the Duck and a small boy named Oscar. They lived in a house made of gingerbread. The whole house was gingerbread; the bricks were gingerbread bricks, the roof was gingerbread, even the chairs and tables were gingerbread. Only the windows were not gingerbread; they were white cake frosting, sliced very thin.

These stories amused my lads, so I wrote down the several that were most successful. *The Gingerbread House* was accepted by Eunice Blake of Oxford University Press, and published in the fall of 1943. In consequence of refusals and delays on *I Find Out*, it was my first published juvenile book. The illustrations were done by Roberta Paflin, an artist who then lived only a few doors from us; she used our second son, Peter, as her model for Oscar. It was a very personal book, dedicated to "Frank, Peter Bruce, and Bryant, Oscar's earliest friends."

The Knight Game

An editor mother and a writer father ensured that we would play games with words. One favorite was the Knight Game, which went like this:

"What Knight do you want when you are hungry?"
(Sir Loin Steak.)
"What Knight might you meet in church?"
(Sir Mon.)

Many years later, as relaxation from sober writing and heavy

administrative duties, I did a zany children's book based on this
Knight Game, consisting almost wholly of dreadful puns. It was:

Dedicated, of course, to
Don Quixote
and his creator
Sir Vantes

Charles Hawes illustrated it with sparkling humor.

It went beyond the Knight Game into other curiosities of our
language and even number system—words that look alike but
are really quite different (e.g. desert: sandy, or quit); words and
whole sentences that can be read forward or backward (step on
no pets); words spelled alike but pronounced differently (the
dove dove); a Number that upside-down is a lie (317); negative
words with positives that are unused and sound strange (preg-
nable, pervious, pecunious, ert); and many others.

For some of these I had the assistance of a learned foundation
friend, Warren Weaver, formerly a vice-president of The Rockefeller Foundation, who makes collections of peculiar words. Our
luncheons were enlivened by word exchanges, and I acknowl-
edge here my indebtedness to him for some of the ideas in my
book, published in 1966 by G. P. Putnam's Sons under the title,
Knights and Daze: A Family Fun Book.

Upside-Down Town

When any belief seems unquestioned, I like to turn it upside
down to see whether the reverse might possibly be true. For a research man, this is a useful and almost essential technique.

It may also help a storyteller. One summer the small daughter
of journeying friends spent several weeks with us up in Vermont.
For her bedtime stories I invented Upside-Down Town, where
everything is backwards. Old folks play while children do all the
fascinating work. Doctors' waiting rooms are rooms where the
doctors wait; they are paid only while patients stay well; they
take temperatures by timing how fast ice cream melts in the
mouth. Teachers give apples to the pupils, and have a course in
elementary forgetting. It proved so useful they planned a course
in advanced forgetting, but a teacher skilled enough in forgetting
to teach it could never remember when or where the course was.

When one of these inventions made my child chuckle, it was
duly noted, and next morning a chapter was written. Soon I had

a book which Little, Brown and Company accepted, and Louis Slobodkin superbly illustrated. *Upside-Down Town* was published early in 1958, but I had an advance copy just in time for a 1957 Christmas present for the young lady, Miss Felicity Russell, who, said the dedication, "was the first to visit Upside-Down Town with me." It was a selection of Junior Literary Guild, and has brought me many amusing letters, often written with some reverse or upside-down twist.

A Teen-Age Novel

I had tried my hand at an adult novel, set in the age of Charlemagne; had indeed gone to Europe to visit the Carolingian sites, refurbishing my Latin and French. After several rejections a perceptive editor, while agreeing with other judgments that as a first novel, and historical, it probably could not be successful financially, pointed out that the earlier chapters, covering the youth of my hero, would make, almost as they stood, a fine teen-age novel. Here the historical background would be pure asset, both in terms of reader interest and with school libraries, eagerly seeking authentic historical material.

I followed his advice. The manuscript was accepted by Harper and Brothers and published under the title *For Charlemagne!* in 1949. I sent a special copy to a beloved high-school teacher, Charles McMullen, who was still living, telling him that the gentle and learned Alcuin, master in the Palace School, had been modeled chiefly after him.

The book was written not only with historical care, but in it I was trying to say to my own then teen-age sons the hard truths about what life is really like which a father finds it difficult to say directly. An example is the farewell the Abbot of Fulda gave Sigmund as he started his long journey:

> "My son," the Abbot said, "tomorrow you are going on a long journey. It is full of danger. But it is a journey every young man must take. I also have been young. A time comes when we feel that all things around us, even those we love, are holding us back. We struggle against even these ties. At last each of us starts alone on the journey toward his own dream. . . ."

At that point the gruff Abbot took from beneath his robe a second loaf of bread from the monastery's dwindling supply, with the harvest months away. He rose, and Sigmund remembered the pressure of his hand on his head and the look in the Abbot's eyes as he spoke his parting words:

"My son, we do not any of us reach in this world the full, bright day of our dream; but we may find the dawn. Many do not find it. Some lose the path. More sit down to rest for a moment, and are too weak to rise again. But you, my son, are strong. Look for the light."[4]

The reviewers were kind. "The story possesses a charm and significance seldom found in such fast-moving tales," said Howard Pease in *The New York Times*. "It is an 'imperative' book for school libraries of the sixth grade up." It was also serialized, published in a Swedish edition, and now, more than twenty years later, still sells well.

Grugan's God

On an autumn walk in 1930 I had an idea for a fable that could be a whole novel. When Grugan the merchant prince opened his window, everyone and everything his eye could see belonged to him. "All mine," he said, "except for the Temple and the loyalty those fools give their imagined god. That's the worm in my fig."

"Well," said his companion, "if you must have everything, you might set up a god of your own in competition."

After a long pause Grugan said in his most matter-of-fact tone:

"You are right. I have done everything else. It is time I try my hand at setting up a god."

The story is what happened after that. In a Foreword that one reviewer called "hair-raising" I said:

In old books we are told how God made man. This is the story of how a man tried to make his own god, and what happened to them both. It took place, however, in a strange country in a forgotten time. Any resemblances to persons or conditions in the second half of the twentieth century are purely intentional.

The characters began taking things in their own hands, with results I had not anticipated. I finished the first draft in Depression year 1932. Nobody was interested in publishing. I resurrected it several decades later, and in 1954 came a letter from Muhlenberg Press saying, "The thought is provocative and the style memorable. We will recommend it to our Board of Publications."

[4] *For Charlemagne!*, pp. 2-3.

Grugan's God was published in February, 1955, and I believe was the first novel published by this religious house. It received a few reviews, usually favorable, but several complaining that its author's theology was not orthodox. Said another: "The more you know of the world, the more vividly you will recognize Mr. Andrews's intricate meanings and the more reasons for salutary uneasiness you will find in this sober, honest, bitter little story."

As a publishing enterprise, it was a dismal failure. It sold a few copies, and is long out of print.

Bibliography

THIS bibliography includes only books of which I was author or co-author. Other publications—pamphlets, chapters in books, magazine articles, even eleven poems—run to the forbidding total of 432, of which 185 deal with philanthropy. Footnotes at the appropriate pages have identified those most important in the present context. A full bibliography is on file in The Foundation Center.

New Numbers: How acceptance of a duodecimal (12) base would simplify mathematics. Harcourt, Brace and Company, New York, 1935. 168 p.

——— Faber and Faber Limited, London, 1936. 163 p.

——— Revised Edition. Essential Books, New York, 1944. 168 p.

The Gingerbread House. Pictures by Roberta Paflin. Oxford University Press, New York, 1943. 48 p.

I Find Out: The Autobiography of Your Child. Pictures by Pelagie Doane. Essential Books, New York, 1946. 44 p.

——— The World Publishing Company, New York, 1951. 44 p.

American Foundations for Social Welfare. (With Shelby M. Harrison.) Russell Sage Foundation, New York, 1946. 249 p.

Russell Sage Foundation, 1907-1946. (With John M. Glenn and Lilian Brandt.) Russell Sage Foundation, New York, 1947. In two volumes, 746 p.

For Charlemagne! Harper & Brothers, New York, 1949. 207 p.

——— Swedish translation. Med Karl den Store. Almquist & Wiksell, Stockholm, 1953. 221 p.

Philanthropic Giving. Russell Sage Foundation, New York, 1950. 318 p.

Corporation Giving. Russell Sage Foundation, New York, 1952. 361 p.

Attitudes toward Giving. Russell Sage Foundation, New York, 1953. 145 p.

Grugan's God. Muhlenberg Press, Philadelphia, 1955. 196 p.

Report of the Princeton Conference on the History of Philanthropy in the United States. (Unsigned.) Russell Sage Foundation, New York, 1956. 84 p.

Philanthropic Foundations. Russell Sage Foundation, New York, 1956. 459 p.

Legal Instruments of Foundations. (Editor.) A Foundation Library Center Study. Russell Sage Foundation, New York, 1958. 318 p.

Upside-Down Town. Illustrated by Louis Slobodkin. Little, Brown and Company, Boston, 1958. 64 p.

The Foundation Directory, Edition 1. (Editor, with Ann D. Walton.) Prepared by The Foundation Library Center. Russell Sage Foundation, New York, 1960. 817 p.

Numbers, Please. Illustrated by Aldren A. Watson. Little, Brown and Company, Boston, 1961. 101 p.

Foundations: 20 Viewpoints. (Editor.) Significant Papers Selected from *Foundation News*, with an Introduction by F. Emerson Andrews. Russell Sage Foundation, New York, 1965. 108 p.

Knights and Daze: A Family Fun Book. Illustrated by Charles Hawes. G. P. Putnam's Sons, New York, 1966. 48 p.

Patman and Foundations: Review and Assessment. Occasional Paper Number Three. The Foundation Center, New York, 1968. 62 p.

The Tenafly Public Library: A History, 1891-1970. The Tenafly Public Library, Tenafly, N.J., 1970. 80 p.

Foundation Watcher. Franklin and Marshall College, Lancaster, Pa., 1973. 321 p.

Trustees of the Foundation Center, 1956-1973

Frederick B. Adams, Jr., April 1962-April 1968
F. Emerson Andrews, June 1956-April 1970[1]
Robert C. Bates, April 1963-April 1969
Wilbur J. Bender, April 1968-March 1969[2]
Julian P. Boyd, May 1956-April 1962
Thomas R. Buckman, July 1971-[3]
John B. Coburn, April 1969-April 1972
Fred C. Cole, April 1971-
Morris D. Crawford, Jr., April 1963-April 1969
Merrimon Cuninggim, April 1963-April 1969
Melvin S. Day, April 1972-
G. Harold Duling, April 1961-March 1964[4]
Marion R. Fremont-Smith, April 1970-
William C. Greenough, April 1961-April 1967[5]
Paul R. Haas, April 1969-
Robert H. Hamlin, April 1961-April 1967
J. George Harrar, April 1969-
Frederick H. Harrington, April 1968-April 1971
Rembrandt C. Hiller, Jr., April 1962-April 1968
J. Kimball Johnson, December 1956-April 1961
Vernon E. Jordan, Jr., April 1971-
Wilbur K. Jordan, April 1962-April 1968
John G. Kemeny, April 1970-
John A. Krout, May 1956-April 1961
W. McNeil Lowry, April 1969-
Robert J. McCracken, December 1956-April 1962

[1] Director, President, June 1956-July 1967; President Emeritus
[2] Deceased, March 1969
[3] President, July 1971-
[4] Deceased, March 1964
[5] Chairman, April 1962-April 1965

Emory W. Morris, May 1956-April 1961
Vernon Munroe, Jr., May 1956-April 1963[6]
Manning M. Pattillo, Jr., July 1967-November 1970[7]
James A. Perkins, May 1956-April 1963[8]
Alan Pifer, April 1968-April 1971[9]
Gordon N. Ray, April 1962-April 1968[10]
John G. Simon, April 1968-
Sydney Stein, Jr., April 1964-April 1967
J. Tyson Stokes, April 1963-April 1969
Richard H. Sullivan, April 1967-April 1973[11]
Robert L. Sutherland, May 1956-April 1963
Walter M. Upchurch, Jr., December 1956-April 1962
Edwin H. Vause, April 1967-April 1973
Martha R. Wallace, April 1971-
Sidney J. Weinberg, Jr., April 1968-
John D. Wilson, May 1956-April 1963
Bernard Wolfman, April 1970-
John E. F. Wood, May 1956-April 1961
William R. Wright, April 1969-
Donald Young, May 1956-April 1962
Arnold J. Zurcher, April 1961-April 1967

[As of April 1973]

[6] Chairman, April 1959-April 1962
[7] President, July 1967-November 1970
[8] Chairman, May 1956-April 1959
[9] Chairman, April 1968-April 1970
[10] Chairman, April 1965-April 1968
[11] Chairman, April 1970-April 1973

INDEX

"Philanthropy in the United States,"
241n
Philippines, 71
Phyfe, Duncan, 28n
Physical Culture, 27
Physical sciences, 153
Pifer, Alan, 306
Pinchot, Gifford, 17, 19
Pitman, Isaac, 292
Pittsburgh Survey, 26
Planning Board, Tenafly, 58-59, 185
*Plans for City Police Jails and
    Village Lockups* (Hart), 25
Player, Gary, 200
Playground Association of America, 31
Playgrounds, 10, 56
Pocantico Hills, 199
"Poetry of Science, The," 262n
Pogany, Willy, 28n
Poland, 28n, 61
Poling, Daniel A., 14
Political and Economic Planning, 129
Pomey, M. Michel, 242
Pony Riding for the Disabled
    Trust, 231
Poor's *Register of Directors and
    Executives*, 119
Pope Leo XIII, 146
Pope Pius XI, 146
Port of New York Authority, 56
Portland, 41
Portugal, 211, 227
Potter, David M., 189n
Prairie chicken foundations, 201
President's (Hoover) Emergency
    Committee for Employment, 40
Press of the Woolly Whale, 65
Price, Don K., 224
Price Fund, 202
Prince George Hotel, 13
Princeton Conference on Philan-
    thropy, 159-160
Princeton University, 127, 155
"Principles of Public Giving"
    (Rosenwald), 18n
"Private Philanthropy and Public
    Institutions," 162n
Protestant giving, 110-111
Provident Loan Society, 9
*Public Accountability of Foundations
    and Community Trusts*
    (Taylor), 149n
Public Assistance Worker, The
    (Kurtz), 47
Publicity for Social Work (Routzahn
    and Routzahn), 26

Purdy, Lawson, 58
Putnam's Sons, G. P., 299

QUEEN Elizabeth I, 231
Queen's Hospital (Honolulu), 206

R S F Bulletin, 35, 66, 92
Rabin, Samuel, 107
Radcliffe College, 164
Raffell, Burton, 192
Ramparts Magazine, 203
Ramsey Corporation, 95
Ransom, Will, 66
Rathbone, Eleanor F., 77, 81
Ray, Gordon N., 306
Raymond Rich Associates, 68, 83
Reader's Digest, 129, 283n
Recreation Department, 30-31, 44
Red Cross. *See* American National
    Red Cross
Red Cross, (Japan), 235
Redman, Sir Harold, 229, 240, 241
Reece, B. Carroll, 142, 145-147
Reece Committee (House), 145-147,
    269
Regent's Park, 229
Regional Plan Association, 54-57, 185
Regional Plan of New York and Its
    Environs, 51-54, 286
Regulation W, 64
Relief abroad, 70-71
Religious giving, 109-112
Remedial Loans Department, 23-25,
    44-46
*Report of the Committee on the
    Law and Practice Relating to
    Charitable Trusts*, 232
*Report of the Joint Legislative
    Committee on Charitable and
    Philanthropic Agencies*, 107n,
    108n
*Report of the Princeton Confer-
    ence on the History of Philan-
    thropy in the United States*,
    160n, 304
Report of the Special (Reece) *Com-
    mittee*, 147
Reporter, The, 181
Revenue Act: of 1894, 268; of
    1950, 95, 224, 249. *See also*
    Tax Reform Act of 1969
Revenue Revisions, 1947-48, 96n
Reverse Notation, The (Johnston),
    294